Visual C++ Database Programming Tutorial

Wendy Sarrett

Wrox Press Ltd. ®

Visual C++ Database Programming Tutorial

Published by Wrox Press Ltd. 30 Lincoln Road, Olton, Birmingham, B27 6PA
Printed in USA
ISBN 1-861002-41-6

Trademark Acknowledgements

Wrox has endeavored to provide trademark information about all the companies and products mentioned in this book by the appropriate use of capitals. However, Wrox cannot guarantee the accuracy of this information.

Credits

Author
Wendy Sarrett

Development Editor
John Franklin

Editors
Victoria Hudgson
Adrian Young

Technical Reviewers
Craig McQueen
Bob Beauchemin
Sing Li
Anil Peres-da-Silva
Curt Krone
Brad Lund
Robert Smith
Simon Robinson
Stephen Rice
Claus Loud

Cover
Andrew Guillaume

Design/Layout
Tony Berry

Index
Andrew Criddle

Cover Photography
STUDIO M/ Toby Marquez

About the Author

Wendy Sarrett graduated from University of Pennsylvania's Wharton undergrad in 1983. After finding out she preferred playing with the computers that did the financial calculations rather than doing them herself, she went back to University of California at Irvine where she received a MS in Information and Computer Science in 1990. After working for four years at FileNet as a test engineer, system administrator and test tool developer, she moved to Minneapolis for a year and a half and then back east to Virginia where she currently works as a software engineer for Careerbuilder Inc. Wendy is both a Microsoft Certified Solution Developer and a Chartered Financial Analyst.

When she's not playing with the computer she's either working out, playing with her pets Marco, a talking parrot, Delenn, a cockatiel, and PC, her long-time feline buddy who has been with her 14 years, and has traveled by plane more than some people. She also enjoys watching sport, talking political heads and of course B5 on TV.

Acknowlegements

I'd like to start with acknowledging the people who worked on the book with me. First, my editors, Victoria Hudgson and Adrian Young, worked extremely hard to turn the raw writing I sent them into a high quality book. I'd also like to thank my reviewers: Craig McQueen, Bob Beauchemin, Sing Li, Anil Peres-da-Silva, Curt Krone, Brad Lund, Robert Smith, Claus Loud, Simon Robinson and Stephen Rice, whose comments were invaluable. Finally, thanks go to John Franklin for giving me the opportunity to write this book despite the fact I've never tried anything like this before.

I'd like to thank my family and friends for there support during this process, my parents who have supported me in every challenge I have undertaken; my brother and sister-in-law, Jeff and Lauren, who always give me encouragement and advice; my Aunt Arlene, Uncle Ira and cousins Heather, Ryan and Scott who put up with me setting up my laptop wherever there was a plug in their house during Thanksgiving. Thanks also to Paula and Mitch who tolerated me being even more impatient than usual and finally, Robin, who encouraged me with her daily emails and listened to the day to day frustrations and victories in working on this project.

Lastly, I can't leave out my pets: Marco, Delenn and PC who had to endure not as much attention as they would have liked.

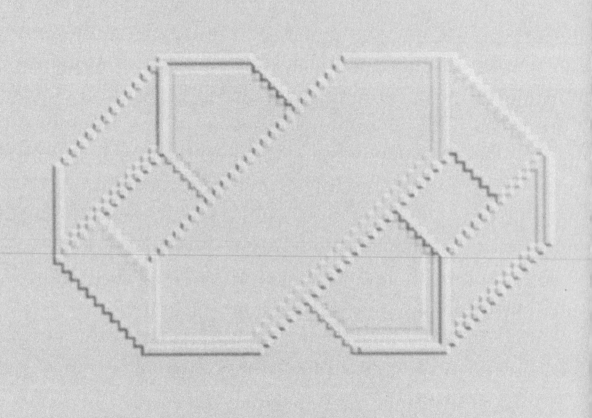

Table of Contents

Introduction   **1**

Chapter 1: Database Theory   **7**
Database Systems   8
    Access   8
    ISAM   8
    FoxPro   8
    Oracle   8
    SQL Server   8
    Btrieve   9
Relational Databases   9
  Storing Data   9
  The Relational Model   10
Key Concepts in Database Design   12
  Relationships   12
  Keys   14
    Candidate Keys and Primary Keys   14
    Foreign Keys   15
    Alternate Keys   16
    Surrogate and Intelligent Keys   17
    Determining the Primary Key   17
  Referential Integrity   18
  The Principles of Data Normalization   19
    Data Redundancy   19
    Anomalies   20
    Functional Dependence   20

Table of Contents

Normal Forms	21
First Normal Form	21
Second Normal Form	21
Third Normal Form	22
Boyce-Codd Normal Form	24
Fourth Normal Form	25
Fifth Normal Form	26
Domain/Key Normal Form	26
Data Normalization — An Example	26
Practical Aspects of Normalization	31
A Word about Object Oriented Databases	32
Indexing	33
Practicalities of Indexing	34
Clustered Indexes	35
Stored Procedures and Queries	35
Triggers	36
Cursors	37
Transactions	37
Designing Your Database	38
Summary	40
Chapter 2: An Introduction to Structured Query Language	**43**
What is SQL?	44
Our Example Database	45
Querying Data: the SELECT statement	46
Introduction to the SQL SELECT Statement	46
The SELECT Element	47
The FROM and WHERE Elements	48
More Advanced Queries: Joins	49
Inner Joins	50
Outer Joins	50
Cross Joins	52
Full Outer Joins	53
Filter Elements	53
More Advanced Elements: GROUP BY and HAVING	55
Aggregate Functions	56
Sorting	57

Updating Your Data: INSERT, UPDATE and DELETE Statements   58
    INSERT   58
    UPDATE   61
    DELETE   61
Defining Databases Programatically   62
    CREATE TABLE   62
    CREATE INDEX   64
    ALTER TABLE   65
    DROP TABLE   66
Tools for Creating SQL   67
Summary   67

Chapter 3: Overview of Data Access Technologies   **71**
A Bit of History   72
Introduction to ODBC   73
The MFC ODBC Classes   75
    The CDatabase Class   75
    The CRecordset Class   76
An Example Using ODBC   77
    Creating an ODBC Connection   77
    The Basic Recordset   79
      The TestRecordset Class   82
      The Document Class   84
      The View Class   85
    A Parameterized Query   94
      The Query-based Recordset   95
      The Vendor Recordset   96
      The Document Class   97
      Creating a View   97
      Switching between Views   100
    Pros and Cons of ODBC   101
Introduction to DAO   102
    DAO versus ODBC   103
The MFC DAO Classes   103
    The CDaoRecordset Class   104
    The CDaoDatabase Class   105
    The CDaoWorkspace Class   105
    The CDaoQueryDef Class   106
    The CDaoTableDef Class   106

Table of Contents

An Example using DAO   107
    The CTestDaoRecordset Class   108
    The Document Class   108
    The View Class   109
    Using a Parameterized Stored Query   114
    Pros and Cons of DAO   118
Universal Data Access, ADO and OLE DB   119
Summary   120

Chapter 4: An Introduction to OLE DB   **123**
A Touch of COM   124
    Advantages of COM   126
The Universal Data Access (UDA) Model   126
What is OLE DB?   128
Design Goals of OLE DB   128
Consumers, Providers and Services   130
    OLE DB Consumers   130
    OLE DB Providers   131
      Available Providers   131
    OLE DB Service Components   132
OLE DB Objects   132
    Data Sources, Sessions, Commands and Rowsets   132
      Connecting to the Data Source   133
      Retrieving Data   134
    Accessors   135
    Error, Transaction and Enumerator Objects   135
    An Overview of the Data Access Process   136
The OLE DB Interfaces   137
    Data Source Object Interfaces   138
    The Session Object Interfaces   139
    The Command Object Interfaces   140
    The Rowset Object Interfaces   142
    The Transaction Object Interfaces   144
Pros and Cons of OLE DB   145
ADO and Templates   146
    ActiveX Data Objects (ADO)   146
    Templates   147
Summary

                                                            147

Chapter 5: OLE DB Consumers   **149**

What is an OLE DB Consumer?   149

The OLE DB Consumer Templates   150

    What are the Consumer Templates?   150

    The OLE DB Consumer Classes   150

        CDataSource   151

        CSession   151

        CTable and CCommand   151

        Accessor Classes   152

        CRowset   153

Creating an OLE DB Consumer Application   154

    Inserting An ATL Object   154

    The Generated Classes   158

    Modifying the Document and View Classes   161

    Adding Delete Functionality   167

    Changing the Rowset Classes   168

More Complex Queries   169

Conclusion   175

Chapter 6: An OLE DB Consumer Example   **177**

Designing the Training Log Application   178

    The Weights Database   178

    The User Interface   182

Creating the Training Log MFC Application   183

Creating Data Access Classes   184

    The Users Classes   185

    A Note on Foreign Keys   186

    The Exercises Classes   187

    Definition of the Remaining Rowset Classes   188

Implementing the Document Class   189

Developing the User Interface   191

    The CUserView Class   191

        The Class Header   192

        Construction   193

        Data Exchange and Validation   194

        Initialization   194

        Adding Functionality for the Buttons   195

        Including Files   200

Table of Contents

The AerobicLog View Class   201
   Referential Integrity   201
   Changes to the Header   202
   Initialization   202
   Command Button Handlers   202
   Helper Functions   207
The Remaining View Classes   211
   The CCommentView Class   211
   Initialization   212
   Button Handlers   212
   Updating the Form   212
   The CMeasurementView Class   213
   The CResLogView Class   214
   The CTrainingView Class   215
Modifying the CMainFrame Class   217
Creating the Report   219
   Selecting the User   220
   Creating the Rowset   221
   The Report View Class   223
Further Issues   226
   Installation Issues   227
   Source Control   227
   Transactions   229
   Multi-User Issues and Security   230
     Security   230
     Visibility   230
Summary   231

Chapter 7: Introduction to ADO   233
   Why Active Data Objects?   234
The ADO Architecture   235
   Higher Level Objects: Connection, Recordset and Command   236
     The Connection Object   236
     The Recordset Object   240
     The Command Object   245
   The Support Objects: Errors, Fields, Properties and Parameters   247
     Errors   247
     Fields   247
     Properties   249
     Parameter   249

Using ADO in C++   250
    Getting Started   250
       An Aside on BSTRs and VARIANTs   251
       The MFC OLE Method   251
       The #import Method   253
    A Practical Example – using the OLE SDK   254
       Creating the Application   254
       The ADO Recordset Class   254
       The Document Class   259
       Viewing the Data   259
    Visual C++ ADO Extensions   263
Summary   264

Chapter 8 Remote Considerations   **267**
Remote Data Objects (RDO)   268
    The RDO Model   269
    Using RDO   270
Remote Data Services (RDS)   270
An Example Using RDS   272
    Setting Up RDS   272
    Setting Up the Database   273
    Security Issues   274
Developing a C++ Application to Use RDS   277
    Initializing RDS   277
    Communicating with the Database   277
    Implementing the View Class   285
Summary   291

Table of Contents

Appendix A: Bibliography   **293**

Appendix B: Using The Active Template Library   **297**
Description of the Main Classes and Templates   298
Module Maps   300
   The Object Map   300
   The COM Map   301
   The Connection Point Map   301
Creating A Project with the ATL AppWizard   301
Inserting the COM Object   305
   Adding Methods   310
Testing the Code   313
Conclusion   314

Index   **317**

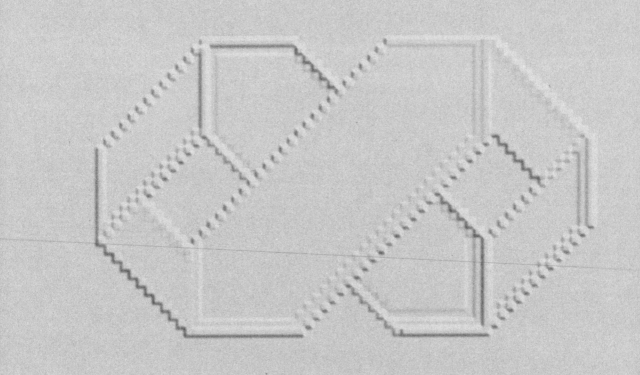

Introduction

Visual C++ Database Programming Tutorial has been designed to provide basic tuition in developing data access applications. It is an introductory book that attempts to cover the common database technologies currently used by presenting an example application for each in turn.

Who's This Book For?

This book is primarily geared towards programmers who have minimal experience in database development in Visual C++, and who now want to learn more about the various database technologies Microsoft offers, with the aim of putting together professional applications using these technologies. This book can also be utilized by experienced database programmers who want to introduce themselves to some of Microsoft's newer technologies, such as ADO (ActiveX Data Objects), RDS (Remote Data Services) and OLE DB.

Our examples are geared towards Visual C++ 6.0, and use MFC to develop the user interfaces. Therefore, some knowledge of C++ is essential and experience in using MFC is very helpful, though instructions are supplied of how to use the MFC Wizards.

For the OLE DB examples, ATL code is used as well. Previous experience of ATL is useful but not necessary, as, once again, there is guidance on the use of the ATL Wizards.

What's Covered In This Book

This book starts with a general overview of database theory and Structured Query Language (SQL). Following this introductory section we discuss specific Microsoft technologies, as follows:

- ❑ Chapter 3 covers the older data access technologies: ODBC and DAO
- ❑ Chapter 4 introduces us to OLE DB
- ❑ Chapter 5 describes OLE DB consumers and presents an example
- ❑ Chapter 6 presents a case study using OLE DB consumers
- ❑ Chapter 7 covers ADO and provides an example of using ADO in Visual C++
- ❑ Chapter 8 covers remote data access, and will present an example of how to develop an RDS application using C++

When you're finished with this book you should be able to write an application in any of these technologies, allowing you to access a database, retrieve a set of records which can be browsed and modified as required.

What You Need To Use This Book

Our examples are based on Visual C++ 6.0 so this version is necessary to successfully implement the examples using the newer technologies, in particular the OLE DB consumer templates.

The databases we will use are Microsoft Access and SQL Server version 6.5. While you can use Windows 95/98 for the Access examples, you have to use Windows NT 4.0 in order to log onto SQL Server. If you don't have the SQL Server 6.5 Enterprise Edition, you can use the Developer Edition supplied along with Visual C++ 6.0.

For the ADO/RDS examples you should download Microsoft's Data Access SDK 2.0 from Microsoft's web site at `http://www.microsoft.com/data`. RDS examples must in addition utilize one of Microsoft's web servers (either the Internet Information Server or the Personal Web Server). These come with the NT Option Pack, which is also available on Microsoft's web site.

Conventions Used

We use a number of different styles of text and layout in the book to help differentiate between the different kinds of information. Here are examples of the styles we use and an explanation of what they mean:

Background information, asides and references appear in text like this.

- ❑ **Important Words** are in a bold type font.
- ❑ Words that appear on the screen, such as menu options, are in a similar font to the one used on screen, for example, the File menu.
- ❑ Keys that you press on the keyboard, like *Ctrl* and *Enter*, are in italics.
- ❑ All filenames are in this style: `Invoices.mdb`.
- ❑ Function names look like this: `OnUpdate()`.
- ❑ Code which is new, important or relevant to the current discussion, will be presented like this:

```
void main()
{
   cout << "Visual C++ Database Tutorial";
}
```

- ❑ Whereas code you've seen before, or which has little to do with the matter at hand, looks like this:

```
void main()
{
   cout << " Visual C++ Database Tutorial";
}
```

Tell Us What You Think

We have tried to make this book as accurate and enjoyable for you as possible, but what really matters is what the book actually does for you. Please let us know your views, whether positive or negative, either by returning the reply card in the back of the book or by contacting us at Wrox Press using either of the following methods:

E-mail: `feedback@wrox.com`
Internet: `http://www.wrox.com/`

Source Code and Keeping Up-to-date

We try to keep the prices of our books reasonable, even when they're as big as this one, and so to replace an accompanying disk, we make the source code for the book available on our web sites:

`http://www.wrox.com/`

The code is also available via FTP:

`ftp://ftp.wrox.com`
`ftp://ftp.wrox.co.uk`

If you don't have access to the Internet, then we can provide a disk for a nominal fee to cover postage and packing.

Errata & Updates

We've made every effort to make sure there are no errors in the text or the code. However, to err is human and as such we recognize the need to keep you informed of any mistakes as they're spotted and amended.

While you're visiting our web site, please make use of our *Errata* page that's dedicated to fixing any small errors in the book or, offering new ways around a problem and its solution. Errata sheets are available for all our books — please download them, or take part in the continuous improvement of our tutorials and upload a 'fix' or pointer.

For those without access to the net, call us on **1-800 USE WROX** and we'll gladly send errata sheets to you. Alternatively, send a letter to:

Wrox Press Inc.,
1512 North Fremont,
Suite 103
Chicago,
Illinois 60622
USA

Wrox Press Ltd,
30, Lincoln Road,
Olton,
Birmingham,
B27 6PA
UK

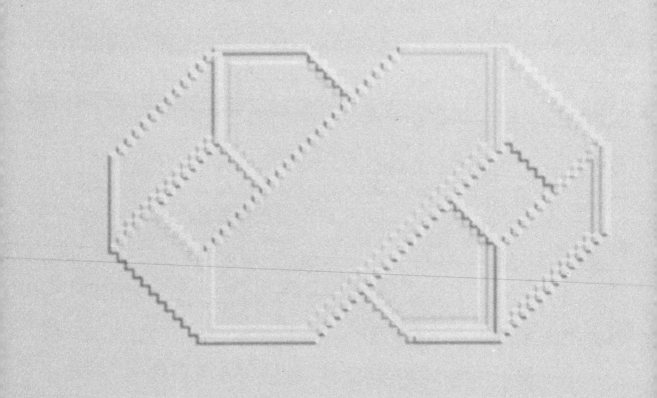

Database Theory

The focus of this book is on writing database applications using Visual C++ 6, but our first priority is to discuss the basics of databases and database theory. In this chapter we will cover the following topics:

❑ An introduction to relational databases — why they are significant and commonly used

❑ Database normalization — how and why

❑ Practical issues in designing databases

❑ What object-oriented databases are

❑ What key values are and how they effect database design

❑ Why indexing is important, and how we determine which index to use

❑ Stored procedures and queries, what they are and how they're used

❑ How we use the information discussed in this chapter to design a database

By the time you have finished this chapter you will have a basic understanding of the theory behind relational databases and how that theory applies to a real database example.

Database Systems

Before we start, however, let's just have a brief run through some of the commercial database systems that are commonly used today.

Access

Access is the desktop relational database system developed by Microsoft as part of its Office suite. It is geared for individual desktop applications but can be applied in a multi-user situation to a certain extent. It takes advantage of Microsoft's JET technology. However, the number of records it can handle is limited compared with enterprise solutions, such as SQL Server. We will be using Access as a number of our examples throughout the book.

ISAM

ISAM stands for Indexed Sequential Access Method. Direct access to records is provided by an index. Note that ISAM is geared for local desktop databases.

FoxPro

FoxPro is a long time ISAM, desktop database that is now part of Microsoft's Visual Studio. It is strictly a Windows based solution. It 's current version, 6.0 has a lot of graphical features. It has developed to a point that one can develop relational DB solutions using FoxPro by collecting the various tables into a "database". This differs from Access and more sophisticated databases as Oracle and SQL Server where one creates a database and within it creates tables. One cannot have a table in these database systems that is not part of a database, but this is possible in FoxPro.

Oracle

Oracle is a powerful server based Relational Database Management System (RDBMS). It is designed to handle very large databases efficiently. It is an enterprise level database solution, as opposed to desktop oriented databases, such as FoxPro and Access. Oracle runs both in the Windows and Unix environments. Oracle has been around for a long time and hence is a very stable well tested and much used RDBMS.

SQL Server

As with Oracle, SQL server is a powerful RDBMS. Again, it is an enterprise level database that runs on Windows NT. It has a number of graphical tools to help one manage their databases and servers. Developed as Microsoft's answer to Oracle, it hasn't been around very long. We will be using SQL server in a number of our examples throughout the book.

Btrieve

Btrieve is what is known as a navigational client/server database. There is both a server and workstation edition of this database available, which is very popular in the field of accounting software. Btrieve was designed especially to be used with 3rd, 4th and 5th generation programming languages. Btrieve is an example of an ISAM database.

Relational Databases

A **Relational Database Management System** (**RDBMS**) is a database that operates by a system based on the Relational Model developed by E.F. Codd. Relational databases are the most common type of database used today — examples ranging from desktop applications such as Microsoft Access to heavy-duty client server databases such as Microsoft's SQL Server and Oracle.

Storing Data

Originally, databases were simply collections of text data and binary records. A classic example is that of an employee list, where employees are represented by employee number, last name, first name, address and so on. The details of each employee are contained in a **record**, with each characteristic occupying a **field** within the record.

A record is essentially a set of attributes representing an object in a list or table and a field consists of a single attribute describing the object in the record.

For our employee example, a simple text file containing the employee data with review dates and ranks would most likely be written out one field at a time, and displayed as follows:

```
1
Smith
John
111 Tree Ln.
3/97
2
3/98
1
2
Jones
Sally
123 First St.
3/98
1
```

The simple database that is most commonly found, however, is a **flat file database**, which is a database consisting of only one table. Often, it might be displayed in a more formal organization such as a simple spreadsheet, and in fact, it is common to turn a spreadsheet that has gotten large, or is very commonly used, into a database of this kind. In a flat file database, the above data can be written out like this:

```
1, Smith, John, 111 Tree Ln, 3/97, 2
2, Smith, John, 111 Tree Ln, 3/98, 1
3, Jones, Sally, 123 First St, 3/98, 1
```

There are several problems associated with flat file databases. First, to insert a record where only a few fields contain new data, the remaining fields have to be filled with duplicate data. In the example above, we had to copy John Smith's full name and address, just to add another review rank. Such databases often have a lot of rows with large amounts of duplicate data, which leads to excess usage of disk space.

A database can get around this problem by using **repeating groups**, where instead of having duplicate data, each new piece of information is added to the end of the record. In our example, the above data would be rewritten as follows:

```
1, Smith, John, 111 Tree Ln, 3/97, 2, 3/98, 1
3, Jones, Sally, 123 First St, 3/98, 1
```

The outcome of using repeating groups is that there will be differing numbers of fields per record. While we have overcome the problem of duplicate data, a second problem has now arisen. If the number of fields varies from record to record, the manipulation of data within the database becomes much more complex. For example, if we want to add a new review period, we need to rewrite the record with the new data added at the end. This is in contrast to the first version of this table, where each review period was contained in one record on one row.

From the above discussion, we can see that the flat file database model — consisting of only one table — can lead to one of two major problems:

❑   Duplicate data and large databases that waste disc space

❑   Complexity in data manipulation and databases that are hard to query

The difficulty of maintaining a balance between these two extremes is the reason why flat file databases are inefficient and restricted in scope. Therefore, a more flexible model needed to be developed — the **relational model**.

The Relational Model

Relational databases have become very important, as they have proved themselves to be a very useful and efficient way of manipulating data. Also they have become popular — the most commonly used databases, such as Access, Oracle and SQL Server, are all relational in nature. They have achieved this level of popularity because they resolve the problems with flat file databases discussed above.

The data model is three-dimensional and the data is divided into a series of **relational tables**, each of which contains a series of fields and records:

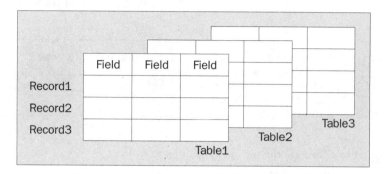

The term *relational* refers to the way the tables and the databases they compose are linked together. In a relational database, this is based on matching fields that distinguish the records.

This organization of the data allows the user to perform queries in various ways: a **query** is a statement that instructs the database to return certain data. Queries can return data from more than one table by using a join on matching fields. Such fields are known as **keys**, and a **relationship** is established between tables based on **key values**. We'll be looking at keys in more detail later on in the chapter.

In order to be relational, a table must have certain characteristics:

- ❑ It must have just one value per row/column pair, where each column represents one characteristic
- ❑ Each column must have a unique characteristic
- ❑ There can be no repeating groups
- ❑ No two rows can be identical
- ❑ The order of rows and columns must be irrelevant

If you want to find out more information about the theory of relational databases, you should check out the work of two gurus of relational databases —E.F. Codd and C.J Date. See Appendix A for more details.

A repeating group, as we saw earlier, is a column (or a combination of columns) which contains several data values for each row. This means that you could have a record with more than one value assigned to a field, which is not allowed if the table is to be relational. Let's look at an example to see what this means.

A table for an invoice could have columns for a number of different items, together with the quantity of each item in the invoice. In the table shown below, the first record has three values in columns titled *Item* and *Quantity*, the second record two. The *Item/Quality* pair forms a repeating group:

Invoice #	Item#1	Quantity1	Item#2	Quantity2	Item#3	Quantity3
00001	002	200	009	100	005	400
00002	001	100	003	200		

This table can be modified to eliminate the repeating groups as follows:

Invoice #	Item	Quantity
00001	002	200
00001	009	100
00001	005	400
00002	001	100
00002	003	200

Key Concepts in Database Design

In this section, we'll be discussing some of the most important concepts that lie behind the design of relational databases. These include:

- ❑ Relationships between tables
- ❑ Key values
- ❑ Referential integrity

Relationships

As we saw earlier, the term *relational* in the phrase relational database refers to the way the tables are linked together — but how does this work in practice? Two tables can be joined if they both contain the same field — this is called a relationship. Let's take an example to see how this works.

Say we have two tables, an employee table containing employee details and an employee/project table listing the projects with which each employee is involved. There is a relationship between the two tables, which are joined by the *EmployeeID* field. Shown below is a screenshot from Microsoft Access, which allows you to graphically display the relationships between the tables in the database:

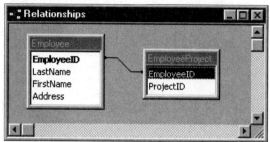

Relationships can be one of three types:

- ❏ One-to-many (1:N)
- ❏ One-to-one (1:1)
- ❏ Many-to-many (M:N)

Relationships are discussed in great detail in many database texts including that of C. J. Date.

As you would expect, a one-to-many relationship between table A and table B means that one entry in table A can be linked to many entries in table B. Take another look at the example above. Each employee can be involved in several projects, so for each employee entry in the employee table, there can be many entries in the employee/project table. The relationship between the employee and employee/project tables is therefore one-to-many.

A one-to-one relationship between tables A and B is also what you would expect. For each entry in table A, there can only be one entry in table B.

While a many-to-many relationship is possible between two tables, it is generally avoided by inserting a third table between the two tables involved in the relationship. This middle table would thus have a 1:N relationship with the first table (joining at the field corresponding to a key value in the first field) and 1:N relationship with the second table (joining at the field corresponding to a key value in the second table).

Let us consider our example again. We can add another table that contains fields for the project ID, the name of the project, its details and so on. The relationships between our three tables are shown below:

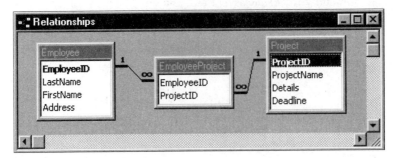

If we only had two tables here — an employee table and a project table, then we'd have to store project information in the employee table and employee information in the project table, with an M:N relationship between the two tables. This is because an employee can be on many projects and a project can have many employees.

However, with the addition of the employee/project table, this relationship is broken into two relationships, a 1:N relationship between the employee and employee/project table and a 1:N relationship between the project and employee project table. This brings the added advantage of simplifying the tables enormously

> *Note that Access uses ∞ rather than N to denote the many end of a one-to-many relationship.*

Keys

Candidate Keys and Primary Keys

A **key** consists of a field (or group of fields) that uniquely identifies a particular record in a table. Generally speaking, such a field or set of fields is known as a **candidate key**. Clearly, we need a method of distinguishing between rows in a table, in order to be able to select a particular row and update it, for example. Candidate keys are the only sure way of finding a particular row in a table. If there are several candidate keys in a table, it is the responsibility of the designer to designate one of them as the **primary key**. If a table has only one candidate key, it is primary by default. It is very important to have a primary key, as without it, updating a table would be impossible.

There are certain criteria that have to be met in assigning a primary key:

- ❑ Its value can never be null (empty)
- ❑ Its value must be unique (no two rows may have the same primary key)

Foreign Keys

A **foreign key** is a primary key from a different table. In other words, it is a key whose value matches the primary key (or a candidate key) in another table. Primary and foreign keys are essential for joining tables together efficiently. Let's look at an example of three tables joined by primary/foreign keys:

The Exercise Table

ExerciseID	Exercise
1	Squat
2	Leg Extension
3	Lunge
4	Dead Lift
5	Leg Press

The Difficulty Table

ExerciseID	weight	Difficulty
1	110	2
1	125	3
2	75	2
3	15	2
4	60	1
5	150	3

Database Theory

The Log Table

PersonID	ExerciseID	Date	Set	Reps	Weight
1	1	5/20/98	1	12	110
1	1	5/20/98	2	12	110
1	1	5/20/98	3	10	110
1	1	5/24/98	4	10	125
1	1	5/24/98	5	8	125
1	1	5/24/98	6	8	125
1	2	5/24/98	1	12	75
1	2	5/24/98	2	12	75
1	2	5/24/98	3	12	75
2	1	5/24/98	1	12	15
2	1	5/24/98	2	12	15
2	1	5/24/98	3	12	15
2	3	5/24/98	1	12	60
2	3	5/24/98	2	12	60
2	3	5/24/98	3	12	60
...	...	...	...	...	...

In this case, the primary key for the exercise table is `ExerciseID`, which is also the foreign key for both the difficulty and log tables. We would then use this primary key to join the exercise table to either the log or difficulty tables.

The difficulty table has a composite primary key of 'ExerciseID and Weight', while the log table has a **composite** primary key of 'ExerciseID, PersonID, Date and Set'. We would join the log table to the difficulty table using 'ExerciseID and Weight'. In this case 'ExerciseID and Weight' would be the foreign key. As you can see, you can have a foreign key whose columns also make up part of the primary key.

Alternate Keys

If we have more than one candidate key, then any that are not designated as primary are referred to as **alternate keys**. Again, the designer makes the distinction between primary and alternate keys. In many cases, there is no alternate key, as only one field or set of fields qualifies as a candidate key.

Surrogate and Intelligent Keys

Finally, we must make a distinction between what are known as **surrogate keys** and **intelligent keys**. Surrogate keys are keys like `ExerciseID`, from the above example, which have no meaning in the real world, but are added to the database to make things work more smoothly. Intelligent keys are keys such as `Date`, which do have a real meaning. Often we won't include surrogate keys in any interaction with the user.

Surrogate keys are generally created for two reasons:

❑   There can potentially be a null value in a primary key field, and this is forbidden

❑   They allow for more efficient joins

For example, if you have a primary key that is a combination of several fields, it's often more efficient to create a surrogate key, so that joins can be done on one field, rather than on several.

In his article *The Case for the Surrogate Key*[1], Mike Lonigro advocates the extensive use of surrogate keys as primary keys. This is based mainly on the additional requirement that the primary key remains stable. The term *stable* means that the key is under the control of the database administrator, which further implies that it is assigned by the system, and not by part of the business logic. The need for stability comes from the fact that the data must be able to be updated without affecting the relationships between tables. This doesn't mean that all tables need a surrogate key, but they do if they are involved in joins with more than one table.

Determining the Primary Key

Well, now that we know what key values are, how do we determine which of our candidate keys should be the primary key? First, it must be restated that in order to be a primary key, a key value must be unique and no subset of the columns making up the key can create a unique key. Once these requirements are met, the relational database model does not distinguish between them. There are however some guidelines we can follow when designating a primary key. The first is simplicity — the simpler the primary key, the better, so composite keys should have as few fields as possible. Also we should consider the kind of joins that will be done on our database. If a particular candidate key is going to be joined frequently, it might very well be a good choice for a primary key. Often, tables only have one candidate key, so this will become the primary key by default. Also recall that a primary key must always be non-null — a requirement that can often lead to the creation of surrogate keys.

---

[1] "The Case for the Surrogate Key", Lonigro, Mike, *Database Programming and Design, Online Extra,* May 1998.

Referential Integrity

One important use of keys is in ensuring **referential integrity**. In a relational database, referential integrity is essentially maintaining consistency between joined tables, such that certain operations are not permissible if they compromise the relationship between the tables.

Databases such as Microsoft Access allow the user to enforce referential integrity, although it is strictly optional. According to the Access documentation, if referential integrity is enforced between two tables, then certain rules have to be observed. Other databases, such as SQL Server, have different means of handling referential integrity —triggers, which we will be looking at later on.

Let's go back to our earlier employee example to see what this all means. Consider two tables:

- ❏ An employee table
- ❏ An employee/project table

EmpID	Name
1	Joe
2	Sally
3	Tom

EmpID	ProjID
1	500
2	400
2	600

EmpID is the primary key in the employee table and the foreign key in the employee/project table. In order to enforce referential integrity, there are several points we must bear in mind:

- ❏ Joe cannot be deleted from the employee table until the records with his empID (empID = 1) are deleted from the employee/project table
- ❏ We cannot add project information about an employee, until he or she has been entered into the employee table
- ❏ We cannot change an EmpID in the employee table

Now, Access does permit us to get around these rules by allowing what is known as 'cascading updates and deletes'. If this option is selected, we can update an EmpID or delete a row in the employee table and the change will automatically be reflected in the employee/project table.

Without ensuring referential integrity, it is possible for a database to get into an inconsistent state. For example, a situation could arise where there are employees listed in the employee/project table who do not exist in the employee table. This would lead to joins with undesirable results, such as querying for employees on a project that joins the two tables, but which wouldn't pick up all the employees on the project.

You should, however, be aware that enforcing referential integrity does affect performance when carrying out bulk inserts and updates. This is due to the fact that each value has to be validated against the acceptable values. In such a situation, it is often more efficient to validate the database after the inserts/updates have taken place.

The Principles of Data Normalization

The efficiency of a relational database is a function of the quality of its design, and the nature of the application or applications using the database. Some applications might do a lot of updates, while others might rarely update the data, but do frequent queries. These differences are critical in database design.

Data Redundancy

One characteristic of a well-designed relational database is that **data redundancy** is minimized, thereby increasing efficiency of updating. Data redundancy, as the name implies, means that the same data has to be repeated in a number of places. To illustrate this, look again at the example that we saw earlier of storing the data about employees and their reviews:

```
1, Smith, John, 111 Tree Ln, 3/97, 2
2, Smith, John, 111 Tree Ln, 3/98, 1
3; Jones, Sally,123 First St,3/98, 1
```

Storing the data in this way means that, for each review, we have to repeat John Smith's full name and address, which is a prime example of data redundancy. If this trend continued, then after ten years there would be a whole list of review dates all containing his name and address, which would affect the speed of updating the database and waste valuable processing time.

Note that it is not possible to eliminate data redundancy totally — at the very least we will need to repeat the foreign key that links the detailed information about the employee to the table containing the employee's review information.

In addition, a database has to be designed in such a way that tables can be joined in an efficient manner, especially when querying data. Based on these requirements, E. F. Codd (see Appendix A) developed the concept of **data normalization**. This is essentially the process of organizing data into tables, in a manner that eliminates the duplication of data and assures that the columns in a table are related by only one **key value**.

Database Theory

Anomalies

Another characteristic of a well-designed database is that there should be no anomalies arising as a result of the modification of the database, or a table within the database. There are three different types of anomaly that can occur:

- Update anomaly
- Deletion anomaly
- Addition anomaly

In a fully normalized database, there should be no situation where modifying the database requires entering one type of information before adding another type, where the first piece of information is not a function of the second. Using the above employee list example, the situation should not occur where the review information is entered before the employee information, since the latter is *not* a function of the former. However, the reverse situation can occur, since review information *is* a function of the employee —the employee's details can be in the database before the review information is entered.

Furthermore, care must be taken when deleting one type of information so that another type is not lost as well. Using our employee/review example once again, we would not want to lose information on an employee if the corresponding review information is deleted. The key here is that the meaning of the employee information does not depend on the review information. On the other hand, if the employee information is deleted, the review information must also be deleted, since its meaning does depend on the employee's details.

Finally, changing one piece of data must not require updating multiple records — if an employee's address changes, several records have to be updated. We will see more of this employee/review example later on.

Functional Dependence

Before discussing data normalization in detail, it is important to understand the concept of **functional dependence** — two columns are functionally dependent when, for any given row, the value of one column implies the value of the other.

In other words, the value of column 1 determines what the value of column 2 will be. When we refer to one column being *dependent* on the other, this is what we mean. A column that determines the value of a second column is quite logically called the **determinate**. Full functional dependency means that if the determinate is a composite of several fields, the dependent column is a function of all of them.

Normal Forms

The degree of normalization can be described by a progression of seven **normal forms**, listed below, and starting with the least normalized:

- ❏ First Normal Form
- ❏ Second Normal Form
- ❏ Third Normal Form
- ❏ Boyce-Codd Normal Form
- ❏ Fourth Normal Form
- ❏ Fifth Normal Form
- ❏ Domain/Key Normal Form

As data is **normalized** it must satisfy stricter constraints on independence and duplication of data. As we've discussed above, all tables in the database can ideally be modified without requiring extra data, losing data or modifying redundant data. We will see this concept in action as we proceed.

First Normal Form

First normal form (1NF) is the initial level of data normalization. Essentially, any table that meets the criteria of a relational table is in 1NF:

- ❏ There are no repeating groups
- ❏ There is only one value in each column/row pair

In addition to these characteristics of 1NF, all relational tables are unordered.

Second Normal Form

Second normal form (2NF) is built upon the 1NF, with the additional constraint that the non-key columns must depend upon (they are a function of) the entire key — that is, all of the columns that make up the key.

Suppose we have a table that has fields for city, state and local income tax rate, as well as some other characteristics of the cities in question:

City	State	Tax Rate	Population	Climate
Columbia	MD	10%	100,000	Moderate
Columbia	MO	5%	65,000	Moderate
Bethesda	MD	10%	110,000	Moderate
Los Angeles	CA	15%	1,000,000	Warm

For the purpose of this example, let's assume that cities cannot implement their own income tax, so local income tax is determined only by the state. The above data is not in 2NF, since the key value would be a composite of city and state — we need to distinguish between Columbia, Maryland and Columbia, Missouri — and income tax is only a function of the state. Hence, both Columbia, Maryland and Bethesda, Maryland have the same tax rate.

The normalization step in this case would be to create a separate table for state and income tax rate, joined to the first table by the `State` column:

State	Tax Rate
MD	10%
CA	15%
MO	5%

The tax rate column can now be eliminated from the original table, thus normalizing it to 2NF.

Third Normal Form

Third normal form (**3NF**) is 2NF with the additional constraint that only the key field can determine all non-key fields. In addition, non-key fields must not depend on each other.

Suppose in an employee table, we not only have the fields `EmpID`, `LastName`, `FirstName` and `Address`, but also fields for `ReviewDate` and `Rating`. The table would not be in 3NF as `Rating` is related to `ReviewDate` as well as `EmpID`. The appropriate change would be to create a new table with the composite key of `ReviewDate` and `EmpID` and the `Rating`, as well as any other fields determined by `EmpID` and `ReviewDate`.

3NF is the most common normal form — most databases are normalized to this level. It is the Industry Standard. Unlike 2NF and 1NF it allows for easy updating, deletion and insertion of data.

To understand this better, let's adapt the employee/review example that we have been referring to. The table in 2NF would be as follows:

EmpID	LastName	FirstName	Address	RewiewDate	Rating
1	Smith	John	111 Tree Ln	3/97	2
1	Smith	John	111 Tree Ln	3/98	1
2	Jones	Sally	123 First St.	3/98	1

In this case, we could not enter employee information without including information on reviews. Similarly, when we add review information, we must include all the other information about the employee. Furthermore, deleting the review information would result in the employee information being deleted. Finally, updating employee information is more difficult than it need be, as the information for each record for a given employee must be updated. If John Smith moves, two records have to be updated.

Now, let's put the table in 3NF:

EmpID	LastName	FirstName	Address
1	Smith	John	111 Tree Ln
2	Jones	Sally	123 First St.

EmpID	ReviewDate	Rating
1	3/97	2
1	3/98	1
2	3/98	1

Notice how structuring the data in this way solves the problems listed above. We can add information about an employee without having any information about the review and we can delete review information without touching employee information. Any change employee information will not affect the review information — we only have to make the change in one place. Notice too that we no longer have duplicate data. The tables are also in the 3NF. In the first table, EmpID determines the other columns — FirstName, LastName and Address, and in the second table EmpID and Date form a composite key which determines Rating.

Boyce-Codd Normal Form

While 3NF is a very practical form, the data may still not be totally normalized. **Boyce-Codd normal form (BCNF)** is very similar to 3NF, but has an additional restriction — all the determinate columns must uniquely identify the record. (Recall that a **candidate key** is a column or columns, which uniquely identifies each row.) As it turns out, our previous example actually is in BCNF. In the employee table above, the EmpID is a determinate and it is also a candidate key, as EmpID uniquely identifies each employee. In the review table that follows, the composite key of EmpID and ReviewDate determines Rating. This composite key is also a candidate key as EmpID and ReviewDate uniquely identify the record.

Consider now a different table, showing students with their exam grades:

StudentID	ClassID	NumberGrade	LetterGrade
1	300	95	A
2	300	85	B
3	400	95	A

In this case, the composite key is StudentID and ClassID. However, although NumberGrade determines LetterGrade, it does not uniquely identify the row. Thus, this table is not in BCNF. To put this table in BCNF, we'd have to break it up and have a separate table mapping the number grade to the letter grade.

StudentID	ClassID	NumberGrade
1	300	95
2	300	85
3	400	95

NumberGrade	LetterGrade
95	A
85	B
75	C

Most databases are never normalized beyond BCNF, and the following descriptions are included for completeness.

Fourth Normal Form

Fourth normal form (**4NF**) is built upon BCNF, but with one more restriction. If there is a non-trivial **multi-valued dependency** (**MVD**) between two columns A and B, all other columns must be functionally dependent on column A. Let's take a moment to see what this means.

A trivial MVD exists where there are two columns A and B, and A implies a set of possible values in B. In other words, for all the rows in the table, the value of B is a function of the value of A.

In the case of a non-trivial multi-valued dependency, column A implies a set of possible values in column B (as in the trivial case already described), but the values of all the other columns in the table are independent of B's dependency on A. Hence the other columns must be functionally dependent only on column A. An alternative definition of non-trivial multi-valued dependency is as follows:

> "In a relation having at least three attributes a MVD exists between two attributes, say X and Y, if the values of Y depends only on the value of X, regardless of the values of the other attributes in the relation."

Therefore, there can be no multi-valued dependency, if a value in column A maps to several values in the column B, and the value for each row in B is determines a value in a third column C.

For example, let us consider again the student/grade table above. The StudentID and ClassID composite key maps to only a small number of letter grades. However, since letter grades are a function of number grades, the other non-key column, this is not an example of a non-trivial MVD.

Suppose we took the normalized version of the student/grades table, and added a non-key column that was the rating they gave the professor:

StudentID	ClassID	NumberGrade	ProfRating
1	300	95	70
2	300	85	60
3	400	95	75

Since ProfRating would not be directly related to NumberGrade, although one could argue there is an indirect relationship, we would have an example of a non-trivial MVD. However, the table is in 4NF since ProfRating is a function of StudentID and ClassID. Note that we're assuming here that a student can only register for a class once. Otherwise, the key of StudentID and ClassID would not uniquely identify each row, thus taking the table out of BCNF, a precondition for 4NF.

Fifth Normal Form

Fifth normal form (**5NF**) deals with a very specific situation where cyclic data may exist. Cyclic data occurs when links exist between multiple tables such that they are all linked together in a cyclic fashion, as shown in the screenshot below:

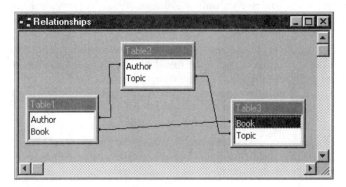

If this happens, one is in danger of decomposing the tables too far, which can lead to inconsistent data. In fact, one definition of 5NF is that a table cannot be decomposed without losing or changing information, leaving the database in an inconsistent state.

Domain/Key Normal Form

The ultimate normal form is **domain/key normal form** (**DKNF**). In this case, there should be no anomalies arising from any modification of the data:

❑ Adding data doesn't require the knowledge of extra data

❑ Deleting one piece of data doesn't delete any extra data

❑ When one row of data is updated other redundant rows don't need to be updated

Data Normalization — An Example

So, now that we've defined the different levels of data normalization, let's look in detail at a real database example. It is often the cases, that a user starts with a simple spreadsheet and only later decides to convert it to a database. In this section, we'll look at an example that does just that, and it will also serve us later on in the book when we go on to our programmatic examples.

Here is our initial spreadsheet, which logs various weight-training activities:

Person	Date	Exercise	Set 1 Weight	Set 1 Reps	Set 2 Weight	Set 2 Reps	Set 3 Weight	Set 3 Reps
Sally	5/20/98	Squat	110	12	110	12	110	10
Sally	5/24/98	Squat	125	10	125	8	125	8
Sally	5/24/98	Leg Extension	75	12	75	12	75	12
Sally	5/24/98	Lunge	15	12	15	12	15	12
Sally	5/24/98	Leg Lifts	60	12	60	12	60	12
Sally	5/24/98	Leg Press	150	12	150	12	150	12

Suppose we want to turn this simple table into a relational database. It is in tabular form, but there are repeating groups (Set 1 Weight, Set 2 Weight, Set 1 Reps, Set 2 Reps, etc.), so it is not relational.

There are also other problems. In the above table, Person, Exercise and Date identify each row, but these don't uniquely define each value, as Weight and Reps can also be related to the Set. You can see that we are going to have a problem with this layout if we decide to include more than three sets. Furthermore, we cannot add information about an exercise without having to include information about the exercise session (that is the person and the date). And suppose we wanted to include a description of each exercise — it would have to be duplicated on every line.

So, let's set about implementing the first step by removing the repeating groups:

Person	Height	PersonWeight	Exercise	Date	Set	Reps	Weight (rep)
Sally	5' 4"	120	Squat	5/20/98	1	12	110
Sally	5' 4"	120	Squat	5/20/98	2	12	110
Sally	5' 4"	120	Squat	5/20/98	3	10	110
Sally	5' 4"	120	Squat	5/24/98	4	10	125
Sally	5' 4"	120	Squat	5/24/98	5	8	125
Sally	5' 4"	120	Squat	5/24/98	6	8	125
Sally	5' 4"	120	Leg Extension	5/24/98	1	12	75
Sally	5' 4"	120	Leg Extension	5/24/98	2	12	75
Sally	5' 4"	120	Leg Extension	5/24/98	3	12	75

Database Theory

Person	Height	PersonWeight	Exercise	Date	Set	Reps	Weight(rep)
Sally	5' 4"	120	Lunge	5/24/98	1	12	15
Sally	5' 4"	120	Lunge	5/24/98	2	12	15
Sally	5' 4"	120	Lunge	5/24/98	3	12	15
Sally	5' 4"	120	Dead Lift	5/24/98	1	12	60
Sally	5' 4"	120	Dead Lift	5/24/98	2	12	60
Sally	5' 4"	120	Dead Lift	5/24/98	3	12	60
Sally	5' 4"	120	Leg Press	5/24/98	1	12	150
Sally	5' 4"	120	Leg Press	5/24/98	2	12	150
Sally	5' 4"	120	Leg Press	5/24/98	3	12	150

In developing the database, we have also added Sally's height and weight. This table now meets the requirements of 1NF — it is in tabular form and there are no longer any repeating groups. The key is a composite of Person, Exercise, Date and Set.

However, the table is not yet in 2NF, as Sally's height and weight only depend on Sally, not the exercise, date and set. Therefore, let's separate out the information about Sally into another table. We now have a new person table:

PersonID	Name	Height	PersonWeight
1	Sally	5' 4"	120
2	John	6' 0"	185

Shown below is the new version of the log table. I've added a column for 'difficulty' and for the purposes of this example, let's assume that difficulty is based on weight.

This is now almost in 2NF as the non-key columns (Rep, Weight) are a function of the entire key.

PersonID	Exercise	Date	Set	Reps	Weight	Difficulty
1	Squat	5/24/98	1	12	110	2
1	Squat	5/24/98	2	12	110	2
1	Squat	5/24/98	3	10	110	2
1	Squat	5/24/98	4	10	125	3

PersonID	Exercise	Date	Set	Reps	Weight	Difficulty
1	Squat	5/24/98	5	8	125	3
1	Squat	5/24/98	6	8	125	3
1	Leg Extension	5/24/98	1	12	75	2
1	Leg Extension	5/24/98	2	12	75	2
1	Leg Extension	5/24/98	3	12	75	2
1	Lunge	5/24/98	1	12	15	2
1	Lunge	5/24/98	2	12	15	2
1	Lunge	5/24/98	3	12	15	2
1	Dead Lift	5/24/98	1	12	60	1
1	Dead Lift	5/24/98	2	12	60	1
1	Dead Lift	5/24/98	3	12	60	1

The `Difficulty` column, however, is a function of `Weight` and `Exercise`. The table is therefore not in 3NF as difficulty is a function of a non-key value. Furthermore, adding this `Difficulty` column takes it out of 2NF since it's not a function of the entire key. Therefore we need to separate out this column. Since we might want to add some information about the exercises, we'll separate that out as well.

Shown below are our new versions of the following:

- ❑   The Exercise Table
- ❑   The Difficulty Table
- ❑   The Log Table

ExerciseID	Exercise
1	Squat
2	Leg Extension
3	Lunge
4	Dead Lift
5	Leg Press

ExerciseID	Weight	Difficulty
1	110	2
1	125	3
2	75	2
3	15	2
4	60	1
5	150	3

PersonID	ExerciseID	Date	Set	Reps	Weight
1	1	5/20/98	1	12	110
1	1	5/20/98	2	12	110
1	1	5/20/98	3	10	110
1	1	5/24/98	4	10	125
1	1	5/24/98	5	8	125
1	1	5/24/98	6	8	125
1	2	5/24/98	1	12	75
1	2	5/24/98	2	12	75
...	...	...	...	...	...

Notice that we can now add more information about the exercises (such as a column for description), without having to change the log table at all. We were also able to add information about John without having any workout information about him yet. Furthermore, you can do as many sets or as few as you'd like without a problem. (Note that we used these three tables earlier in this chapter when we were discussing primary/foreign keys.)

In the log table, PersonID, ExerciseID, Date and Set form the composite key for, and uniquely identify each set of Rep/Weight. This table is in 2NF, because the Weight and Reps depend upon the entire key. For example, with ExerciseID of value 1, you need to know the person doing the exercise, the date, and the set to get the values of for the reps and weight. For 3NF, each set of attributes must be only a function of the key. Clearly, this is the case here, because by having the key information, you can find the reps and weight.

Our database actually goes beyond the normal requirement to be normalized to 3NF. In each of the tables, the key uniquely identifies each row. The exercise and difficulty tables have only a trivial MVD, so the table is normalized to 4NF. There is a potential non-trivial MVD in the user table (since you can have two Johns that are 6'), but as all the attributes are directly related to the PersonID, *the table is still in 4NF. In the log table, the* Weight *and* Reps *columns are determined by the combination of* PersonID, ExerciseID, Date *and* Set.

Practical Aspects of Normalization

In an ideal world, you would always seek to normalize a database to the maximum level, that is, to DKNF. In the real world, however, this hardly ever occurs, as a balance has to be made between the competing requirements of the ease and speed of updating and the efficiency of the querying process. In practical terms, this limits the level of normalization that can be achieved.

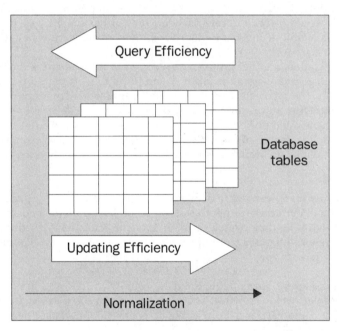

The main benefit of normalization is that it leads to databases that are extremely easy to modify. However, the main drawback of normalization is reduced performance when querying data. In designing a database, we should initially normalize the data as fully as possible, before looking to see if it is appropriate to undo some of the normalization by merging tables back together.

In a relational database, the cornerstone of querying data is the joining of tables. However, there are costs incurred in doing joins — such as complex joins which consume processor time. Therefore, if many data queries involve the same complex join, we should consider redesigning the tables so that such a join is unnecessary. The process of modifying tables in this way is known as **denormalization**. The purpose of denormalization is to improve efficiency by avoiding time consuming or common joins. However, it should be noted that there are always tradeoffs. While denormalization might improve query speed and efficiency, it may make updating more complex or clumsy. So, in addition to considering what queries and joins are commonly done, we have to consider how frequently updates are carried out, relative to queries.

Another possible situation can be demonstrated using our weight training example. We may decide to create a non-normalized table, if we are certain that there will only ever be three `Weight/Reps` sets. A better example might be that of a bowling sheet, where there are a fixed number of frames per game. In cases like these, it is probably more efficient to retrieve a person's performance during a bowling match or training session from a non-normalized table. The reason for this is that there are far fewer rows to be searched when carrying out a query than in a normalized table. However only simple queries can be carried out on non-normalized tables. In the case of the bowling sheet, it would be hard to select when a bowler has scored, say, three or more strikes in a single game. This would be much simpler in a suitably designed normalized table.

When considering denormalization, another issue you may need to think about is the type of report that you might wish to generate from the tables. In addition to merging normalized tables back together, it might make sense to create a separate table, optimized for the report in question, which would allow quick and efficient printing. However, modifying the database would make it more complex, as the extra table must be kept up to date. Another possibility is to use the report you wish to generate to guide the design of the tables. Finally, some databases, such as SQL Server, enable the creation of views, which are defined as virtual tables that internally query the database tables.

As you can tell, there are many instances where denormalization is necessary for performance reasons. However, a decision to denormalize a series of joined tables has to be made carefully as it could lead to problems in modifying data, which could give rise to the anomalies discussed earlier in the chapter. Also, while denormalization can improve performance in one type of data access, it can hurt performance in a different type.

As a rule, you should always start by normalizing the data, usually to 3NF, and then denormalize as necessary to resolve these performance issues. The reason we do this is that we don't want to denormalize unless we need to and carrying it out in the early stages of database development is better than having to do it later.

A Word about Object Oriented Databases

While the relational database model is currently the most popular one in practice, there is another model that is becoming increasingly important. This is the **object-oriented database model**.

In a typical relational database system, there are different models implemented for the database and the programs that search them. These programs might be written in C++, Visual Basic, C, or some other programming language. However they will all use **SQL (Structured Query Language)** to interface between the database and the program.

One common way a program interfaces with the data is to use SQL to retrieve the desired data by placing it in a special data structure known as a **recordset**, the structure of which is directly related to the structure of the table or join that it represents. You can move through the records in the recordset by using operations such as `Next` and `Previous` and select various fields within the records. The program then extracts data from the recordset and operates upon it. It should be noted that the data in the database is persistent, while that in the program is considered transient. Thus there is a separation between how data in the database is operated upon, through SQL, and how it is stored.

We will be discussing SQL in more depth in the next chapter.

The idea of an objected-oriented database is that the program and the data should be integrated seamlessly. This integration means that the program and the data are based on the same object model. In other words, the program should manipulate data inside the database and in the program, using the same object-oriented (OO) model, for example C++. In essence, versions of C++ and Smalltalk have been developed that operate upon the data in the database in the same way they would on a class/object within the program. One example of an OO databases is the Object Designs' Object Store (see: `http://www.odi.com`). Object Store has been around for 10 years.

In practice, pure OO databases are not used very frequently. It is a far newer technology that has not been as tried-and-tested as the relational model. However, many commonly used databases that use the OO model are what are known as hybrid object-relational systems. Applications are written using OO languages, such as C++, but access standard relational databases. They operate by mapping the database into classes, which the C++ code goes on to manipulate.

We will see example of a hybrid system when we use Microsoft Foundation Classes (MFC) in Chapter 3.

Indexing

Indexes are extremely important in database design. An **index** is basically an ordering of the rows in a table of a relational database. This ordering is based on one or more columns in the table. Usually it is a logical ordering, not the physical order of the rows. However, some databases, such as SQL Server, permit the creation of **clustered indexes**, where the database is physically ordered on the index values. If each value of the index comprises a unique value then it is known (not surprisingly) as a **unique index**.

Once the basic design for the database has been completed and the data is normalized, the most important thing to do next is to determine what your indexes will be. This is crucial, because if you query a field that is not indexed when it should be, or indexed when it should not be, then performance will be affected. Most modern databases maintain statistics on cardinality and distribution to determine whether or not to use indexes in a search.

Practicalities of Indexing

As with many things in the database world, indexing is a tradeoff between the speed of updates and the efficiency of queries. You do not want to have an excessive number of indexes, as each index slows down modification routines. Thus, if the database is queried frequently but modified infrequently, it would make sense to have more indexes. As you might imagine, indexing becomes extremely important in a large database where the search and sorting algorithms have to wade through hundreds of thousands (if not millions) of records.

You should also consider the distinction between single field and multiple field (compound) indexes. Single field indexes are usually more efficient than compound indexes, as the latter typically incur a large memory overhead. However, this is not always the case, if you take the number of bytes per column into account. A compound index of two four-byte fields will be more efficient than an index consisting of a fifty-byte character string, as far as minimizing disk I/O. Consequently, it is best to restrict indexing to columns of narrow width.

One of the most important issues choosing the fields to index. Obviously, if you are sorting or searching on a field, then indexing this field should increase the efficiency of these operations. As a general rule of thumb, you should consider indexing the following fields:

❑   Primary keys

❑   Foreign keys

❑   Fields that are to be used in joins

❑   Fields being searched upon

❑   Fields on which the data is to be sorted

This doesn't necessarily mean you should index all of the above — remember that each index you add carries an additional overhead. In general, indexes work best on fields with a high ratio of possible values compared to the number of rows. If a field is indexed which has a value that is replicated frequently throughout the records, it is less useful as an index. The primary key, on the other hand, has a unique value for each record by definition. The ratio for the number of different values to the number of rows is therefore 1:1, making it the ideal field on which to index. If you are using an Access database, then the primary key is indexed by default.

It is very important to carry out tests on the speed of querying and updating if you are planning a large database, as this will help you optimize performance. You can test the time taken for certain operations and adjust indexes based on the results of these tests.

If you are using Access, this can be done most easily using Access VBA code to run queries and updates over large volumes of data, and the time taken measured with different fields indexed each time. Some systems have tools that can help you here. SQL Server, for example, has a very useful feature called SHOWPLAN, which allows you to run a query, after which the Query Optimizer informs you of the efficiency of that query, such as whether a particular index was used or not. It will also indicate any changes that you might need to make. Oracle and Informix have similar facilities.

Clustered Indexes

When dealing with enterprise databases such as SQL Server, a distinction is made between clustered and non-clustered indexes. In a **clustered index**, the records are arranged physically in order, according to the indexed field, and as a result there can only be one in any given table. A clustered index is often more efficient than a non-clustered index, when a range of values is being searched. On the other hand, a non-clustered index is generally better for single-value or point searches. Thus, it is important to choose carefully which index will be a clustered index. As with choosing any index, you should look at what fields are frequently used for joins or regularly searched upon.

Stored Procedures and Queries

There are many cases where operations such as queries are performed on a frequent basis. Rather than have the database interpret these instructions each time, most modern databases allow some means of saving these instructions in the database, so that they can be accessed quickly. These are known in some databases as **stored procedures**, or in the case of Access, stored queries known as **QueryDefs**. Some databases such as SQL Server allow us to write stored procedures and execute them programmatically, and Access allows us to execute the QueryDefs programmatically. Note, however, that these two definitions are not equivalent.

The difference between stored procedures and QueryDefs is that stored procedures are actual procedures that operate on a database, rather than simply an SQL query. (A SQL query in a QueryDef can, however, modify the database.) These stored procedures are actually compiled as **execution plans**, which further reduce the work that needs to be done on each call. In the case of stored procedures, a lot of processing can be done on the server, thus reducing the work that needs to be done on the client.

There are several other advantages of stored procedures:

❑ The client only needs to know which procedure to invoke. It doesn't have to be aware of the details of implementing the procedure on various database platforms. This is a classic example of **information hiding**.

❑ Any client that can access the database can share the stored procedure.

❑ Security can be implemented on the server, preventing the client from directly accessing the data. This is analogous to private data members of a C++ class, and is another example of information hiding.

❑ Development of applications can be made easier as the stored procedures only need to be written once. This avoids both redundant coding and errors in programming.

❑ If we're dealing with an interpreted system, we can optimize the procedure at the time of creation, rather than at runtime.

Information hiding is keeping the internals of a module hidden from other modules, and only allows them to access the module from well-defined interfaces — in this case the stored procedure becomes a well-defined interface.

In the Oracle system, stored procedures take advantage of that database's particular memory model. The Oracle8 Server Concepts, which can be downloaded from `http://www.oracle.com` is a good reference.

One limitation of using stored procedures is that they tend not to be portable between different database systems, which is a problem if you are using software that has to deal with multiple databases. As part of your database design strategy, you should examine stored procedures/QueryDefs for yourself and carry out tests of their efficiency, as you would do for indexes.

Finally, in higher level databases such as Oracle, the native programming language is so robust that procedures can be organized into packages as an entire unit. In fact, Oracle's language PL/SQL is so sophisticated that it can be used to write an entire application. Even the Access VBA language can be used to write an application. However, the performance and flexibility may be limited.

Triggers

To complete our discussion of stored procedures, we should also look at **triggers**. Triggers are simply stored procedures that are set off when certain conditions are met. One use of triggers is to maintain the database in a consistent state, although their usefulness is not limited to this. They can also be used for such things as:

❑ Auditing database statistics

❑ Generating values for certain derived columns

❑ Validation statistics

In designing a database, using triggers, you must take into account the fact that they can be overused, making the database overly complex. Triggers can lead to other triggers being executed, if you tell them to, which can make it hard to tell exactly what's going on. A disadvantage of using triggers is that they tend to be non-portable.

A mainly desktop database like Access doesn't have triggers. However, it does have options for cascading updates and deletes, which are essentially triggers. ('Cascading' comes from 'cascading triggers' — i.e. triggers that set off other triggers.) This can be a very useful feature for handling database integrity, as was discussed earlier in the section on referential integrity.

Note that there are several types of integrity associated with databases:

- ❑ Referential (as we've discussed)
- ❑ Entity (unique rows, enforced by primary keys)
- ❑ Domain integrity (data values, format and type)

We've seen the concept of domain integrity when referring to foreign keys, which enforce the possible values a particular column can contain.

Cursors

There are two more aspect of relational databases that we should look at briefly — cursors and transactions. Whereas queries and stored procedures access several records at once, sometimes you might want to access and process just one record at a time. This is achieved by using **cursors**, which are structures that can be programmed to navigate around a recordset.

An important property of a cursor is that it stores the position of the next record to be accessed. The simple cursor operations include moving to the next row, and updating and deleting records. More sophisticated cursor operations permit scrolling forwards and backwards through the recordset, moving to the first or last record, and accessing a record that meets specific criteria.

All the major enterprise databases such as SQL Server and Oracle implement cursors. They are also implemented in the major data access methodologies, such as ODBC, DAO and OLE DB.

Transactions

Another common term that is often used in the database world is **transaction**. The concept of a transaction is a very straightforward one. There are cases where one database operation automatically leads to a second operation being carried out (for example changing a value of a field followed by an update on the modified record). Failure to carry out the second operation would leave the database in an inconsistent state. We can group such operations together in a transaction.

Within a transaction two actions are possible. Either all required operations must be carried out and then **committed**, i.e. written, to the database, or, if an operation fails, the entire group of operations is canceled, known as **rollback**. Transactions can be simple as the previous example or a highly complex sequence of commands. In some databases transactions can be nested — that is, there can be transactions within transactions.

Designing Your Database

Throughout this chapter we have talked about various design considerations. In particular we've discussed normalization, denormalization, key values and indexing. For basic databases, these methods are sufficient to allow you to produce a satisfactory database design.

However, for a large or complex database following these methods may not be sufficient to produce an efficient database. However, there are more formal methods for designing databases that are very helpful, for example the **Entity-Relationship Model** or **ER Model**, introduced in 1976[2].

Basically this models the database in terms of **entities** and the **relationships** between them. By *entity* we mean either a physical entity, such as a person, or an abstract entity, such as a set in a workout. (An entity is also known as an **object**.) Entities can be regular entities, as already described, or what is known as 'weak' entities. A **weak entity** is simply an entity whose existence depends on the existence of another — for example an exercise log record is dependent on the existence of the person who is exercising.

Entities contain **properties**, which can be **simple** (like `PersonID`) or **composite**. A property can be designated a **key property**. As with a key value in a table, a key property implies a unique value for each entity. An example of a property would be a person's last name or first name.

Relationships are expressed in terms of the **cardinality** between one entity and another. Consistent with database theory, relationships can be one-to-one (1:1), one-to-many (1:N) or many-to-many (M:N), though we don't usually tend to have many of the third type of relationship. The ER model also includes the term **subtype**, which can be described in terms of an *'is-a'* relationship (for example, exerciser *is a* person). In C++ terms, this is the equivalent of public inheritance.

---

[2] Chen, P.P., *The Entity-Relationship Model – Towards a Unified View of Data*, ACM TODS 1:1, 1976

The figure below is an example of an ER diagram, based on our earlier exercise log example:

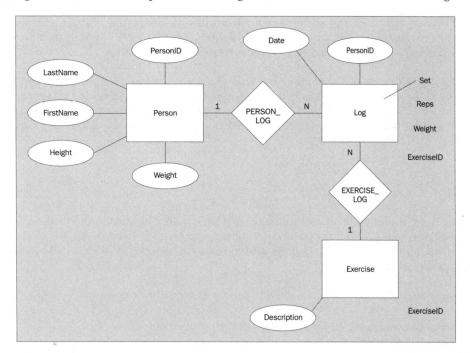

Notice how the entities map on to the normalized tables and how the relationships between them are based on the relationships between primary and foreign keys, although this diagram doesn't state which field we'll actually be joining on.) It also shows whether there is a 1:1, 1:N or M:N relationship between the entities.

Access has the capacity to produce similar diagrams of the tables you create:

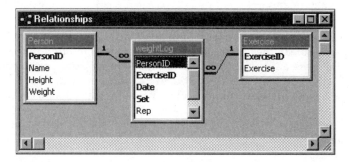

Of course, you should first diagram your database design and then implement it. You can use Access itself as a design tool and either refine the initial design in Access until we have production database, or port it to a more robust system such as Oracle or SQL Server.

From the definitions above we can get a broad idea of how ER modeling is used. After carefully determining ER modeling requirements (which is a topic of it own and is outside the scope of this book), you need to identify the entities in the system, determine the properties of these entities as well as the relationships between them, including whether they are 1:1, 1:N or M:N. If they are M:N an intermediate table should be used to model the relationship.

It should be noted that ER modeling is not the only type of what is termed 'semantic modeling or extended models'. These are simply models that are designed to capture the meaning inherent in the database being designed. ER modeling is popular and there are now tools designed to support it, thus making it easier for a designer to create his or her design and produce a database directly from it.

Summary

In this chapter we have discussed the basics of database design including data normalization, selecting keys, indexing, using stored procedures to improve performance and modeling your data. These techniques are important in facilitating the design of an efficient database that will be easy to work with programmatically.

To conclude, when designing a database, we need to carry out the following steps:

- ❑ Normalize your database based on the definitions presented in this chapter
- ❑ Use the principles presented in this chapter to select your primary keys
- ❑ Choose sensible fields to index on
- ❑ Experiment with the design to optimize performance, adding and removing indexes, designing stored procedures (or in the case of access, stored queries) and denormalize as required
- ❑ Test the design thoroughly

By following these guidelines, you should produce a high quality design for your database. In practice, this doesn't necessarily mean the end of the process. You may well find that when the database is actually in use there are adjustments that can be made to improve performance. In fact, the way the database is actually used may differ from the use anticipated when it was created. However, by employing these methods you will hopefully avoid any major database bottlenecks.

In the next chapter we will move on to examine a very important aspect of database programming – Structured Query Language, or SQL.

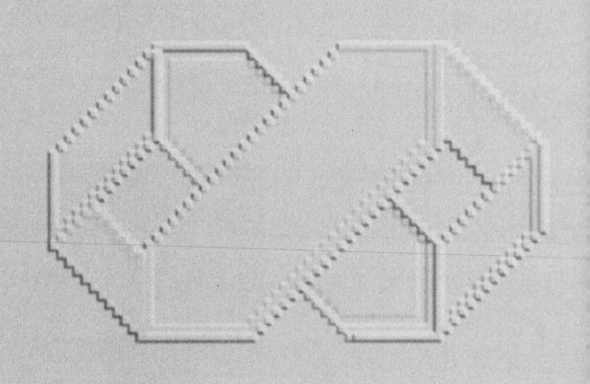

2

An Introduction to Structured Query Language

In this chapter, we'll be covering the **Structured Query Language (SQL)**, which forms an interface between the programmer and the database. In particular, we'll be looking at:

❑   What SQL is and why we need it

❑   How to perform basic queries and using the SELECT statement

❑   How to perform more advanced queries, including joins and sorts

❑   Basic data manipulation, that is, inserting, deleting and updating records

❑   An introduction to **Data Definition Language (DDL)**

SQL is, however, a very large subject, and we shall just be getting a taste of it in this chapter. You should learn enough here to allow you to understand the practical examples we'll be looking at later in the book, but if you want to learn about it in more detail, you should check out one of the references listed in Appendix A

What is SQL?

SQL is the principal language by which computer users communicate with a relational database. It was originally called 'Structured English Query Language' and is usually pronounced *sequel*. It is now standardized, as ANSI X3.135-1992 (or 'SQL-92' for short) and is used, with some minor differences, on most, if not all, relational databases. If you are going to work with databases, it is absolutely essential you become familiar with SQL.

SQL is very powerful because it allows you to:

❑   Manipulate the database itself

❑   Query data in the database

❑   Manipulate data in the database

The part of SQL that deals with manipulating the database itself (rather than the data therein)is known as **DDL**, or **Data Definition Language**. The part that deals with manipulating and querying the data in the database is known as **DML**, or **Data Manipulation Language**. Most modern relational databases running on Windows-based operating systems allow users to utilize both DDL, as well as a graphical interface to manipulate the database. This is also true for UNIX systems that possess a MOTIF GUI, which may be of importance as many databases are hosted on UNIX systems. Furthermore, most of these databases provide the user with an interface for data manipulation. The graphical interface used by Microsoft Access is a good example of this:

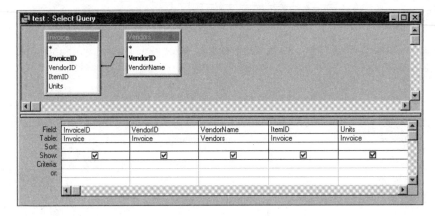

Notice how the tables we wish to be included in the query can be added to the interface, and then the required fields selected by a simple drag and drop procedure. You can also limit the records returned, such as including selection criteria and sorting the included fields. The equivalent query in SQL would take the form:

```
SELECT Invoice.InvoiceID, Invoice.VendorID,
       Vendors.VendorName, Invoice.ItemID,
       Invoice.Units
FROM Invoice
INNER JOIN Vendors ON Invoice.VendorID=Vendors.VendorID
```

Don't worry about the syntax used in this statement just yet — we'll be finding out exactly what this means as we go through the chapter.

Our Example Database

In this chapter, we will focus on an example database in order to learn about SQL. This database is very simple, consisting of only three tables:

❑   A vendor table

❑   An invoice table

❑   An item table

The screenshot below shows the relationships between the three tables as shown in Access:

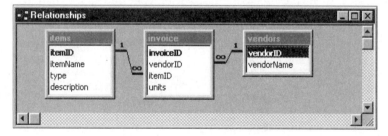

The symbol 1 : • signifies a '1-to-many' relationship. In our invoice database, this means that one item can be in many invoices and one vendor can have many invoices. The three primary keys of the tables shown above are `VendorID`, `InvoiceID` and `ItemID` — these are set as `AutoNumbers` in Access, which means they are generated automatically by Access to ensure that each record in a table contains a unique value for the primary key. Each time a new record is added, Access increments the number for the ID by 1.

> *If you want to try out some of the SQL statements demonstrated in this chapter, you can download the sample database from the Wrox Press web site, at `http://www.wrox.com`.*

Querying Data: the SELECT statement

The most widely used statement in SQL is the SELECT statement, which allows you to access the data in a database in a very flexible manner. In addition to simply returning the required data, you can also have some control over how it is returned, by sorting, grouping and labeling the columns.

SELECT is what is known as a **reserved word** — that is, it is recognized by SQL as having a special meaning. Other examples of reserved words in SQL are FROM, WHERE and INSERT, which we'll see more of later in the chapter. They are called reserved words because they cannot be used outside of their SQL-defined context — they cannot be used as variable names.

Introduction to the SQL SELECT Statement

The SELECT statement has the following syntax:

```
SELECT [ALL|DISTINCT] <[table].columnA, [table].columnB>
FROM <tables>
WHERE <filters>
GROUP BY <columns used to combine records based on column value>
HAVING <filter on grouped records>
ORDER BY <columns to be sorted on>
```

Note the syntax used to specify the required columns. The brackets indicate something that can be optional. It is only necessary to specify the table name ([table].columnName) if there are multiple tables containing the same specified field. If, on the other hand, there is only one table making up the query, you only need specify the column name. We'll see what the rest of this statement means as we go through the chapter.

Consider our vendor table:

VendorID	VendorName
1	Joe's Parts
2	Part Store
3	Widget City
4	Pete's Place
5	All Parts

The following line shows an example of a simple query on this data:

```
SELECT * FROM Vendors WHERE VendorID = 3
```

This statement would return all the fields (the * means all fields) from the vendor table for the record with a VendorID of 3. This is an example of a **filter**.

The output from this statement is as follows:

VendorID	VendorName
3	Widget City

SELECT, FROM and WHERE are the most basic elements of the SELECT statement. In the rest of this section, we'll be looking in greater detail at these and the other elements that make up the SELECT statement.

The SELECT Element

The SELECT element has two parts. The first part states whether you want all rows returned (ALL) or just non-duplicate rows (DISTINCT). While each row in a given table must be unique, often one only returns a subset of the columns. Hence there is the possibility of duplicates and the need for DISTINCT. The second part lists the columns to be returned. As we saw above, the columns can either be specified by their name only, or by their table and name (Table.ColumnName). This becomes necessary in queries using multiple tables where two or more tables share the same column name.

When listing the columns, we can also specify a title for the output. For example, in Access we can specify <ColumnName> AS <Output Title> which will be used as the header in the resulting table. (Note that the angled brackets here represent what is essentially a variable.) In a query, the <ColumnName> will be replaced by in the output by the specified <Output Title>.

An example of this is shown below, where the string Item replaces the more cryptic ItemID:

```
SELECT Invoice.InvoiceID, Invoice.ItemID AS Item FROM Invoice
```

The result of this query is the following:

InvoiceID	Item
1	1
19	3
22	1
3	2
4	5
20	2
21	3
2	3
...	...

The FROM and WHERE Elements

The FROM element simply lists the tables in the database that are involved in the query. We can specify one or more tables from which we wish to retrieve data. In the example above, we simply selected two fields from one table. Let's take a look now at how we might select data from more than one table.

To illustrate this, let's return to our invoice example. Consider the vendor and invoice tables:

VendorID	VendorName
1	Joe's Parts
2	Part Store
3	Widget City
4	Pete's Place
5	All Parts

InvoiceID	VendorID	ItemID	Units
1	1	1	300
2	4	3	4000
3	2	2	6000
4	2	5	3000
5	5	2	2000
...	...	...	...

So, to look at a vendor's invoices, we could write the following query:

```
SELECT Vendors.VendorID, Vendors.VendorName,
       Invoice.InvoiceID, Invoice.ItemID, Invoice.Units
FROM Vendors, Invoice
WHERE Invoice.VendorID = Vendors.VendorID
```

This would result in the following table output:

VendorID	VendorName	InvoiceID	ItemID	Units
1	Joe's Parts	1	1	300
1	Joe's Parts	19	3	4000
1	Joe's Parts	22	1	3000

VendorID	VendorName	InvoiceID	ItemID	Units
2	Part Store	3	2	6000
2	Part Store	4	5	3000
3	Widget City	20	2	4000
3	Widget City	21	3	4000
4	Pete's Place	2	3	4000
...	...	...	...	...

Earlier we saw the WHERE element being used as a filter, but here it is being used to join the two tables. In order to obtain a consistent recordset, we only select records where the VendorID fields in each of the tables have matching values. As you might expect from the SELECT clause in our query, the resulting table includes the VendorName field from the Vendor table, the InvoiceID, ItemID and Units fields from the Invoice table and the VendorID field from both tables.

There is, however, another method for joining tables, and we'll be looking at this in the next section.

More Advanced Queries: Joins

Whenever two or more tables are brought together for the purpose of returning data from those tables, a **join** is the point at which the tables are linked. These tables are joined on key fields, as outlined in the previous chapter. In the above example, we joined the Invoice and Vendor tables on the VendorID field — the primary key of the Vendors table and a foreign key in the Invoice table.

In total, there are five types of join:

- ❑ **Inner join** — returns all rows where the key column value in table A is equal to the key column value in table B

- ❑ **Left outer join** — returns all rows from the table on the left side of the join operation and the rows from the table on the right side of the join operation that match

- ❑ **Right outer join** — returns all rows from the table on the right side of the join operation and the rows from the table on the left side of the join that match

- ❑ **Cross join** — returns the set of all possible combinations of rows from the joined tables, which is known as a **Cartesian product**

- ❑ **Full outer join** — returns the set of all the rows from the joined tables, even when there is no match

Some of these are not supported by all database vendors, and you should consult the vendor's documentation for the supported join types.

In this section, we'll describe each of these joins in full and look at some examples of how we use them.

Inner Joins

Inner joins are joins based on matching values in columns that are common to both tables, and rows from each table are only selected where these columns match. There are two ways of performing inner joins. The first, as we have already seen, is to use a WHERE clause:

```
SELECT Vendors.VendorID, Vendors.VendorName,
       Invoice.InvoiceID, Invoice.ItemID, Invoice.Units
FROM Vendors, Invoice
WHERE Invoice.VendorID = Vendors.VendorID
```

The more modern syntax, approved by the ANSI Standards Board, is now more commonly used:

```
SELECT Vendors.VendorID, Vendors.VendorName,
       Invoice.InvoiceID, Invoice.ItemID, Invoice.Units
FROM Invoice
INNER JOIN Vendors ON Invoice.VendorID = Vendors.VendorID;
```

Note that there is also a slight difference in the syntax of the two FROM elements — in the first example we need to specify both tables in the FROM element, whereas in the second example, we only specify one, as the second table with which it is joined is specified by the INNER JOIN element.

This query produces exactly the same result as the previous example, so you may be wondering what the advantage is in using it. Well, when using the latter syntax clearly separates the join from the filter — the INNER JOIN element specifies the join, leaving the WHERE element to specify the filter conditions. It is therefore good practice to use the INNER JOIN syntax.

Outer Joins

Outer joins between two tables are those where one table includes rows, regardless of whether or not they have a matching value in the other table, but the other table only includes those rows with matching values. In the resulting output, NULLs are used for fields from the first table where there is no match with the second table. (Recall that NULL, in terms of databases, means that the field is empty.) Since we are dealing with an output set, the restriction on NULL values doesn't apply.

There are two types of outer join:

❑   LEFT JOIN

❑   RIGHT JOIN

A LEFT JOIN is one where all rows are included from the table from the left of the join clause and only matching rows are included from the table on the right of the join clause. A RIGHT JOIN is just the opposite — all rows from the right hand table are included and only matching rows from the left.

Going back to the invoice example above, consider the following query:

```
SELECT Invoice.InvoiceID, Invoice.VendorID, Invoice.ItemID,
       Invoice.Units, Vendors.VendorID, Vendors.VendorName
FROM Invoice
LEFT JOIN Vendors ON Invoice.VendorID = Vendors.VendorID;
```

Note that VendorID is included twice to show exactly what is coming from which table. This is an example of a LEFT JOIN. The resulting output is shown below:

InvoiceID	Invoice. VendorID	ItemID	Units	Vendors. VendorID	VendorName
1	1	1	300	1	Joe's Parts
3	2	5	3000	2	Part Store
4	2	3	4000	2	Part Store
2	4	2	6000	4	Pete's Place
6	4	6	4000	4	Pete's Place
8	4	4	2000	4	Pete's Place
5	5	1	3000	5	All Parts
7	5	2	2000	5	All Parts

In this case, this query is essentially equivalent to an INNER JOIN, since all the Invoice records have a matching Vendor record.

Now let us look at the RIGHT JOIN. The query would look like this:

```
SELECT Invoice.InvoiceID, Invoice.VendorID, Invoice.ItemID,
       Invoice.Units, Vendors.VendorID, Vendors.VendorName
FROM Invoice
RIGHT JOIN Vendors ON Invoice.VendorID = Vendors.VendorID;
```

The resulting output is the following:

InvoiceID	Invoice. VendorID	ItemID	Units	Vendors. VendorID	VendorName
1	1	1	300	1	Joe's Parts
3	2	2	6000	2	Part Store
4	2	5	3000	2	Part Store
				3	Widget City
2	4	3	4000	4	Pete's Place
6	4	1	3000	4	Pete's Place
8	4	6	4000	4	Pete's Place
5	5	2	2000	5	All Parts
7	5	4	2000	5	All Parts

Notice that since Widget City doesn't have a matching invoice, its record has NULLs in the columns that come from the invoice table.

Cross Joins

A **cross join** is essentially the product of two or more joined tables. The output is every combination of rows from each table. For example, if table A has 4 rows (A1...A4) and table B has 4 rows (B1...B4). The output would consist of 16 rows, (A1B1, A1B2, A1B3, A1B4...A4B1, A4B2, A4B3, A4B4).

In the older syntax it is equivalent to including two or more tables in a SELECT statement, but excluding a WHERE element requiring matching values in key columns. The new ANSI-approved syntax is the CROSS JOIN element.

Note that not all databases support this syntax. In Access, for example, the syntax would be:

```
SELECT Invoice.InvoiceID, Invoice.VendorID, Vendors.VendorName,
       Invoice.ItemID, Invoice.Units
FROM Invoice, Vendors
```

In SQL Server 6.5, the more sophisticated syntax would be used:

```
SELECT Invoice.InvoiceID, Invoice.VendorID, Vendors.VendorName,
       Invoice.ItemID, Invoice.Units
FROM Invoice
CROSS JOIN Vendors
```

It should be noted that a cross join rarely produces useful results — it just dumps the contents of the tables into one very large table, and is very expensive in terms of query optimization. Thus their use is not recommended.

Full Outer Joins

Finally, we have the **full outer join**, where we include all the records of two or more tables, even where there are no matching fields. This is *not* the same as a cross join, as each row from each table is only included once. In other words, all the records from table A are included in the result set, and if there is no corresponding row in table B, the columns from table B are filled with NULLs. The rows from table B are included regardless of whether there is a corresponding row in A — the empty fields from table A are also filled with NULLs. This is essentially the same as the result of an inner join plus all the non-matching rows from each table.

The modern syntax is the following:

```
SELECT Invoice.InvoiceID, Invoice.VendorID, Vendors.VendorName,
       Invoice.ItemID, Invoice.Units
FROM Invoice
FULL OUTER JOIN Vendors ON Invoice.VendorID = Vendors.VendorID
```

This syntax is supported by Enterprise databases, such as SQL Server, but not Access. You should check the documentation on the specific database you are using.

Filter Elements

Filters are a critical part of the SELECT statement. They allow the user to limit the records returned to only those in which they are specifically interested. We saw a simple filter earlier, when we wanted to retrieve information about a specific vendor. There, we simply required that a particular field must equal a particular value.

The WHERE element is used to specify the criteria that have to be met, if a row is to be included in the selection.

These filters can be written using:

- ❑ Comparison operators
- ❑ Keywords

An Introduction to Structured Query Language

The comparison operators supported by SQL are shown in the table below:

Operator	Meaning
>	Greater Than
<	Less Than
=	Equal To
>=	Greater Than or Equal To
<=	Less Than or Equal To
<>	Not Equal To

The keywords summarized below in the following table:

Keyword	Meaning
AND	Logical AND
OR	Logical OR
BETWEEN	The element's value is between the two specified values
NOT BETWEEN	The element's value is not between the two specified values
IN	The element's value is in a list of values
NOT IN	The element's value is not in a list of values
LIKE	Similar to =, but allows wildcards
NOT LIKE	Similar to <>, but allows wildcards

If for example, we wanted to select just those invoices from Joe's Parts where the total number of units was greater than 1000, we could use the following command:

```
SELECT Invoice.InvoiceID, Invoice.VendorID, Vendors.VendorName,
       Invoice.ItemID, Invoice.Units
FROM Invoice
INNER JOIN Vendors ON Invoice.VendorID = Vendors.VendorID
WHERE (Vendors.VendorID = 1) AND (Units > 1000);
```

When using VendorID *in the* WHERE *clause, we need to specify which table we're referring to, as* VendorID *is a field in both of the tables involved in the query.*

The IN keyword is rather interesting. It can be used not only in the filter clause, but also (in Access at least) in the FROM clause to specify the database from which the specified table comes.

> *There are other keywords (*EXISTS *for example) that are supported by some enterprise databases, such as SQL Server, Oracle and Informix, but not by desktop systems, such as Access. It is best to check the documentation for your particular database system.*

More Advanced Elements: GROUP BY and HAVING

Sometimes we might want to aggregate our results based on a particular output row, and this is the purpose of the GROUP BY element. For example, suppose you are querying order data and you want aggregate totals based on Vendor.

The query might look something like this:

```
SELECT VendorName AS Vendor, Vendors.VendorID,
       SUM(Invoice.Units) AS [Total Units]
FROM Invoice
INNER JOIN Vendors ON Invoice.VendorID = Vendors.VendorID
GROUP BY VendorName, Vendors.VendorID
```

SUM([Invoice.Units]) in the above statement is an example of an **aggregate function**. Here, were are using the SUM() function to calculate the total number of units for each vendor, which is then output in the Total Units column. We'll see some more aggregate functions later.

Note that each column in the SELECT element has to either be in the GROUP BY element (that is the values which you're aggregating upon) or be an aggregate computation, such as the SUM(invoice.Units) statement above.

The first few records of the resulting output are the following:

Vendor	VendorID	Total Units
Joe's Parts	1	25373508
Part's and Stuff	10	24701508
Many Parts	11	24844560
Widget City	12	25170402
Widget Haven	13	24151487
Washington Widgets	14	25072414
...	...	...

Suppose we only want a list of some of the vendors, such as those with a `VendorID` of less than 10. This is an example of where you would use a `HAVING` element. This query would now have the following form:

```
SELECT VendorName AS Vendor, Vendors.VendorID,
       SUM(invoice.Units) AS [Total Units]
FROM Invoice
INNER JOIN Vendors ON Invoice.VendorID = Vendors.VendorID
GROUP BY VendorName, Vendors.VendorID
HAVING Vendors.VendorID < 10
```

The output you would obtain from such a query is shown below:

Vendor	VendorID	Total Units
Joe's Parts	1	25373508
Part Store	2	24490863
Widget City	3	24852363
Pete's Place	4	24994098
All Parts	5	25437413
Sixth and Lex	6	24754839
NY Parts	7	25879349
CA Parts	8	24250630
Midwest Parts	9	24925132

You may be wondering what the difference between the `HAVING` and `WHERE` elements is, as they appear to be doing very similar things. Technically speaking, `WHERE` applies the filter *before* the data is grouped or aggregated, while `HAVING` applies the filter afterwards. Therefore, if you wish to apply a filter to `Total Units`, `HAVING` would be the element to use. However, if one wishes to filter a non-aggregate value, either can be used. It should be pointed out that `HAVING` has little meaning separate from the `GROUP BY` clause.

Aggregate Functions

SQL supports a number of **aggregate functions**. These are functions that are used in `GROUP BY` elements to calculate the aggregate values. They are implemented on the server, thus avoiding unnecessary network traffic. We saw an example of an aggregate function earlier, when we used the `SUM([ColumnName])` function in the previous example.

Other commonly used aggregate functions include:

- ❑ COUNT([ColumnName]) — counts the number of records in the aggregate
- ❑ MAX([Expression]) — returns the highest value among the records in the aggregate
- ❑ MIN([Expression]) — returns the lowest value among the records in the aggregate

In addition to aggregate functions, most enterprise and desktop SQL applications implementations have mathematical functions, string functions, date functions and so on. These functions can be applied to return columns with calculated values.

Sorting

Often when we're doing a query, we want the data returned in a particular order. We can do this using the ORDER BY element to select any of the returned columns to sort upon. We can even sort on more than one column. Let's look again at the aggregation example we saw above. Suppose we wanted to see the results based on units —the query would look something like this:

```
SELECT Vendors.VendorName AS Vendor, Vendors.VendorID,
       SUM(Invoice.Units) AS [Total Units]
FROM Invoice
INNER JOIN Vendors ON Invoice.VendorID = Vendors.VendorID
GROUP BY Vendors.VendorName, Vendors.VendorID
ORDER BY SUM(Invoice.Units);
```

The resulting output would be the following:

Vendor	VendorID	Total Units
...	...	...
27th Street Parts	27	24318157
Ace Parts	21	24375128
Part Store	2	24490863
Lots of Parts	71	24543811
Cheap Parts	88	24567768

Vendor	VendorID	Total Units
Mays Parts	24	24587988
Main Line Parts	67	24588582
...	...	...

Updating Your Data: INSERT, UPDATE and DELETE Statements

Up until now, we have been concentrating on the various methods of retrieving, sorting and displaying our data using the SELECT statement. Now we turn to another important aspect of database usage — the modification of data using SQL's INSERT, UPDATE and DELETE statements.

INSERT

The INSERT statement is used to add records to the database. There are actually two types of INSERT statement. The first adds a single record to the table. The SQL syntax is as follows:

```
INSERT INTO <table> (<field1>, <field2>) VALUES (<value1>, <value2>)
```

Here, we simply give the values we want to insert into the specified fields.

The second INSERT statement adds records from an existing table. Its syntax looks like this:

```
INSERT INTO <table> [IN <external database>]
SELECT [source].<field1>, <field2>
FROM <table>
WHERE <filter clause>
```

Let's see how we'd use the INSERT statement in our Invoice database example. Here is how we'd add a record into the invoice table:

```
INSERT INTO Invoice (VendorID, ItemID, Units) VALUES (5, 100, 3000)
```

Note that we don't actually specify a value for the invoice ID here — this is a primary key with a unique value that is created automatically by the database.

The invoice table now looks like this:

InvoiceID	VendorID	ItemID	Units
1	1	1	300
2	4	3	4000
3	2	2	6000
4	2	5	3000
5	5	2	2000
6	4	1	3000
7	5	4	2000
8	4	6	4000
9	5	1	3000

The highlighted record is the one that has been added by the INSERT INTO statement above.

Now let's add multiple records to the Invoice table using a SQL statement — we can duplicate all of the Pete's Place orders (VendorID = 4) with the following statement:

```
INSERT INTO Invoice (VendorID, ItemID, Units)
SELECT VendorID, ItemID, Units
FROM Invoice
WHERE VendorID = 4
```

The invoice table now has three new records:

InvoiceID	VendorID	ItemID	Units
1	1	1	300
2	4	3	4000
3	2	2	6000
4	2	5	3000
5	5	2	2000

InvoiceID	VendorID	ItemID	Units
6	4	1	3000
7	5	4	2000
8	4	6	4000
9	5	1	3000
10	4	3	4000
11	4	1	3000
12	4	6	4000

Note that the SQL processing engine has a certain amount of intelligence. If we leave out the `ItemID` field from the `SELECT` element, it still completes the query.

```
INSERT INTO Invoice (VendorID, ItemID, Units)
SELECT VendorID, Units
FROM Invoice
WHERE VendorID = 4
```

The above `INSERT` statement will produce the following output, if the default value for `ItemID` is set to zero:

InvoiceID	VendorID	ItemID	Units
...	...	...	...
7	5	4	2000
8	4	6	4000
9	5	1	3000
10	4	3	4000
11	4	1	3000
12	4	6	4000
13	4	0	4000
14	4	0	3000
15	4	0	4000

Note that omitting fields in this way does not guarantee successful inserts in all circumstances. The `INSERT` statement would fail if, for instance, the omitted field was a string field that did not allow NULLs.

UPDATE

The UPDATE command is used to modify existing data in the database. An UPDATE statement takes the following form:

```
UPDATE table
SET <field1> = <value1>, <field2> = <value2>, ...
WHERE <filter statement>
```

Suppose we want to change the invoice with InvoiceID of 12 to be ItemID 700 and 5000 Units. The appropriate statement would be:

```
UPDATE Invoice
SET ItemID = 700, Units = 5000
WHERE InvoiceID = 12
```

The resulting table is shown below, where the updated record is highlighted:

InvoiceID	VendorID	ItemID	Units
...	...	...	...
9	5	1	3000
10	4	3	4000
11	4	1	3000
12	4	7	5000
13	4	0	4000
...	...	...	...

Note that if the WHERE clause does not uniquely identify a row, then multiple rows can be updated with a single UPDATE statement. Suppose we wanted to increase all of the orders for Joe's Parts (VendorID of 1) by 100. We could do this with the following SQL statement:

```
UPDATE Invoice
SET Units = Units + 100
WHERE VendorID = 1
```

DELETE

The DELETE statement, as its name suggests, removes the specified rows. It has the following syntax:

```
DELETE
FROM table
WHERE <filter statement>
```

Suppose we want to remove all the records without any `ItemID`, since such records are invalid. The `DELETE` statement we would need to do this is shown below:

```
DELETE FROM Invoice WHERE ItemID = 0
```

Defining Databases Programatically

So far in this chapter, we've been discussing elements of SQL's Data Manipulation Language (DML), and we've seen how to use this to query data in our database, add new data, update existing data and also delete records.

We'll now briefly discuss the Data Definition Language (DDL).
The major statements in DDL that we'll discuss are:

❑ CREATE TABLE

❑ CREATE INDEX

❑ ALTER TABLE

We will be focusing on the DDL syntax used in Microsoft Jet. Note that this is the database engine for Access only, and though Jet allows access to other databases, its DDL is only supported when working with Access databases. Enterprise databases, such as Oracle and SQL Server, have greater capabilities and hence have more parameters and reserved words in their DDL commands. You should look at the specific DDL syntax of the database you are using.

CREATE TABLE

As its name suggests, the `CREATE TABLE` statement is used to compose a database table. It takes the following syntax:

```
CREATE TABLE <tablename>
   (<field1> <type>[(size)] [CONSTRAINT <constraint clause>],
    <field2> <type> [CONSTRAINT <constraint clause>], ...)
```

A **constraint clause** specifies the limits of the values in a column. For example, a common constraint is `NOT NULL`, which means that no values in the column can be empty. Note that the constraint can be added either on the individual fields, or on a group of fields. As shown above, the `CONSTRAINT` element would appear at the end of the field listing.

The `CONSTRAINT` clause is specified in the following ways. For a constraint on an individual field, the syntax is as follows:

```
CONSTRAINT name
   {PRIMARY KEY | UNIQUE | NOT NULL | IDENTITY [(seed, increment]}
```

For a constraint on multiple fields, the statement becomes more complex:

```
CONSTRAINT name
   {PRIMARY KEY (field1 [, field2, ...]) |
    UNIQUE (field1 [, field2, ...]) |
    NOT NULL (field1 [, field2, ...]) |
    FOREIGN KEY (field1 [, field2, ...] )
    REFERENCES (foreigntable1 [, foreigntable2, foreigntable3, ...]) }
```

We can use the CREATE TABLE statement outlined above, with CONSTRAINT clauses, to create an Items table in our database. The code to do this is as follows:

```
CREATE TABLE Items
   (ItemID counter CONSTRAINT pkconst PRIMARY KEY,
    ItemName text, Type text, CONSTRAINT un1 UNIQUE (ItemName))
```

Note that ItemID of type counter, which is a counter that is incremented every time a new record is added. This is a Jet database SQL data type that produces an AutoNumber field in an Access database that is automatically set by the system to produce a unique value for the primary key. These values cannot be changed by the user.

Bear in mind that these types will vary from system to system and you should consult the relevant documentation for details.

The labels pkconst and un1 are the names of the constraint clauses. pkconst refers to the PRIMARY KEY constraint on ItemID and un1 refers to the UNIQUE constraint on ItemName. The outcome of this statement is the Access table shown below:

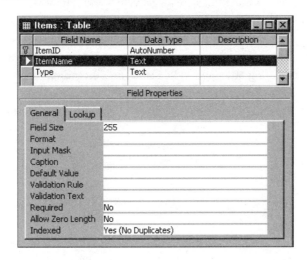

Note that since we didn't specify a size for ItemName, the system gave it the maximum size of 255.

Note that all the DDL operations we will demonstrate can be carried out using the Access GUI, without needing to know the underlying SQL statement. You do not really need to know DDL to be able to create a database.

SQL Server 6.5 also has some graphical support for creating databases, which is much improved in SQL 7.0. One useful thing SQL Server provides is the ability to generate the DDL statements for a given database in a text file. This is especially useful as the generated file can be used to recreate the database elsewhere. (We'll be using such SQL text files in later chapters to generate SQL Server databases.) Also, if you are frequently changing a database structure during a development cycle, you can simply modify this file manually and recreate the database.

CREATE INDEX

The CREATE INDEX statement allows you to add an index to an existing table. The statement takes the following form:

```
CREATE [UNIQUE] INDEX <name>
ON <table> (<field1> [ASC | DESC] [, <field2> [ASC | DESC],...)
[WITH { PRIMARY | DISALLOW NULL | IGNORE NULL} ]
```

There are a few things to note about this definition:

- ❑ The PRIMARY reserved word implies that the created index will be designated the primary key and will be invalid if a primary key already exists

- ❑ DISALLOW NULL means that NULLs are illegal values and cannot be added to the indexed column

- ❑ IGNORE NULL means that while NULLs are legal values, they will not be included in the index

- ❑ ASC stands for ascending order and DESC stands for descending order

Suppose we wanted to put an index on the VendorID field of the invoice table. The statement would be the following:

```
CREATE INDEX Vend
ON Invoice (VendorID ASC)
WITH DISALLOW NULL
```

The table now has the following format:

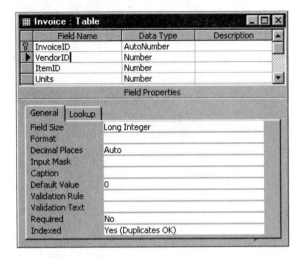

Note that because we did not specify the parameter UNIQUE in the CREATE INDEX statement, VendorID now has an index where duplicate entries are allowed. In fact, in this example we are creating an index on the foreign key, VendorID, which does have duplicate entries in the invoice table. However, in the general case, you can easily create a unique index, either by using the UNIQUE keyword in the CREATE INDEX statement, or by using the Access GUI to change the **Indexed** field to read **Yes (No Duplicates)**.

ALTER TABLE

The ALTER TABLE command does exactly what it suggests — it allows you to change the structure of an existing table. The command has the following syntax:

```
ALTER TABLE <table>
    {ADD COLUMN <field1> <type> [(size)]
    [CONSTRAINT <single index statement> |
    ADD CONSTRAINT <multi-index statement> |
    DROP {COLUMN field1 | CONSTRAINT <single index>}]}
```

This command allows us to do a number of things to a given table. We can add a column, or add a constraint to a column (such as a primary key, foreign key, etc.) or even drop a column or a constraint. DROP is the SQL command used to remove an *object* (that is a column, index, constraint, etc.) from a database. Recall that *data* is removed from the tables using the DELETE command.

Here's how we would add a column to the Items table:

```
ALTER TABLE Items ADD COLUMN Description text(60)
```

The table now has the description field:

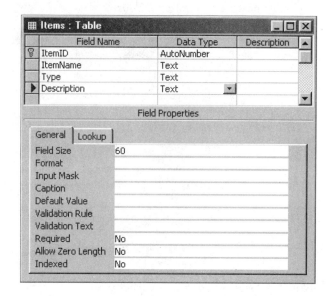

If we now want to drop the index on VendorID that we added earlier using CREATE INDEX, we would use the following command:

```
ALTER TABLE Invoice DROP CONSTRAINT Vend
```

If you take a look at the Invoice table after running this statement, then you'll see that there is no longer an index on VendorID. Note that you can also use the DROP INDEX statement to accomplish the same thing. The syntax for this statement is:

```
DROP INDEX <single index> ON <table>
```

To drop the index on VendorID in the Invoice table above, the statement would be:

```
DROP INDEX Vend ON Invoice
```

DROP TABLE

It is also very straightforward to remove a table using DDL. The DROP TABLE command has the following syntax:

```
DROP TABLE <table>
```

So to remove the items table from the database, the command would be:

```
DROP TABLE Items
```

Tools for Creating SQL

Many of the newer databases include tools that that you can use to create queries with a graphical user interface (GUI). In this chapter, we have seen the user interface that Access provides for creating queries. Other Windows-based databases have similar interfaces. The advantage of graphically creating a query is that you can view the actual SQL code that is being generated. Thus it becomes easy to copy the SQL code directly into your program. Alternatively, you can call stored procedures from the program. In that case the SQL is stored in the database rather than explicitly written into the code.

SQL Server 6.5 uses MS Query for its graphical capabilities. While it is not as sophisticated as the Access GUI, you can still view the SQL code.

As well as defining queries, the GUI can be used to create and modify databases as we have already demonstrated using Access — creating and dropping tables, adding and removing indexes, inserting columns and so on. Other databases have similar UI capabilities. SQL Server's Enterprise Manager, for example, allows you to carry out exactly the same operations.

However, not all queries can be carried out by means of the user interface. You may wish to perform a more complex and sophisticated query, which is beyond the scope of the GUI, and thus requires manual SQL programming. For this reason, an understanding of SQL syntax is recommended.

Summary

In this chapter, we have discussed the basics of SQL, including:

- ❏ How to use the SELECT statement
- ❏ What joins are and how they work
- ❏ How to use SQL to modify the data in the database using DML
- ❏ How to modify the database itself using DDL

To find out more information on the DDL for your database, you should consult the appropriate documentation.

In addition, we have seen, in the case of Access, how the task of querying and modifying databases is made easier by using graphical interfaces. Once again, you should consult the documentation for the user interface capabilities of your database.

Finally, while some aspects of SQL are ANSI standards, remember that there are differences between the way databases implement these standards. For example, join statements such as RIGHT JOIN, LEFT JOIN and INNER JOIN are all implemented by the common databases. However, some databases, such as Access, do not support the related CROSS JOIN and FULL OUTER JOIN commands. There are differences also in the syntax of the various SQL statements. For example the CREATE TABLE and CREATE INDEX commands vary considerably from one database to another. You should be aware of what is the standard SQL, as using it will avoid problems if you need to port your system to another database (see references listed in Appendix A for more details).

In the next chapter, we'll be moving on to looking at exactly how we can go about accessing a database from a C++ program, and at the different technologies around that enable you to do this. Many tools exist that make this job easier, and we'll be looking at a couple of examples using some MFC classes specially designed for data access.

3

Overview of Data Access Technologies

Over the years Microsoft has created a number of technologies to facilitate database access. The goal has been to allow developers to access data in a variety of data stores with just one set of commands. Over the past few years, Microsoft have been presented a number of access technologies, namely:

- ❑ Open Database Connectivity (ODBC)
- ❑ Data Access Objects (DAO)
- ❑ OLE DB
- ❑ ActiveX Data Objects (ADO)

Note that these are not the only technologies for accessing data using a common set of methods or functions. For example, in the UNIX/Linux world, an access technology known as DBI/DBD has been popular. This is similar to ODBC and allows users to access a number of databases using the Perl programming language, including Oracle.

We'll start this chapter by looking at a brief overview of these Microsoft technologies, and then we'll go on to focus in more detail on ODBC and DAO. Along the way, we'll try out some practical examples demonstrating how to use the MFC wrapper classes for these technologies.

A Bit of History

Over the years Microsoft have developed a number of data access technologies, and in this section, we'll be examining these technologies, how they have come about and where they are going in the future. The aim has been to develop a common interface for client applications to access a variety of different database systems. In the context of database access, the word *interface* is used to mean the access technology itself.

The first interface that Microsoft introduced to make data access easier was called **VBSQL**. This was designed to allow Visual Basic programmers to access both Microsoft's and Sybase's SQL Servers. (Microsoft is limiting future support for VBSQL and in SQL Server 7.0 will no longer support any new features. Sybase dropped support for this feature a number of years ago.)

After VBSQL, Microsoft introduced **ODBC**, which is an API designed for use by C programmers. Over time, this has become very widely accepted, and today all important databases now have drivers that support it. In addition, there are ODBC drivers for such data sources such as Excel and text files. This means that we can write programs accessing a wide variety of data using a common set of function calls. ODBC was a big advance in data access technology, as it now has almost universal database support. We will discuss this interface in greater detail later on in this chapter.

The next development was the introduction of **DAO** or **Data Access Objects**. This C++ interface was designed to allow a number of database front-end applications to access the **Jet database engine**, which is the data access engine of Microsoft Access, separated from the Access GUI. (Access, along with several other major database systems, was discussed briefly in chapter 1.). DAO has a somewhat different purpose from ODBC. Rather than provide a general, extensible mechanism for accessing any data source, it is intended for fast local-machine access. Nowadays, mainly Visual Basic and Access programmers use DAO, but other databases can also be accessed using DAO, including:

- ❑ ISAM (Indexed Sequential Access Method) databases
- ❑ Oracle
- ❑ Btrieve

RDO (Remote Data Objects) has also been introduced within the last few years. It is more geared to server bases databases that are designed to handle a large volume of data and transactions, such as SQL Server. A variation on DAO is DAO/ODBCDirect, which allows the programmer to use a lot of RDO functionality. You can use existing DAO code to access remote data sources efficiently by passing DAO function calls to their RDO equivalents. We will talk about RDO later on in the book, when we discuss remoting issues in Chapter 9.

Finally, **OLE DB** and **ADO** are the latest in the series of data access interfaces. OLE DB is a set of COM interfaces, and can access the same SQL-based systems as ODBC. However, this is only a tiny fraction of what OLE DB can do. It is a completely different technology from ODBC and is a prime example of how COM (Microsoft's Component Object Model) is used effectively in the real world. Using the OLE DB interfaces, we can access many different kinds of data sources, from file systems and spreadsheets, to Microsoft Exchange and ASP (Active Server Pages).

ADO, built on top of OLE DB, is an automation server that presents a high-level set of objects to the client. Unlike OLE DB, ADO can be called by scripting languages such as VBScript, in addition to Visual Basic and Java. RDO is related to ADO but is designed for remote database access.

Because of the importance of both OLE DB and ADO, much of the rest of this book is devoted to exploring these technologies from a C++ programmer's point of view. In this chapter, however, we'll be focussing mainly on ODBC and DAO.

Introduction to ODBC

ODBC was Microsoft's first attempt to allow access to any database that includes an appropriate driver. Since ODBC has been around for a while, a number of efficient drivers have been developed and all the commonly used databases are supported, including:

❑   Microsoft SQL server

❑   Oracle

❑   Sybase SQL Server

❑   Microsoft Access.

*You can easily see what ODBC drivers you have installed on your machine by double-clicking on the **ODBC (32 bit)** icon on your control panel, and then clicking the **Add** button. A dialog box will appear showing you all the available drivers.*

ODBC attempts to hide the differences between various databases by having three layers between the data and the application program requiring the data. These three layers are:

❑   The ODBC API (Application Programming Interface),

❑   The driver manager

❑   The driver

Overview of Data Access Technologies

This is illustrated in the diagram below:

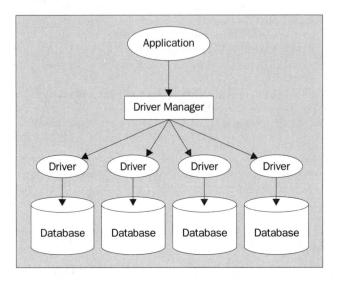

The **ODBC API** is a set of function calls that enables the program to communicate with the **driver manager**. The driver manager essentially accepts the commands from the program and passes them on to the appropriate **driver** for the database being used. The driver handles the communication between the driver manager and the actual data source. The application makes a connection to a particular database using a **connection string**. This string specifies the database by its **data source name** (or **DSN**), and can also contain user ID and password information.

The ODBC API can be used to write single applications that can access different types of databases. In carrying out advanced operations, however, you are likely to require a great deal about of knowledge about the database you're attached to, so you can generate the proper dialect of SQL. As we saw back in Chapter 2, there are variations in the SQL used by different databases. (A good example is Access's crosstab query[1], which SQL Server and Oracle do not support. Thus when porting code from Access to one of these databases any code that includes a crosstab query will have to be rewritten.) This means that whilst writing an ODBC application to communicate with to any single database is fairly straightforward, writing an application that can communicate with arbitrary data sources is much more difficult, as even the conventions for quoting table names vary from one database to another. ODBC provides some useful tools that make such programming possible, but it is not trivial. Scaling an application up from a desktop database (such as Access) to an enterprise database (such as Oracle or SQL Server) is also a non-trivial undertaking, as the SQL used in the two systems is often very different. It is possible to achieve with only limited changes to the code, if the stored procedures use ANSI standard SQL and all target databases support the same level of ODBC that the application is programmed in.

---

[1] This is described in the Access online documentation.

However, Microsoft has developed technologies allowing the user to create working programs with minimal direct use of the API. We'll take a look a practical example of this using the Microsoft Foundation Classes (MFC). Additionally, higher level languages such as Visual Basic insulate the programmer from the API almost entirely.

The MFC ODBC Classes

The purpose of MFC is to put a layer of abstraction on top of raw Windows programming. The MFC Wizards generate a great deal of routine code, which enables the developer to focus on the functionality of a particular application. We won't look at the details of the MFC here — there are a number of good books that do this, such as Mike Blaszczak's *Professional MFC Programming with Visual C++ 5.0*. However, there are a few basics of MFC you will need to understand before we develop our example.

First, the MFC operates on the basis of its **Document/View architecture**, which specifies how work is split up in the application. For our database example, the *document* manages the application's data and the *view* manages how the data is presented to the user. Data is passed from the document to the view for display, and any queries or modifications are passed back to the document for processing.

Second, the MFC Wizards create **wrapper classes** for the ODBC API, which thus becomes almost completely hidden from the user. This is very similar to the way that the MFC creates wrapper classes to hide the complexity of the Win32 API. The two main wrapper classes involved are:

❑   The database class — creates an object representing the database in use, and is the point of contact between the user and the database

❑   The recordset class — creates an object representing the data itself, upon which queries and updates may be performed

MFC also provides a corresponding series of DAO classes, providing additional objects for working with table structure, saving queries for reuse and so on. We'll see more about the classes for DAO later on in this chapter.

MFC makes database programming easier, which is especially true if you are writing small, relatively simple applications

We will now look at the support MFC has for ODBC.

The CDatabase Class

The CDatabase class is responsible for establishing and maintaining a connection to the ODBC data source. The CDatabase object communicates with the ODBC driver manager and with the network, opens the data source and manages the connection thus made. It is responsible for monitoring whether a query is being executed, whether cursors are being used or whether the data source is in read-only mode.

Microsoft describes an ODBC data source as an instance of data residing on a DBMS (Database Management System), and the information required to access that data. It is specified by the data source name.

The CDatabase class implements the following functionality:

- ❑ Creating the database object and connecting to the database.

- ❑ Getting and setting database connection attributes. For example, verifying that the connection is open, obtaining the name of the database and setting the number of seconds ODBC has to wait before timing out a query.

- ❑ Implementing database operations, such as starting transactions, executing SQL statements and binding parameters to a query.

- ❑ Setting the database options

The CRecordset Class

Probably the class you'll encounter most often is CRecordset, which is always used in conjunction with CDatabase. Whereas CDatabase handles all communication between the database and the application, CRecordset essentially represents the data itself. A CRecordset object will contain the records retrieved from the database, which can be manipulated one record at a time, in a number of ways.

The functionality implemented by CRecordset includes:

- ❑ Creating and opening the recordset.

- ❑ Obtaining information about the recordset. For example, getting the SQL statement associated with the recordset, verifying that the recordset has been opened, determining whether the recordset supports transactions and so on.

- ❑ Modify the data in the recordset, deleting records and adding new ones.

- ❑ Traversing the data in the recordset.

- ❑ Exchanging data (in both directions) between the field data members of the recordset and the corresponding record on the data source.

- ❑ Obtaining the connection string and the SQL statement.

- ❑ Obtaining information about the recordset itself – for example, its size, the field types and values and so on.

In customizing your application you would normally derive your classes from CRecordset rather than from CDatabase. Many CRecordset objects can be created for each CDatabase object.

If you use the the MFC class wizard to create your recordset class based on a table, then you'll find that the wizard does virtually all of the work for you. Similarly, the wizard allows you to create a recordset class based on a QueryDef or stored procedure (which were discussed in Chapter 1). However, if you want to create a recordset based on a more complex query (not stored on the server), then you must manually put that query in and adjust the column variables accordingly. We'll see some practical examples of this later on in the chapter.

An Example Using ODBC

Now that we've been through a bit of the theory, let's try putting it into practice with a coded example using these MFC classes. This application uses the invoice table that we saw in the previous chapters and we will provide a form that the user can use to browse through the database and update and insert records. We'll be using the MFC classes in the code and the Wizards to help create the application, but before we start, we need to create an ODBC connection to the sample database.

> *The sample database and the source code for the example can both be downloaded from the Wrox Press Web site:* http://www.wrox.com.

Creating an ODBC Connection

Before you can connect to a database via ODBC, you first have to create an ODBC connection though the Control Panel. The steps to create this connection are outlined below.

1 Go to the Control Panel and double click on ODBC. You will see the ODBC Data Source Administrator dialog:

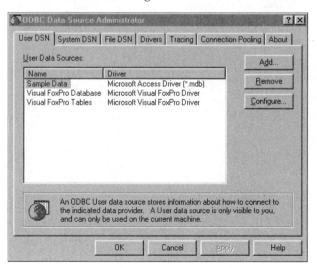

Overview of Data Access Technologies

You can create your connection as either a User DSN, where only a particular user can access the data, a System DSN, where anyone can access it, or a File DSN, which can be used by all users sharing the same DSN file directory. (Recall that DSN stands for Data Source Name, and is used by the client application to connect to the database.)

We will be creating a System DSN, so select the **System DSN** tab.

2   Click on Add... and you'll see the following screen:

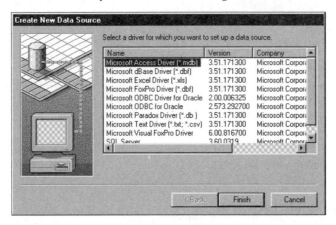

Select the appropriate driver for the database you wish to use. In our case we'll use Access.

3   Click on **Finish** and you will see a screen like the one shown here:

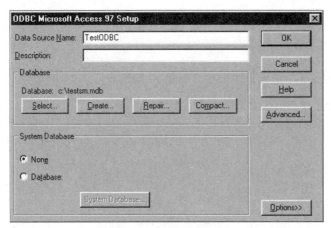

If you click on **Select**, you will see a file selection dialog. You use this select the database. We shall be using the database called `testsm.mdb`.

4   Type in a data source name (in our case `TestODBC`) and optionally a description, then click on **OK**. You are now done!

Note that the dialog in step 3 might vary depending on the particular ODBC driver. For example, if you were creating a connection to a SQL Server database, the dialog would be the following:

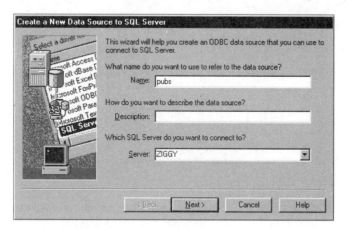

With the data source configured you can now connect to a database from your MFC application.

The Basic Recordset

What you will find when you start using ODBC is that you don't need necessarily to implement a `CDatabase` class. `CRecordset` has the ability to create the `CDatabase` object internally, the default version being good enough for most projects. However, by creating and opening the database object yourself you can control certain options, for example whether or not the database is read-only. See the online documentation for `CDatabase` for more details.

In order to see how ODBC is implemented in MFC, we will create a simple MFC application using the MFC AppWizard.

1   Select the **Project** tab from the Visual C++ **File | New** menu, and then the **MFC AppWizard (exe)** option from the list of Wizards. Type in the project name (call it `TestODBC`).

2   In the first step of AppWizard check the **Single Document Interface** box. The next step allows us to select database support, but here you should select **None** — we'll see why shortly.

3   Click Next> for the steps 3 through 5 as we are accepting the default values set by AppWizard.

4   In the final step, change the view class from CView to CFormView:

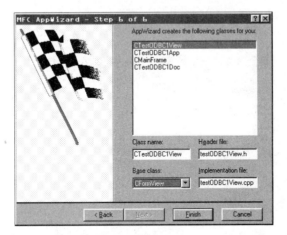

Finally, press Finish and the OK button to let AppWizard construct the project's skeleton code. You will be presented with a blank dialog box, but don't worry about that just yet —we'll see what the form looks like later on.

Let's start by creating our recordset class. We'll add a new class to our application using the MFC ClassWizard. Derive this class from CRecordset, and call it CTestRecordset.

Because we have selected CRecordset as the base class, the wizard automatically prompts us for a data source with a new dialog box, as shown here:

Now it is clear why we needed to set up the database connection in the ODBC manager before creating this class — the connection shows up in the drop-down list. Confirm the connection by selecting TestODBC from the list and then select the Invoice field from the following list. Press OK to complete the operation.

Note that there are two possible options for the recordset type:

❑ Snapshot

❑ Dynaset

A **snapshot** maintains an exact copy of what the data was when the query was executed. It is essentially static in nature and in order to update the snapshot recordset, the Requery() method needs to be called on it.

On the other hand, a **dynaset** is to a limited extent synchronized to the actual data in the database, in that a user immediately sees the changes made to the data on which the recordset is based, provided that the user has made those changes. However, in a multi-user environment other users can delete, add records or update data in your recordset, and you will not see any of these changes reflected immediately. You will only see updated records in your recordset, if you move to another record and then back to the original one. Deleted records are always skipped by MFC code whether you or another user deleted them. To see records inserted by another user, you have to call the Requery() function.

We'll be using the **Dynaset** recordset option in our example, so you should check this option.

So why create the recordset class separately rather than select the database options in AppWizard? Well, by default, the Wizard creates the data class *inside* the view class, which means that any data is contained in the view rather than in the document. This goes against the whole spirit of the Document/View architecture, where a program's data is normally stored in the document class. We want the CRecordset object and its data to be contained in the document, which will do the job of processing the data for display, before passing it to the view. Thus the view does not directly access the recordset.

The TestRecordset Class

Let's take a look at this class now. The header file `TestRecordset.h` is generated by ClassWizard for us and is listed as follows:

```
// TestRecordset.h

class CTestRecordset : public CRecordset
{
public:
    CTestRecordset(CDatabase* pDatabase = NULL);
    DECLARE_DYNAMIC(CTestRecordset)
// Field/Param Data
    //{{AFX_FIELD(CTestRecordset, CRecordset)
    long    m_InvoiceID;
    long    m_VendorID;
    long    m_ItemID;
    long    m_Units;
    //}}AFX_FIELD

// Overrides
    // ClassWizard generated virtual function overrides
    //{{AFX_VIRTUAL(CTestRecordset)
    public:
    virtual CString GetDefaultConnect();      // Default connection string
    virtual CString GetDefaultSQL();          // Default SQL for Recordset
    virtual void DoFieldExchange(CFieldExchange* pFX);  // RFX support
    //}}AFX_VIRTUAL

// Implementation
#ifdef _DEBUG
    virtual void AssertValid() const;
    virtual void Dump(CDumpContext& dc) const;
#endif
};
```

We can see from this file that the `CTestRecordset` class inherits from `CRecordset` as we'd expect. At the top of the class definition, the constructor appears. It has one parameter, `pDatabase`, which is a pointer to `CDatabase` and has a default value of `NULL`. When the `CTestRecordset` class is created, this pointer is passed to the constructor for the `CRecordset` class, which then creates the `CDatabase` object automatically for you.

Next, we have some member variables declared, which represent the fields from the invoice table in the database. These are added automatically for us by ClassWizard.

Two member functions of particular interest are `GetDefaultConnect()` and `GetDefaultSQL()`. This is where we can change the connection to the database and the SQL statement that will be applied to the database. By changing these functions, you can change the SQL statement the class is based upon as well as which ODBC connection is being accessed.

Note that the definition of the CRecordset class is contained in the header file, afxbd.h, so you'll need to add a #include for this at the top of the file:

```
#include <afxdb.h>
```

The implementation of this class is in the TestRecordset.cpp file as shown below:

```
// TestRecordset.cpp

IMPLEMENT_DYNAMIC(CTestRecordset, CRecordset)

CTestRecordset::CTestRecordset(CDatabase* pDatabase)
    : CRecordset(pDatabase)
{
    //{{AFX_FIELD_INIT(CTestRecordset)
    m_InvoiceID = 0;
    m_VendorID = 0;
    m_ItemID = 0;
    m_Units = 0;
    m_nFields = 4;
    //}}AFX_FIELD_INIT
    m_nDefaultType = dynaset;
}
```

IMPLEMENT_DYNAMIC() is a macro that generates an instance of a class that inherits directly from CObject, that is CRecordset. (Most MFC classes inherit directly or indirectly inherit from CObject). At run time, the macro can access the class name and its place within the object hierarchy. It must be in the .cpp file since it should only be evaluated once at compile time. The corresponding macro DECLARE_DYNAMIC() appears in the header file.

The implementation of the constructor for CTestRecordset does two things:

- ❑ Initializes the member variables that correspond to the fields of the invoice table

- ❑ Sets the m_nDefaultType variable to dynaset (recall that we selected this option earlier when creating the class)

This is followed by the implementation of the member functions GetDefaultConnect() and GetDefaultSQL(), which are very straightforward:

```
CString CTestRecordset::GetDefaultConnect()
{
    return _T("ODBC;DSN=TestODBC");
}

CString CTestRecordset::GetDefaultSQL()
{
    return _T("[invoice]");
}
```

`GetDefaultConnect()` returns the ODBC connecting string, consisting of the DSN that we specified at the very beginning of the exercise when me made our ODBC connection. Note that the connection string is prefixed by "ODBC" which is used to indicate that we are connecting to an ODBC data source.

`GetDefaultSQL()` returns the name of a table that we specified earlier, but it could also be the name of a stored query/procedure or a SQL statement.

In practice, AppWizard limits you to just a table or stored query/procedure.

The implementation of `DoFieldExchange()` is as follows:

```
void CTestRecordset::DoFieldExchange(CFieldExchange* pFX)
{
    //{{AFX_FIELD_MAP(CTestRecordset)
    pFX->SetFieldType(CFieldExchange::outputColumn);
    RFX_Long(pFX, _T("[invoiceID]"), m_InvoiceID);
    RFX_Long(pFX, _T("[vendorID]"), m_VendorID);
    RFX_Long(pFX, _T("[itemID]"), m_ItemID);
    RFX_Long(pFX, _T("[units]"), m_Units);
    //}}AFX_FIELD_MAP
}
```

This is a very important function. Its job is to map the values in columns that make up the tables to member variables in the `CTestRecordset` class. The function `SetFieldType()` tells the system whether you're dealing with columns, input parameters or output parameters. Here, we're dealing with columns.

Input parameters are used in either **stored procedures** or **parameterized queries**. You may recall that a stored procedure is a set of query criteria that are stored in the database so that they can be accessed quickly. A parameterized query is a type of query that takes input values, which are set when the query is run. These input parameters make recordsets far more flexible. Output parameters are the return values of stored procedures.

The Document Class

Now that we've examined the `CTestRecordset` class itself, let's see how it's used in the program. The first thing that we need to do is include an instance of `CTestRecordset` in the document class. The header for this class can be found in `TestODBCdoc.h`:

```
#include "TestRecordset.h"

class CTestODBCDoc : public CDocument
{
protected: // create from serialization only
    CTestODBCDoc();
    DECLARE_DYNCREATE(CTestODBCDoc)
```

```
// Attributes
public:
   CTestRecordset m_TestRecordset;

...
```

The additional lines are highlighted in the above code. Note that we also need to #include the header file containing the definition for the CTestRecordset class.

The constructor and destructor are implemented in TestODBCDoc.cpp:

```
// CTestODBCDoc construction/destruction

CTestODBCDoc::CTestODBCDoc()
{
   m_TestRecordset.Open();
}

CTestODBCDoc::~CTestODBCDoc()
{
   m_TestRecordset.Close();
}
```

In this simple example, we need only put an Open() and Close() statement in the constructor and destructor of the document class. Note that we don't need to implement these methods ourselves, as we inherit them from the CRecordset class. The Open() method actually performs the query encapsulated by the recordset, which in our example is:

```
SELECT 'invoiceID', 'vendorID', 'itemID', 'units' FROM 'invoice'
```

Close() simply releases the recordset.

The View Class

In Microsoft's Document/View architecture, we use the document class in the view class — this is where the recordset is most heavily used. The form view we are going to create will have the following features:

- ❑ Edit boxes to display the data for each record
- ❑ Buttons to permit the user to browse through the data, add a new record, or update the current record displayed in the view.

This is what our form will look like:

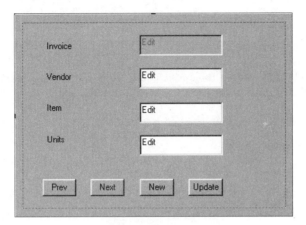

Add these edit boxes and buttons to the form, changing their ID's to IDC_INVOICE, IDC_VENDOR, IDC_PREV and so forth. It is a good idea to make the edit box for the invoice ID read-only, as this is the primary key for the invoice table — each value is unique and set by the database, so you do not want the user changing these values and corrupting the data.

We can add member variables to the view class corresponding to each of the edit boxes very simply by double-clicking on the edit box while holding down the *Ctrl* key. Call these variables m_Invoice, m_Vendor, m_Item and m_Units:

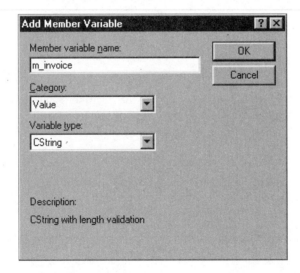

Next, double-click on the buttons to add message handlers for them:

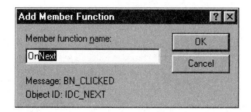

One thing to note here is that we've called the handler for the **Update** button `OnUpdateDB()`, rather than the slightly more obvious `OnUpdate()`. The reason for this is that `CTestRecordset` actually inherits a method called `OnUpdate()` from `CRecordset`, which we need to override. We'll see the implementation for this function later on.

Now we have created our form, let's look at the code generated for the view class. We start with the class declaration, found in `TestODBCView.h`. The first key area is the `AFX_DATA` section:

```
public:
    //{{AFX_DATA(CTestODBCView)
    enum { IDD = IDD_TESTODBC_FORM };
    CString    m_Invoice;
    CString    m_Item;
    CString    m_Units;
    CString    m_Vendor;
    //}}AFX_DATA
```

These are the variables that will contain the data as displayed in the form view. The other item to note is the line, `enum { IDD=IDD_TESTODBC_FORM }`, which indicates that the form view is mapped to the `CTestODBCView` class.

In the remainder of the header file, there are two additions to make to the code. First, we need to add a declaration for the `OnUpDate()` method that we're going to override. You can do this very easily by right-clicking on the `CTestODBCView` in ClassView and selecting **Add Virtual Function** from the drop-down menu. We'll use the method to fill in the values of the current database record.

```
    virtual void OnEndPrinting(CDC* pDC, CPrintInfo* pInfo);
    virtual void OnPrint(CDC* pDC, CPrintInfo* pInfo);
    virtual void OnUpdate(CView* pSender, LPARAM lHint, CObject* pHint);
    //}}AFX_VIRTUAL

// Implementation
public:
    virtual ~CTestODBCView();
#ifdef _DEBUG
    virtual void AssertValid() const;
    virtual void Dump(CDumpContext& dc) const;
#endif
```

Finally, we insert a protected data member m_bNew — this variable will help us keep track when a new record is being added:

```
protected:
    bool m_bNew;

// Generated message map functions
protected:
    //{{AFX_MSG(CTestODBCView)
    afx_msg void OnNew();
    afx_msg void OnNext();
    afx_msg void OnPrev();
    afx_msg void OnUpdateDB();
    //}}AFX_MSG
    DECLARE_MESSAGE_MAP()
};
```

The implementation of the view class is in TestODBCView.cpp. It is in this class that the majority of work in the program is done. Here, we will add functionality that allows us to:

- ❑ Move through the invoice table
- ❑ Update the data
- ❑ Add new records

Note that this is very simple example and there is no validation of input data.

Much of generated code we can leave just as it is, for example the DoDataExchange() function, which is called automatically to exchange data between the dialog and member variables, and the constructor, which initializes the member variables as NULL strings. In this case, we also don't need to change OnInitialUpdate().

Firstly, we need to make a minor addition to the constructor to initialize the m_bNew member to false:

```
CTestODBCView::CTestODBCView()
    : CFormView(CTestODBCView::IDD)
{
    //{{AFX_DATA_INIT(CTestODBCView)
    m_Invoice = _T("");
    m_Item = _T("");
    m_Units = _T("");
    m_Vendor = _T("");
    //}}AFX_DATA_INIT
    m_bNew = false;
}
```

We now need to implement our four message handler functions. Let's start with the one for adding a new record, OnNew():

```
void CTestODBCView::OnNew()
{
    // set initial values of new record and allow updating of form
    m_Item = "";
    m_Units = "";
    m_Vendor = "";
    m_Invoice= "tbd";
    UpdateData(FALSE);
    m_bNew = true;
}
```

In the handler for the **New** button, we simply clear the form and enter "tbd" for the **Invoice** field, since its value is determined by the system. (In fact, the value is set in the database when the record is updated with the OnUpdateDB() handler.) The remaining fields are set to NULL ready for input by the user.

UpdateData() is called to update the form with the values we have just set. This method takes one of two arguments:

- ❑ TRUE if you're passing data from the form to the variables
- ❑ FALSE if you're passing data from the variables to the form.

In this case, we want to update the form with the values in the variables, so we call UpdateData() with an argument of FALSE. In turn, it calls DoDataExchange() where the exchange actually takes place.

Finally, we need to set the m_bNew member to true. We'll use this later in the handler for the **Update** button, because we need to do different things depending on whether the update involves editing an existing record or adding a new one.

Now we implement OnNext():

```
void CTestODBCView::OnNext()
{
    // create a string buffer
    char tres[MAX_LENGTH];

    // get a pointer to the recordset
    CTestRecordset* pTestRecordset = &GetDocument()->m_TestRecordset;

    // Check it's not EOF before stepping fwd thru recordset
    if(pTestRecordset->IsEOF())
    {
        MessageBox("At end of file",
                   "File Warning",MB_OK | MB_ICONINFORMATION);
    }
```

```
    else
    {
        // move to the next record, but if it's EOF move to the
        // last record
        pTestRecordset->MoveNext();
        if(pTestRecordset->IsEOF())
        {
            MessageBox("At end of file",
                    "File Warning",MB_OK | MB_ICONINFORMATION);
            pTestRecordset->MoveLast();
        }
    }

    // fill in fields
    m_Invoice = ltoa(pTestRecordset->m_InvoiceID,tres,10);
    m_Item = ltoa(pTestRecordset->m_ItemID,tres,10);
    m_Units = ltoa(pTestRecordset->m_Units,tres,10);
    m_Vendor = ltoa(pTestRecordset->m_VendorID,tres,10);
    UpdateData(FALSE);
}
```

We start the OnNext() function by creating a buffer for the string output. The value of the symbol MAX_LENGTH is set by the following statement, which is inserted at the top of the file:

```
#define MAX_LENGTH 10
```

Next we get a pointer to the recordset:

```
CTestRecordset* pTestRecordset = &GetDocument()->m_TestRecordset;
```

The function GetDocument() returns a pointer to the document class, which is then used to access the recordset. The key to the view class is the interaction between the class variables m_Invoice, m_Item, m_Units and m_Vendor and the form. Data is passed from the form to these variables, and then to the document class, which ultimately handles storage and retrieval of the data.

We then check that we're not at the end of the recordset, and if not, we move to the next record by calling MoveNext() (a member function of CRecordset that is inherited). It's important to call IsEOF() before MoveNext() — if the recordset is empty, then you'll be at the end of the file before stepping forward even once. (Note that it's perfectly valid to have a recordset object with no data in it. You could use such an object to allow the user to populate a table with data, for example.) We call IsEOF() again after stepping forward, and if we've moved to the end of the recordset, we simply set the current record as the last one in the recordset.

Finally, we set the member variables of the view class to the current values for the fields in the table (converting to strings as we do so) and then update the form by calling UpdateData().

The OnPrev() function is very similar to OnNext(), only it gets and displays the data for the previous record:

```
void CTestODBCView::OnPrev()
{
   // create a string buffer
   char tres[MAX_LENGTH];

   // get a pointer to the recordset
   CTestRecordset* pTestRecordset = &GetDocument()->m_TestRecordset;

   // check it's not BOF before stepping backward thru recordset
   if(pTestRecordset->IsBOF())
   {
      MessageBox("At beginning of file",
               "File Warning",MB_OK | MB_ICONINFORMATION);
   }
   else
   {
      // move to the previous record, but if it's BOF move to the
      // first record
      pTestRecordset->MovePrev();
      if(pTestRecordset->IsBOF())
      {
         pTestRecordset->MoveFirst();
         MessageBox("At beginning of file",
                  "File Warning",MB_OK | MB_ICONINFORMATION);
      }
   }

   // fill in fields
   m_Invoice = ltoa(pTestRecordset->m_InvoiceID,tres,10);
   m_Item = ltoa(pTestRecordset->m_ItemID,tres,10);
   m_Units = ltoa(pTestRecordset->m_Units,tres,10);
   m_Vendor = ltoa(pTestRecordset->m_VendorID,tres,10);
   UpdateData(FALSE);
}
```

The only differences here are that we have to check for the beginning of the file rather than the end, and use the MovePrev() method on the recordset object.

The final message handler is the OnUpdateDB() function:

```
void CTestODBCView::OnUpdateDB()
{
   // create a string buffer
   char strTmp[MAX_LENGTH];

   // get a pointer to the recordset
   CTestODBCDoc* pDoc = GetDocument();
   CTestRecordset* pTestRecordset = &pDoc->m_TestRecordset;
```

```
// is the record a new one?
if(m_bNew)
    pTestRecordset->AddNew();
else
    pTestRecordset->Edit();

// update the recordset
UpdateData(true);
pTestRecordset->m_ItemID = atol(m_Item);
pTestRecordset->m_Units = atol(m_Units);
pTestRecordset->m_VendorID = atol(m_Vendor);
pTestRecordset->Update();

// insert invoice ID of new record
if(m_bNew)
{
    pTestRecordset->MoveLast();
    m_Invoice = ltoa(pTestRecordset->m_InvoiceID,strTmp,10);
    UpdateData(FALSE);              // update form view
    m_bNew = false;                // record no longer 'new'
}
}
```

The `OnUpdateDB()` handler is called when the **Update** button is pressed. Its purpose is to take data from the form and pass it to the recordset. If the **New** button has been pressed, that is `m_bNew` is `true`, then the recordset's `AddNew()` function is called before the data is passed to the recordset. Otherwise, the `Edit()` function is called before passing the data.

`AddNew()` and `Edit()` are both methods of the `CRecordset` class, which, as you might expect, prepare a new empty record and prepare the current record for changes respectively.

In either case the data is converted from strings to long integers and passed back to the member variables of the recordset class. Once this has been done, we call `Update()` on the recordset class, which is necessary in order to save the changes in the database itself. If we don't do this, then all changes would be lost as soon as the user moved away from the record being edited.

The final part of the **Update** handler is dealing with the invoice ID of a new record. Recall that this is the primary key for the invoice table and is set automatically by the database when a new record is added. So, we need to pass the value of the invoice ID from the recordset class to the view class and then update the form.

Finally the implementation of the virtual function `OnUpdate()` is as follows:

```
void CTestODBCView::OnUpdate(CView* pSender, LPARAM lHint, CObject* pHint)
{
    // create a string buffer
    char tres[MAX_LENGTH];

    // get a pointer to the recordset
    CTestRecordset* pTestRecordset = &GetDocument()->m_TestRecordset;
```

```
// convert each long integer value returned to a char string and set
// it to its corresponding variable
m_Invoice = ltoa(pTestRecordset->m_InvoiceID, tres, 10);
m_Item = ltoa(pTestRecordset->m_ItemID, tres, 10);
m_Units = ltoa(pTestRecordset->m_Units, tres, 10);
m_Vendor = ltoa(pTestRecordset->m_VendorID, tres, 10);

// update the view - FALSE indicates that the updated variables should
// be passed to the form.
UpdateData(FALSE);
}
```

The OnUpdate() method is called on the view object after the document object has been modified. It is a standard MFC function that is called whenever there is a change to the view's document. In our case, the data from the document — or more specifically the data from the current record in the recordset — is converted to strings, which are then passed to the member variables of the view class.

Now you can build and run the code, and the form you created will appear on the screen with the data of the first record filled in. You can step back and forth through the records in the database, as well as add new records and update existing ones:

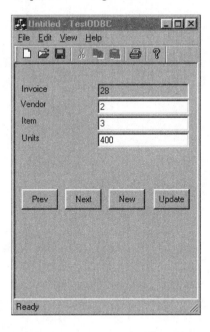

To summarize, in this section we have generated a simple MFC database access application with an ODBC connection to our test database and created a form view to display the data therein. We used ClassWizard to create our `CTestRecordset` class and added message handlers to carry out the requirements of our view class — to browse the data as well as add new records and update existing ones.

A Parameterized Query

As you can see from the last example, creating a recordset class based on a table is very straightforward. The MFC wizards do all the hard work for us. Indeed, the query the recordset was based on was simply:

```
SELECT * FROM [TableName]
```

Now, let's extend the example to look at a more complex recordset — one that is based on a parameterized query. We will add a form that allows the user to select a vendor and return a list of their invoices. The new form is shown below:

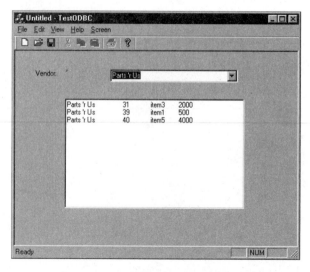

In order to extend the example, we'll need to carry out the following steps:

1   Create a recordset class based on a query that selects data from the vendor, item and invoice tables to allow the user to list the invoices of a particular vendor.

2   Create a second recordset class from the vendor table to display the possible vendors in a combo box, as shown in the form above.

3   Add these classed as member variables in the document class.

4   Implement a view class that allows us to display the data

5   Make the appropriate changes to the main form and to the application class that allows us to switch between the two views.

The Query-based Recordset

So, let's start with the recordset class based on the parameterized query. The simplest way to do this is to create a new class, CQueryRec using Class Wizard — derived from CRecordset and based on the invoice table — as we did in the last example. The only difference here is that we'll be using a snapshot recordset, because the simple report we're creating will not allow the users to modify the data. The all we need to do is change the SQL statement for the desired query and modify the list of column bindings accordingly.

The query we'll be using is shown below:

```
SELECT Vendors.VendorName, Invoice.invoiceID, Invoice.ItemID,
       Items.ItemName, Invoice.Units
FROM Vendors
INNER JOIN (Items INNER JOIN Invoice ON Items.ItemID = Invoice.ItemID)
ON Vendors.VendorID = Invoice.VendorID WHERE ((Vendors.VendorID)= ?);")
```

The only new aspect of this SLQ statement is the ? in the WHERE element. This is here because it is a *parameterized* query, so the database will be expecting a value to be supplied for the vendor ID in order to execute to execute the query. This value is supplied (indirectly) by the user, when they select a particular vendor name from the drop down list in the form shown above.

First, we need to change the member variables of the CQueryRec class to match the fields selected by the SQL statement:

```
// Field/Param Data
  //{{AFX_FIELD(CQueryRec, CRecordset)
  long    m_InvoiceID;
  long    m_ItemID;
  long    m_Units;
  CString m_VendorName;
  CString m_ItemName;
  //}}AFX_FIELD
  long m_nVenID;
```

Note that since we're using a parameterized query, we also need to add a member variable for the parameter itself, that is, the vendor ID. And that's all the changes there are in the header file.

In the .cpp file, we need to alter those methods that use the above data members. Firstly the constructor:

```
CQueryRec::CQueryRec(CDatabase* pdb)
    : CRecordset(pdb)
{
    //{{AFX_FIELD_INIT(CQueryRec)
    m_VendorName = _T("");
    m_InvoiceID = 0;
    m_ItemID = 0;
    m_ItemName = _T("");
    m_Units = 0;
    m_nFields = 5;
    //}}AFX_FIELD_INIT
    m_nDefaultType = snapshot;
    m_nParams = 1;
    m_nVenID = 0;
}
```

We don't need to change the `GetDefaultConnect()` function, as this simple returns the connection string that we need. However, we're going to change the `GetDefaultSQL()` method, so that it supplies the parameterized query:

```
CString CQueryRec::GetDefaultSQL()
{
    return _T("SELECT Vendors.VendorName, Invoice.InvoiceID, Invoice.ItemID, \
        Items.ItemName, Invoice.Units FROM Vendors \
        INNER JOIN (Items INNER JOIN Invoice ON Items.ItemID = Invoice.ItemID) \
        ON Vendors.VendorID = Invoice.VendorID WHERE (((Vendors.VendorID)= ?));");
}
```

The `DoFieldExchange()` method is shown below:

```
void CQueryRec::DoFieldExchange(CFieldExchange* pFX)
{
    //{{AFX_FIELD_MAP(CQueryRec)
    pFX->SetFieldType(CFieldExchange::outputColumn);
    RFX_Text(pFX, _T("[VendorName]"), m_VendorName);
    RFX_Long(pFX, _T("[InvoiceID]"), m_InvoiceID);
    RFX_Long(pFX, _T("[ItemID]"), m_ItemID);
    RFX_Text(pFX, _T("[ItemName]"), m_ItemName);
    RFX_Long(pFX, _T("[Units]"), m_Units);
    //}}AFX_FIELD_MAP
    pFX->SetFieldType(CFieldExchange::param);
    RFX_Long(pFX, _T("[venID]"),m_nVenID);
}
```

As well as changing the columns here, we also need add an exchange command for the parameter, after calling the `SetFieldType()` function to tell it that we are now setting a parameter.

The Vendor Recordset

Before making the necessary changes to the document class, which we'll look at next, you'll need to create another recordset class, `CVendorRec` — this will also be a snapshot, but this time based on the vendor table. The wizard generated code will be sufficient here, and we won't need to make any changes to it.

Don't forget to add a #include for afxdb.h at the top of the headers for the two recordset classes.

The Document Class

The changes to the document class are very simple. In the header, we add variables for the query recordset (m_QueryRec) and the table of vendor information (m_VendorRec):

```
// Attributes
public:
    CTestRecordset m_TestRecordset;
    CQueryRec m_QueryRec;
    CVendorRec m_VendorRec;
```

Remember to add the header files defining these classes to TestODBCDoc.h.

In addition, we open the vendor recordset in the document constructor and close it in the destructor:

```
CTestODBCDoc::CTestODBCDoc()
{
    m_TestRecordset.Open();
    m_VendorRec.Open();
}

CTestODBCDoc::~CTestODBCDoc()
{
    m_TestRecordset.Close();
    m_VendorRec.Close();
}
```

We don't handle opening and closing the parameterized query there as it will be opened and closed each time we use it. The reason for this is that we will be setting the parameter value each time we execute the query.

Creating a View

Now it's time to create the view class that's needed for displaying the data from the recordset classes we've just created. Select **New Form** from the **Insert** menu and fill in CQueryView as the name of the class. Lay out the form as shown above give the IDs for the combo box and edit box as IDC_VENDOR and IDC_QRES respectively. (Note that the edit box is multiline.) You'll also need to add member variables for the controls on the form (*Ctrl*, double-click on control). For each control add one variable for the control and one for the string it will contain:

```
// Form Data
public:
    //{{AFX_DATA(CQueryView)
    enum { IDD = IDD_QUERYVIEW_FORM };
    CComboBox   m_ctlVendor;
    CEdit    m_ctlQres;
    CString     m_qres;
    CString     m_Vendor;
    //}}AFX_DATA
```

We need to override the inherited `OnInitialUpdate()` method, in which we empty the combo box and then step through the vendor recordset to populate the combo box with all the available vendor names:

```
void CInvoiceView::OnInitialUpdate()
{
    CFormView::OnInitialUpdate();

    int iRes;
    m_ctlVendor.ResetContent();

    // get pointer to vendor recordset class
    CVendorRec* pRec = &GetDocument()->m_VendorRec;
    pRec->MoveFirst();

    // populate combo box
    while(!pRec->IsEOF())
    {
        iRes = m_ctlVendor.AddString(pRec->m_VendorName);
        m_ctlVendor.SetItemData(iRes,pRec->m_VendorID);
        pRec->MoveNext();
    }
}
```

Note that while stepping through the recordset, we also associate the vendor ID with each vendor name in the combo box with a call to `SetItemData()`.

Next, we need to implement a handler, `OnSelchangeVendor()`, where we call upon the parameterized query. This method is used to obtain the vendor ID from the combo box, which is then used to set the parameter so we can open the query-based recordset. The recordset is then scrolled through and fills the edit control line by line:

```
void CQueryView::OnSelchangeVendor()
{
    // get pointer to query recordset class
    CQueryRec* pRec = &GetDocument()->m_QueryRec;

    m_ctlQres.SetWindowText("");
    CString strLine;
    char cRes[10];
    int i = 1;
```

```
    // set the parameter value and open the recordset
    pRec-> m_nVenID = (int)m_ctlVendor.GetItemData(m_ctlVendor.GetCurSel());
    pRec-> Open();
    strLine = "";

// fill the edit box with invoice info
    while(!pRec-> IsEOF())
    {
        strLine = strLine + pRec->m_VendorName;
        strLine = strLine + "\t";
        strLine = strLine + itoa(pRec->m_InvoiceID,cRes,10);
        strLine = strLine + "\t";
        strLine = strLine + pRec->m_ItemName;
        strLine = strLine + "\t";
        strLine = strLine + itoa(pRec->m_Units,cRes,10);
        strLine = strLine + "\r\n";
        pRec->MoveNext();
    }

    this->m_ctlQres.SetWindowText(strLine);
    pRec->Close();
}
```

Notice how the record set's parameter is set with a call to `GetItemData()`, in contrast to `SetItemData()` above:

```
    pRec-> m_nVenID = (int)m_ctlVendor.GetItemData(m_ctlVendor.GetCurSel());
    pRec-> Open();
```

A while loop is then used to append the values to the string buffer for each record in the record set. At the end of each record, we append a `"\r\n"` (<CR>, linefeed) in order to move to the next line in the edit control. Finally, we fill the edit box with the string we have just created and then close the recordset.

> *Note that you'll need to #include the headers for the two recordset classes and the document class in QueryView.cpp.*

There is one final change we need to make to the view class, and that is to add the `GetDocument()` method. This was actually added to our first view class, `CTestODBCView`, when it was created by AppWizard. We need this method, because it is used in the above code to obtain pointers to the recordset classes, which are member variables of the document class. Add the declaration for this method to the header file for `CQueryView`, and then simply copy-and-paste the implementation from `CTestODBCView`.

Switching between Views

The last thing we need to do to complete this example is make the appropriate changes to the main form so that it allows one to switch between the original table-based form and the new one. We'll add a <u>S</u>creen menu to the form that allows us to select either <u>I</u>nvoice or <u>R</u>eport. Two handlers, OnScreenReport() and OnScreenInvoice() are added to the CMainFrame class and are used to switch to the report view and then back again, respectively.

The implementation for OnScreenReport() is shown below:

```
void CMainFrame::OnScreenReport()
{
    CRuntimeClass* pNewView;

    CView *pCurrView = this->GetActiveView();

    pNewView = RUNTIME_CLASS(CQueryView);

    CCreateContext cContext;

    cContext.m_pNewViewClass = pNewView;
    cContext.m_pCurrentDoc = GetActiveDocument();

    CView* pView = STATIC_DOWNCAST(CView, CreateView(&cContext));

    if(pView != NULL)
    {
        pView->ShowWindow(SW_SHOW);
        pView->OnInitialUpdate();
        SetActiveView(pView,TRUE);
        this->RecalcLayout();
        pCurrView->DestroyWindow();
    }
}
```

The implementation of the handler for the **Report** menu item first selects the active view and then creates a new view based on the CQueryView class. A context is created and the view and document classes set to the new view class and current document respectively (we only have one document class).

We then set a new view equal to the new view created using the context. Note that STATIC_DOWNCAST simply casts the object created by CreateView() (which is a CWnd) to a CView pointer:

```
CView* pView = STATIC_DOWNCAST(CView, CreateView(&cContext));
```

Finally, the current view is set to the new view and the old view is destroyed.

The handler for the Invoice menu item, to select the original form, is virtually identical, so the code won't be repeated here. We will use this same function in the DAO example later on in this chapter and extensively in the case

> *You'll need to #include the definitions of the two recordset class, the two view classes and the document class to the top of CMainFrame.cpp.*

Note that you'll need to remove the first block of code in CTestODBCApp::InitInstance() that was generated on the addition of the second view class. You need to do this, or the program will not know which view to display on initialization. The basic code covered in this section can be found in MFC references.

Pros and Cons of ODBC

ODBC is a flexible data access technology that has very widespread use. We can access any major DBMS in a relatively consistent manner, from desktop applications to large mainframe databases. Since it is an older technology, it is relatively stable. Many commonly used ODBC drivers have been extensively tried and tested, and are now largely bug-free. It is also very easy to reconnect to a different data source — by simply creating a new connection in the Control Panel as we saw earlier.

However, there are some limitations to ODBC. First, the programmer has to use standard SQL for queries if ODBC is to have truly cross-platform applicability. Using more complex SQL statements ultimately restricts the number of accessible data sources. Even though it is possible can access many different data sources, ODBC is not optimized for any particular type of database. For instance, it is not particularly well suited for use with ISAM (Indexed Sequential Access Method) databases, examples of which include FoxPro, Paradox and dBase. Thus ODBC is generally used with relational/SQL types of data sources. Also, in ODBC, you do not directly connect with the database, relying instead on the driver manager to do the work. Thus there is potential loss of efficiency.

Introduction to DAO

DAO is a data access technology that facilitates access to Microsoft's Jet database engine, which is shipped with Access. Thus DAO is geared towards Access, but can also access ISAM databases and Lotus and Excel spreadsheets. However, it is possible for DAO to access enterprise databases through ODBC drivers, although with limited efficiency. DAO is comprised of objects organized in a hierarchical fashion. The object model of DAO (for the Jet engine) is illustrated in the diagram below:

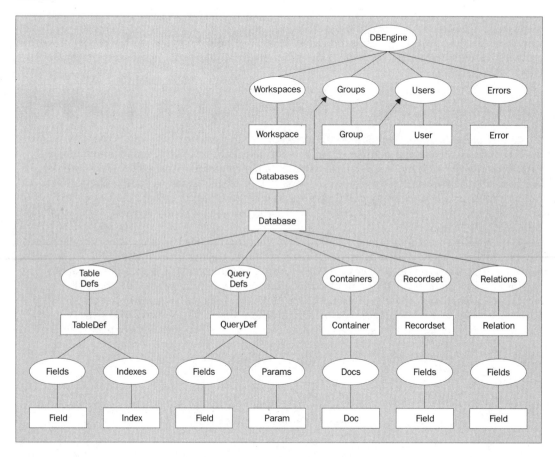

This might look a bit complicated at first, so let's see what all the objects are, one at a time. The first thing to note about DAO is that it is organized in terms of objects and **collections** of objects. In fact, all objects are part of a collection, apart from the top-level **Database Engine** object.

On initialization, the database engine object creates a **Workspace** object, which contains a **Database** object. A database engine can support a group (or collection) of database objects each in its own workspace.

A **TableDef** object defines a set of rows and columns in a database, so you can manipulate the definition of a table using this object. A **QueryDef** object contains predefined SQL statements. Both TableDefs and QueryDefs are stored in files on the database itself and are known as **persistent objects**. Other persistent objects include **Field** and **Index** objects.

As in ODBC, **Recordset** objects contain the records returned by either a table or query and are stored in RAM as virtual tables. A recordset is not persistent.

DAO versus ODBC

Using DAO to access an ODBC database does not provide full functionality when managing stored procedures and when using multiple result sets. Also DAO is not as flexible as ODBC in accessing multiple types of DBMS, or remote data, but it excels at fast local database operations. Like ODBC, DAO is limited to mostly relational/SQL types of data sources.

So, when would you want to use DAO? Whenever an application needs to use a database engine to store its own data efficiently, DAO is a good option, as the Jet engine is quite efficient. If you're using Access or an ISAM database, then DAO is also the preferred option.

When using DAO, there is no need to configure an ODBC connection as you had to in the ODBC example. This becomes advantageous when distributing an application, because in an ODBC application, the install program has to handle creating the connection programmatically, which involves making modifications to the registry. While not especially difficult to do, this does add complexity to the installation. However, if you're using a server-based database such as SQL Server or Oracle, DAO is not the best choice. In client/server programming ODBC provides better performance.

The MFC DAO Classes

As we've just seen, DAO is a set of hierarchical objects that permit access to various databases, most notably Jet and ISAM databases. In order to make is easier to access data via DAO in an MFC application, MFC has provided wrapper classes to for the DAO objects. Note that the object model of the MFC classes has a flatter hierarchy than the DAO object model — while it encapsulates all the functionality of DAO, it does so in fewer classes.

There are seven MFC classes that are used to access DAO functionality, and these are summarized in the table below:

MFC DAO Class	Description
CDaoRecordset	Stores data in a recordset, which can be of three types — snapshot, dynaset (as in ODBC) and table
CDaoDatabase	Establishes and maintains a connection to the database itself
CDaoWorkspace	Defines the session for the user, initializing the database engine, creates a default workspace and providing a space where transactions are applied to all open databases
CDaoQueryDef	Gets and set QueryDef information
CDaoTableDef	Gets and sets Tabledef information
CDaoException	Handles exceptions generated in DAO MFC classes
CDaoFieldExchange	Gets the values from the database fields and assigns them to the recordset's member variables

Let's take a moment to examine these classes in a bit more detail.

The CDaoRecordset Class

This is very similar to the CRecordset class in ODBC — it is the class that essentially represents the data itself, and allows you to perform various manipulations on the data. This class supports a large amount of functionality for working with the data in the recordset and has a huge number of member functions.

The functionality supported by CDaoRecordset includes:

- Creating the recordset.
- Getting and setting various recordset properties — for example, obtaining the SQL statement on which the recordset is based or setting an index on a table-type recordset, whether or not the recordset supports transactions and so on
- Modifying the data in the recordset, adding new records and deleting records
- Traversing the records in the recordset.
- Obtaining information about the types and values of fields in a recordset, as well as the number of fields

❏ Obtaining information about a particular index and the total number of indexes

❏ Refreshing the recordset

❏ Exchanging data between the fields in the recordset object and in the database itself

❏ Obtaining the name of the default data source and the SQL string

The CDaoDatabase Class

As with the ODBC `CDatabase` class, this class maintains the connection to the database itself. Unlike ODBC, the database is usually specified simply by it's name with the full path.

The `CDaoDatabase` class supports the following functionality.

❏ Creating and initializing the database object, and opening and closing the connection to the database itself

❏ Getting information on TableDefs, QueryDefs and relations between database tables

❏ Retrieving the properties of the open database — for example the name and the version, the number of seconds before a query times out (can also set this), whether or not a connection has been made

The CDaoWorkspace Class

The purpose of the DAO workspace is to control a database session that is both named and password protected. Note that you usually don't need to use this class, since the `CDaoDatabase` and `CDaoRecordset` will use the default workspace implicitly.

However, one reason why one might need to access the workspace explicitly is to do things like compact a database. This class also manages transactions over multiple connections to the same database. In other words, unlike the transaction management in the `CDaoRecordset` class, all open database connections are within a single transaction.

The functionality implemented by `CDaoWorkspace` is summarized below:

❏ Creating opening and a new workspace object and closing the workspace

❏ Retrieving information about the workspace attributes, including the name of the workspace and the owner

❏ Beginning, committing and aborting transactions

❑   Compacting and repairing the database object

❑   Obtaining information about a specific databases as well as the total number of databases

❑   Getting and setting database Engine Properties — for example, the version number, the location of the initialization settings, the default password and so on

The CDaoQueryDef Class

This class represents a query that is stored on the database, as opposed to being provided by the program. In addition to using pre-saved QueryDefs, the CDaoQueryDef class can be used to create new QueryDefs or temporary queries. QueryDefs can be used to handle native SQL in databases that are not Jet-based (such as SQL Server and Oracle). There are three groups of functions in this class:

❑   Creating, opening and closing a QueryDef object

❑   Getting and setting the attributes of a QueryDef. — for example, the SQL string which is specified by the QueryDef, the name of the QueryDef, the date of creation, whether or not it can update the database and so on

❑   Executing the query defined by the QueryDef

❑   Retrieving information about the stored Querydefs, including the number of fields, the number of parameters and so on

The CDaoTableDef Class

The DAO database object maintains all the tables stored in the database in a collection, and the definition of each table is represented by a TableDef object. The purpose of the CDaoTableDef class is to allow you to access these definitions and create new ones.

The functionality implemented by CDaoTableDef includes:

❑   Creating, opening and closing a TableDef

❑   Altering or retrieving the attributes of the TableDef — for example, the name, creation date, number of records, and information about the indexes and fields

❑   Modifying a TableDef, for example, creating and deleting both fields and indexes

An Example using DAO

Now that we've looked at the MFC DAO classes, let's have a look at a practical example that uses some of these classes. We'll create an MFC application as before, using the same example database (testsm.mdb) and creating the same kind of form view to display the data. However, this time, we will access the database using DAO rather than ODBC.

So, create a new AppWizard (EXE) project and call it TestDAO. Select the very same options as we did before, that is, Single Document Interface in Step 1, and changing the view's base class from CView to CFormView in the final step. As with the ODBC example, we won't use the Microsoft database options in the AppWizard.

Before creating the form, use ClassWizard to create a new class called CTestDaoRecordset, which will inherit from CDaoRecordset. It is at this point, we confirm that we are going to use DAO. As soon as you specify CDaoRecordset, the following dialog box is shown:

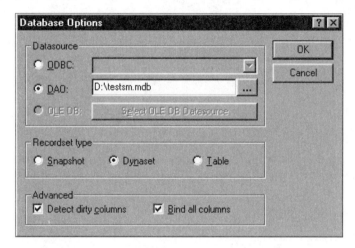

Note that the dynaset button is checked, which is what we want. Now press the ellipsis (...) button and select first our data source "testsm.mdb" and then the Invoice table from the next drop-down list. Pressing OK will create the class with the connection to the invoice table in place.

Now we have the new class, we can create the form, in exactly the same way as before. In fact, we'll use the same form as we did for the ODBC example. Remember that there were four edit boxes for the invoice ID (read-only), item ID, units and the vendor ID. There are also four buttons — Next and Prev for moving through the recordset, New for adding a record and Update for updating a record.

The CTestDaoRecordset Class

The definition of the `CTestDaoRecordset` can be found in `TestDaoRecordset.h`. It is almost exactly the same as what we have seen before. The main difference here is that the class is derived from `CDaoRecordset` rather than `CRecordset`. Note also that, as with the ODBC file, the database object (`CDaoDatabase`) is created in the constructor. This means that the default database object is created automatically for us.

At the top of `TestRecordset.h`, you will need to add a `#include` for the header file that defines the MFC DAO classes, `afxdao.h`.

You can find the default implementations for the constructor, and the member functions in the file `TestDaoRecordset.cpp`. The constructor simply initializes the member variables that correspond to the fields in the table to zero:

```
CTestDaoRecordset::CTestDaoRecordset(CDaoDatabase* pdb)
    : CDaoRecordset(pdb)
{
    //{{AFX_FIELD_INIT(CTestDaoRecordset)
    m_InvoiceID = 0;
    m_VendorID = 0;
    m_ItemID = 0;
    m_Units = 0;
    m_nFields = 4;
    //}}AFX_FIELD_INIT
    m_nDefaultType = dbOpenDynaset;
}
```

Note the difference between this and the ODBC example in the `GetDefaultDBName()` function. Instead of providing the name of the ODBC connection, it returns the path to the database itself:

```
CString CTestDaoRecordset::GetDefaultDBName()
{
    return _T("C:\\testsm.mdb");
}
```

...

Now let's see how we can use this class to retrieve and modify the data set.

The Document Class

The document and view classes are also almost identical. The only change we need to make to the header for the document class, `TestDAODoc.h`, is the addition a member variable, `m_TestDaoRecordset`, which is an instance of the `CTestDaoRecordset` class, which will contain the recordset data:

```
// Attributes
public:
   CTestDaoRecordset m_TestDaoRecordset;

// Operations

...
```

Obviously, you'll also need to #include the header containing the definition of the CTestDaoRecordset class:

```
#include "TestDaoRecordset.h"
```

In the implementation file for this class, TestDAODoc.cpp, we need to add some code for the constructor and destructor, and also for the OnNewDocument() member function:

```
// CTestDAODoc construction/destruction

CTestDAODoc::CTestDAODoc()
{
   m_TestDaoRecordset.Open();
}

CTestDAODoc::~CTestDAODoc()
{
   m_TestDaoRecordset.Close();
}

BOOL CTestDAODoc::OnNewDocument()
{
   if (!CDocument::OnNewDocument())
      return FALSE;

   m_TestDaoRecordset.MoveFirst();
   return TRUE;
}
```

The View Class

For the CTestDAOView class, we need to carry out the following steps:

❑ Add data members corresponding to the four edit boxes using ClassWizard

❑ Add message handlers for the four buttons on the form, remembering to name the handler for the **Update** button OnUpdateRec()

❑ Add an override for the OnUpdate() method of CTestDaoView using ClassWizard

❑ Add a Boolean data member, m_bNew, to the protected part of the class header

Now let's look at the implementation of this class. First, we need to add a line to the constructor to initialize our m_bNew data member:

```
CTestDAOView::CTestDAOView()
    : CFormView(CTestDAOView::IDD)
{
    //{{AFX_DATA_INIT(CTestDAOView)
    m_Invoice = _T("");
    m_Item = _T("");
    m_Units = _T("");
    m_Vendor = _T("");
    //}}AFX_DATA_INIT
    m_bNew = false;
}
```

The rest of the changes we need to make to this file are concerned with the implementation of the message handlers for the four buttons we have on our form, and the OnUpdate() member function that we are overriding. Let's take a look at that first:

```
void CTestDAOView::OnUpdate(CView* pSender, LPARAM lHint,
                            CObject* pHint)
{
    // create string buffer
    char tres[MAX_LENGTH];

    // get a pointer to the recordset
    CTestDaoRecordset* pTestRecordset = &GetDocument()->m_TestDaoRecordset;

    //we convert the long values returned to a char string and set it
    //to the associated variable
    m_Invoice = ltoa(pTestRecordset->m_InvoiceID,tres,10);
    m_Item = ltoa(pTestRecordset->m_ItemID,tres,10);
    m_Units = ltoa(pTestRecordset->m_Units,tres,10);
    m_Vendor = ltoa(pTestRecordset->m_VendorID,tres,10);

    // update the screen - FALSE indicates that the updated
    // variables should be passed to the form.
    UpdateData(FALSE);
}
```

Note that this is very similar to the implementation we saw in the previous example. Here are the implementations for the message handlers. First, the **Prev** button:

```
void CTestDAOView::OnPrev()
{
    // create string buffer
    char tres[MAX_LENGTH];

    // get a pointer to the recordset
    CTestDaoRecordset* pTestRecordset = &GetDocument()->m_TestDaoRecordset;
```

```
    // check it's not BOF before stepping backward thru recordset
    if(pTestRecordset->IsBOF())
    {
        pTestRecordset->MoveFirst();
        MessageBox("At beginning of file",
                    "File Warning",MB_OK | MB_ICONINFORMATION);
    }
    else
    {
        // move to the previous record, but if it's BOF move to the
        //first record
        pTestRecordset->MovePrev();

        if(pTestRecordset->IsBOF())
        {
            pTestRecordset->MoveFirst();
            MessageBox("At beginning of file",
                        "File Warning",MB_OK | MB_ICONINFORMATION);
        }

        m_Invoice = ltoa(pTestRecordset->m_InvoiceID,tres,10);
        m_Item = ltoa(pTestRecordset->m_ItemID,tres,10);
        m_Units = ltoa(pTestRecordset->m_Units,tres,10);
        m_Vendor = ltoa(pTestRecordset->m_VendorID,tres,10);

        UpdateData(FALSE);
    }
}
```

Notice how we use the constant MAX_LENGTH again here — don't forget to #define this at the top of the file.

And now the **Next** button:

```
void CTestDAOView::OnNext()
{
   // create string buffer
   char tres[MAX_LENGTH];

   // get a pointer to the recordset
   CTestDaoRecordset* pTestRecordset = &GetDocument()->m_TestDaoRecordset;

   // check it's not EOF before stepping fwdward thru recordset
   if(pTestRecordset->IsEOF())
   {
      MessageBox("At end of file",
               "File Warning",MB_OK | MB_ICONINFORMATION);
   }
   else
   {
      pTestRecordset->MoveNext();
      if(pTestRecordset->IsEOF())
      {
         MessageBox("At end of file",
                  "File Warning",MB_OK | MB_ICONINFORMATION);
         pTestRecordset->MoveLast();
      }

      m_Invoice = ltoa(pTestRecordset->m_InvoiceID,tres,10);
      m_Item = ltoa(pTestRecordset->m_ItemID,tres,10);
      m_Units = ltoa(pTestRecordset->m_Units,tres,10);
      m_Vendor = ltoa(pTestRecordset->m_VendorID,tres,10);

      UpdateData(FALSE);
   }
}
```

And now the **New** button:

```
void CTestDAOView::OnNew()
{
   m_Item = "";
   m_Units = "";
   m_Vendor = "";
   m_Invoice= "tbd";
   UpdateData(FALSE);
   m_bNew = true;
}
```

And finally the **Update** button:

```
void CTestDAOView::OnUpdateRec()
{
    // create string buffer
    char strTmp[MAX_LENGTH];

// get a pointer to the recordset
    CTestDAODoc* pDoc = GetDocument();
    CTestDaoRecordset* pTestRecordset = &pDoc->m_TestDaoRecordset;

    if(m_bNew)
        pTestRecordset->AddNew();
    else
        pTestRecordset->Edit();

    UpdateData(true);
    pTestRecordset->m_ItemID = atol(m_Item);
    pTestRecordset->m_Units = atol(m_Units);
    pTestRecordset->m_VendorID = atol(m_Vendor);
    pTestRecordset->Update();

    if(m_bNew)
    {
        COleVariant varBK =
            pTestRecordset->GetLastModifiedBookmark();
        pTestRecordset->SetBookmark(varBK);
        m_Invoice = ltoa(pTestRecordset->m_InvoiceID,strTmp,10);
        UpdateData(FALSE);
        m_bNew = false;
    }
}
```

The code for the above functions is virtually identical to that of the ODBC example. This gives the impression that ODBC and DAO operate by very similar methods. However this is not true — DAO and ODBC are very different indeed. However, the differences between them are handled inside MFC itself and it works hard to present a fairly uniform interface to the user. MFC provides such a wrapper around the object-oriented DAO model, whereas in the case of ODBC, MFC provides an abstraction of an object-oriented implementation.

Note the differences in the message handlers for the **Update** button in our two examples. There is a difference in the way new records are added to the recordset in ODBC and DAO. In ODBC, a new record is appended to the recordset. However, in DAO we must get the bookmark of the last modified record, set the recordset to that location and then retrieve the invoice ID.

Using a Parameterized Stored Query

In our last example, we used a simple recordset based on a table, but it is also possible to use stored procedures or QueryDefs in your recordset (depending on the data source).

In this section, we'll extend the last example with another recordset class, this time based on a QueryDef, using a stored query in Access. As you will see, this example is very similar to the parameterized query example we saw earlier using ODBC.

First, we have to set up the QueryDef. Shown below is a screenshot from Access, showing graphically the lay out of the query:

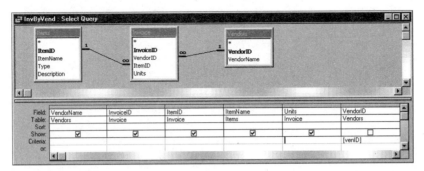

The SQL for this query is:

```
PARAMETERS venID Short;
SELECT vendors.vendorName, invoice.invoiceID, invoice.itemID, items.itemName,
      invoice.units
FROM vendors INNER JOIN (items INNER JOIN invoice ON items.itemID = invoice.itemID)
ON vendors.vendorID = invoice.vendorID
WHERE (((vendors.vendorID)=[venID]));
```

Now, we create the recordset class using the wizard, just as we did earlier. Call the class CQueryRec. However, this time we need the stored query InvByVend. This example is actually much easier than using the parameterized query with ODBC, as the recordset class generated for us by the wizard does not require any alteration. Lets' just take a quick look at some of the code it has generated for us.

Here, you can see that the wizard has generated a member variable, m_venID, for the parameter we declared in the SQL statement, as well as the usual member variables for the appropriate columns:

```
// Field/Param Data
//{{AFX_FIELD(CQueryRec, CDaoRecordset)
CString    m_VendorName;
long    m_InvoiceID;
long    m_ItemID;
CString    m_ItemName;
long    m_Units;
//}}AFX_FIELD
// ...
// ...
short m_venID;
```

We will need to set this `m_venID` variable in order to set the parameter for the query, before we can open the recordset.

Look at the implementation of the recordset class in the .cpp file. The key difference in the constructor is the fact that the number of parameters (`m_nParams`) is initialized to 1 and the parameter (`m_venID`) is initialized to 0:

```
CQueryRec::CQueryRec(CDaoDatabase* pdb)
    : CDaoRecordset(pdb)
{
    //{{AFX_FIELD_INIT(CQueryRec)
    m_VendorName = _T("");
    m_InvoiceID = 0;
    m_ItemID = 0;
    m_ItemName = _T("");
    m_Units = 0;
    m_nFields = 5;
    //}}AFX_FIELD_INIT
    m_nDefaultType = dbOpenDynaset;
    m_nParams = 1;
    m_venID = 0;
}
```

Again, there's no need to change the implementations of `GetDefaultDBName()` and `GetDefaultSQL()`. These simple return the full pathname for the database and the name of the Access QueryDef respectively:

```
CString CQueryRec::GetDefaultDBName()
{
    return _T("C:\\Books\\2416\\TestODBC\\testsm.mdb");
}

CString CQueryRec::GetDefaultSQL()
{
    return _T("[InvByVend]");
}
```

The `DoFieldExchange()` method will also access (set and retrieve) the parameter, as well as the column data. Note that the `SetFieldType()` method is used to specify the fact that `m_venID` is a parameter:

```
void CQueryRec::DoFieldExchange(CDaoFieldExchange* pFX)
{
    //{{AFX_FIELD_MAP(CQueryRec)
    pFX->SetFieldType(CDaoFieldExchange::outputColumn);
    DFX_Text(pFX, _T("[VendorName]"), m_VendorName);
    DFX_Long(pFX, _T("[InvoiceID]"), m_InvoiceID);
    DFX_Long(pFX, _T("[ItemID]"), m_ItemID);
    DFX_Text(pFX, _T("[ItemName]"), m_ItemName);
    DFX_Long(pFX, _T("[Units]"), m_Units);
    //}}AFX_FIELD_MAP
    // ...
    // ...
    pFX->SetFieldType(CDaoFieldExchange::param);
    DFX_Short(pFX, _T("venID"), m_venID);
}
```

You'll need to create another DAO recordset class now, `CVendorRec` — this time based on the vendors table. Again, the generated code is sufficient and does not require any changes.

Now, let's look at how it is used. We can use the same form as we did the ODBC example:

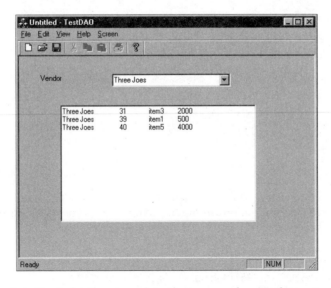

As before, the important methods for the view class that we need to implement are:

- ❑ `OnInitialUpdate()` — the function called when the view is initialized

- ❑ `OnSelchangeVenlist()` — called when one selects a vendor from the combo box

These functions are very similar to those from the ODBC example. The implementation for `OnInitialUpdate()` is shown below:

```
void CQueryView::OnInitialUpdate()
{
    CFormView::OnInitialUpdate();

    int iRes;
    m_ctlVendor.ResetContent();

    // get pointer to vendor recordset
    CVendorRec* pRec = &GetDocument()->m_VendorRec;
    pRec->MoveFirst();

    // populate combo box
    while(!pRec->IsEOF())
    {
        iRes = m_ctlVendor.AddString(pRec->m_VendorName);
        m_ctlVendor.SetItemData(iRes,pRec->m_VendorID);
        pRec->MoveNext();
    }
}
```

In this function, we go step through the recordset containing the vendors information. For each record, we add the vendor name as the string (using `AddString()`) and the vendor ID as the data item (using `SetDataItem()`). This allows us to later retrieve the correct vendorID of the currently selected item in the combo box (or more accurately, dropdown list box).

The implementation of `OnSelchangeVenlist()` uses the parameterized query:

```
void CQueryView::OnSelchangeVenlist()
{
    // get pointer to query recordset
    CQueryRec* pRec = &GetDocument()->m_QueryRec;

    m_ctlQres.SetWindowText("");
    CString strLine;
    char cRes[10];
    int i = 1;

    // set parameter and open recordset
    pRec->m_venID = (int)m_ctlVendor.GetItemData(m_ctlVendor.GetCurSel());
    pRec->Open();
    strLine = "";
```

```
// fill edit box with invoice info
while(!pRec->IsEOF())
{
    strLine = strLine + pRec->m_VendorName;
    strLine = strLine + "\t";
    strLine = strLine + itoa(pRec->m_InvoiceID,cRes,10);
    strLine = strLine + "\t";
    strLine = strLine + pRec->m_ItemName;
    strLine = strLine + "\t";
    strLine = strLine + itoa(pRec->m_Units,cRes,10);
    strLine = strLine + "\r\n";
    pRec->MoveNext();
}
this->m_ctlQres.SetWindowText(strLine);
pRec->Close();
}
```

First, we need to set the parameter value from the data in the combo box, before we can open the recordset. We then simple scroll through the recordset, filling the edit box line by line. This is also virtually the same as the ODBC function we saw earlier.

The changes to the document class, `CMainFrame` and `CTestDAOApp` classes are identical as described earlier in the ODBC case. Once you've made these changes, you should be able to build the example and try it out!

Pros and Cons of DAO

In accessing common desktop databases such as Access, FoxPro and other ISAM databases on local servers, DAO has better performance than ODBC. It also has the advantage of not requiring any extra user configuration — no ODBC-like connection to the data source needs to be made. DAO objects can attach directly to a table in a database where you can carry out modifications to the data. You can also use DAO to create database tables from, and modify a database itself by performing DDL calls.

However, DAO also has its limitations. It does not have the ability to connect directly with remote servers such as SQL Server and Oracle. Recall that DAO can be used to access the ODBC driver manager, allowing indirect access to these databases, but this is not an efficient process. With DAO connecting directly to databases rather then data sources, as in the case of ODBC, a DAO object has to be configurable if it is to be used with more than one database.

Universal Data Access, ADO and OLE DB

The idea behind Microsoft's **Universal Data Access (UDA)** is to provide a common means of accessing all types of data *regardless of what form it is in*. Among the technologies that fall under the UDA umbrella are:

- ODBC
- OLE DB
- ADO
- RDS (Remote Data Services)

In this chapter, we have seen ODBC and how easy it is to access an ODBC connection in Visual C++, using the MFC. ODBC has many advantages, due to the fact that it is a well tested and widely used technology, offering access to all major DBMSs.

We introduced and briefly described OLE DB and ADO at the beginning of this chapter. In this closing section we will prepare ourselves to delve into these newer technologies in the coming chapters, where they will be more thoroughly explained. OLE DB and ADO have been designed as the next generation of data access technologies, eventually replacing ODBC and DAO. The beauty of these technologies is that they are built upon COM and therefore have all the advantages that COM offers. We'll see more about this in the next chapter. OLE DB and ADO to access a far wider range of data sources —either in a desktop, client/server or web-based applications. This provides a great deal of flexibility to programers.

OLE DB lies at the heart of the Universal Data Access strategy. The reason for this is that it can be used to access any data source. Unlike ODBC, it is not limited to relational data and ISAM databases. ADO, built upon OLE DB, can be accessed in a wide variety of environments, including Visual Basic, ASP and scripting languages.

ADO and OLE DB are important technologies — they are the future of data access in the Microsoft environment. They are, however, quite complex technologies, so we will devote the next few chapters to examining them in detail.

Summary

In this chapter we have shown how data can be accessed using two well-established Microsoft technologies: ODBC and DAO. With ODBC you can access any data source, providing the appropriate driver software exists for the required database. On the other hand, DAO is designed to access the Jet database engine and is optimized for use with desktop and ISAM databases. For remote server-based databases, such as SQL Server and Oracle, ODBC is the better option.

We also created simple database applications using the MFC ODBC classes and the corresponding DAO classes, and have shown that as far as MFC is concerned, there is little difference between them. However MFC hides the substantial differences between the two technologies. We also saw how to base recordset classes on parameterized queries, and how simple it is to use an Access QueryDef with the MFC DAO classes.

We now leave ODBC, DAO and MFC and discuss the new COM-based technology OLE DB.

An Introduction to OLE DB

At the end of the last chapter, we looked briefly at Microsoft's strategy for **Universal Data Access**, or UDA. Let's take a moment to consider why this is so important. Accessing data is a key part of many applications in today's world, and that data is stored in many different formats in many different places. What kind of data is important to businesses? Well, it could be files stored in a FAT or NTFS file system, graphical data, emails, Web-based text files, hierarchical data, as well as data stored in a more traditional DBMS. Rather than search for a common format in which to store a wide variety of data, UDA seeks to find a common way of *accessing* that data, so that it may remain stored in the place that is most suitable for it.

ODBC was a first step along this road, creating a common interface to a wide variety of DBMSs. As we saw in the last chapter however, this has its limitations, particularly regarding the kind of database that can be accessed using it. All ODBC drivers had to at least implement a layer that mimicked SQL. On the other hand, OLE DB has been developed to handle a much wider range of data sources, including hierarchical data. OLE DB takes the aim of generic data access further by creating an interface, based not on a C API (as in ODBC), but on Microsoft's **Component Object Model**, or **COM**. More specifically, OLE DB is a set of *COM interfaces*. This further abstraction allows us to create access to almost any data source, as well as bringing with it all the advantages of COM, namely reusability, extensibility and maintainability.

In this chapter, we'll be taking an introductory overview of OLE DB. In particular, we'll be looking at:

- ❑ What OLE DB is
- ❑ How OLE DB came about
- ❑ OLE DB consumers, providers and service components
- ❑ The OLE DB object model
- ❑ The interfaces of OLE DB
- ❑ Technologies that make OLE DB easier to use

Since OLE DB is built upon COM, we'll start this chapter with a brief look at COM, and why it is so useful.

A Touch of COM

Several years ago Microsoft developed the **Component Object Model** or **COM**. The idea behind COM is to provide a binary model for interface-based programming, supplying code that can be used and reused by many different applications. Since it is a binary specification, it is language neutral and so you can write a COM component in a variety of different languages and any program can, through interfaces, interact with the component and use it.

Code reuse has been the goal of software developers for many years. However the problem with earlier methods of code reuse, such as C++ classes and libraries, is the level of reusability they provide. For instance, MFC consists of many classes that can only be used by C++ programmers — they are not available to Visual Basic and Java users. COM addresses the issue of reusability by moving from a monolithic model of software development to creating software using prewritten, precompiled portions of code called **components**.

Object-oriented programming (OOP) is a well-established method of reusing code, utilizing, for example, C++ classes. The problem with OOP and C++ is that you need to have knowledge of the class or classes your object inherits from. Recall that OOP is based on, among other things, an "is a" hierarchy. For example, a bear "is a" mammal, and generally speaking mammals give birth to live young. This would be one property of the mammal that would be defined in the base class. A bear class can therefore be derived from the mammal class. However, a duck-billed platypus is a mammal that lays eggs rather than gives birth to live young. A platypus class would thus not have all the characteristics of the mammal class and as a result the "is a" relationship does not hold. As far as OOP is concerned, a platypus is not a mammal. To be consistent with the principles of OOP, you should not derive this class solely from the mammal base class. This simple example illustrates that OOP, as a code reuse technology, does not work very well — the platypus class requires code which the mammal class cannot supply.

Another means of reusing code that is extensively used in the Windows world is the **DLL** or **Dynamic Link Library**. This provides for much greater reusability than OOP, as the libraries can be loaded into any Windows program and their functions called as and when required. DLLs contain precompiled code that can be shared by a number of applications simultaneously.

However, there are disadvantages to using DLLs. If you're familiar with Windows systems, you will be aware of the problems that can result if you install a program that puts a DLL on the system that upgrades an existing one. Often there will have been changes made to the new DLL that make it incompatible with the previous version. Any applications requiring the older version of the DLL will then cease to work.

Another problem arises from the fact that an operating system can, and often does, contain different DLLs with the same name, which makes it possible to call the wrong one. If the DLL doesn't contain the function you want, the results can be unpredictable.

In order to use DLL functionality, you have to load the entire library and even then you might not find what you want. DLLs allow a certain amount of code reuse, but can be inefficient in terms of time and memory usage.

COM, however, takes code reusability to a higher level altogether, by completely separating the interface from the function implementation. You do not need to load a component into memory to search for the functionality you require. Instead you query the component's *interfaces*, and COM itself informs you whether or not what you want is available. Only if the query is successful does the component load itself into your application. The component's functionality is never directly exposed to the user, only the interfaces.

For any COM component, its interfaces have to be immutable. If any changes are made to the functionality of a component, you cannot change the interface to accommodate these changes — a brand new interface has to be defined. This is important because this means that any particular interface will always work the same way — it is truly reusable. Functions cannot be removed from a component, nor the calling interface to those functions changed. Therefore, upgrading a COM object should never cause a program already using that object to fail.

Since COM is based on pure virtual functions, there is no pre-existing base implementation to cause concern. Furthermore, COM avoids the naming problem associated with DLLs. In COM, every object and every interface has a unique ID (known as a **Globally Unique Identifier** or **GUID**) that the system uses to locate it. Therefore, installation of a new COM object cannot affect existing programs.

As COM defines a binary standard, all programs can potentially utilize it whether they're written in C, C++, Java, Visual Basic and scripting languages. All interfaces take the form of a vtable — an array of function pointers. Theoretically, any language that can dynamically create a vtable can be used to create a COM object.

Advantages of COM

What is it about COM that makes it so useful to us? Apart from its language neutrality, already described, it allows us to create COM components, which become integrated into our applications. In essence, we're applying to software what hardware manufacturers have been employing for decades. A COM object is not unlike a piece of hardware — it can be "plugged" into an application when certain functionality is required and "unplugged" when it is finished with.

COM itself keeps track of component usage by means of **reference counting**. For every method call on an interface, the count is incremented (the COM function `AddRef()` is called) and every time a function returns, the count is decremented (the COM function `Release()` is called). Once the count reaches zero, the component itself is released.

With COM taking care of the functionality contained within components, we are free to develop our application to suit our own needs. A component exists as a separate binary object (a DLL or an EXE) that exposes a set of pre-defined, unchangeable COM interfaces to the user. It is therefore COM that sets the rules for interface implementation. It is our task to supply the code to suit the requirements of our project. One of the strengths of COM is its consistency. It will not allow you to implement an interface inappropriately or wrongly, unlike ordinary C++ classes which can be 'made to work'.

Before we move on, there is one more advantage of COM that should be mentioned — support services. COM has a number of such services available to it such as security, transactions and message queuing. These, however, are beyond the scope of this book.

> *You'll need to be familiar with the basics of COM, in order to understand OLE DB, so if you're completely new to the subject, it might be a good idea to check out one of the books on the subject listed in Appendix A. Among the topics you should understand are interfaces in general, the `IUnknown` interface, composition and aggregation. The first two chapters from* Professional COM Applications with ATL *provide an excellent introduction to COM, and are available for download from the Wrox Press Web site at* `http://www.wrox.com`.

The Universal Data Access (UDA) Model

In the past, most data would be accessed either from a desktop computer or via a client/server architecture. The data would be stored in spreadsheets, desktop databases or server based databases, mainly on a local machine or a mainframe. However, with the advent of the Internet, things have changed. The ability to access remote data sources across a network is now essential. The Internet allows access to data from any Web browser. No other special software is required.

This is where the UDA model comes in. The beauty of UDA is that an enterprise is not limited to using one type of data source. A department within a large corporation might store all its data on spreadsheets, another might use SQL Server. A third might use Oracle, and a fourth, Access. With various departments using different databases, there has to be an application that can access all of them. Thus, each department can choose the database that meets its own needs, but still allow for data to be available to the rest of the corporation. ODBC does allow for multiple data source access, but OLE DB carries out this task in a much more efficient manner. OLE DB providers can be simpler than ODBC drivers since they do not have to fit a non-SQL data source into a SQL format and can take advantage of reusable components.

For example, in order to do analysis of certain data, you might want to create a spreadsheet using data which resides in a SQL Server database. OLE DB would provide the means to do this in a very efficient manner. Indeed, OLE DB was designed two solve two major downsides of ODBC. The first is efficiency, which becomes much more important when we're dealing with data that can even be distributed over the Internet. The second concerns configuration management issues, for example, there can be versioning problems associated with ODBC drivers, a problem eliminated when using COM-based OLE DB providers.

The UDA model is illustrated in the following diagram:

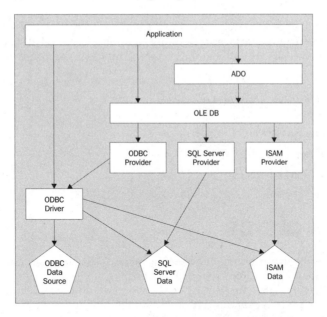

At the heart of UDA is OLE DB, with ADO (ActiveX Data Objects) inserted as an additional layer on top. There are two main motivations behind the creation of ADO. Firstly, there are many languages that cannot directly use OLE DB, Visual Basic being a prime example. Languages like these must work at the ADO level to harness the power and flexibility of OLE DB. Secondly, ADO hides some of the more complicated details of OLE DB, and makes the life of the programmer a little easier. ADO is described more fully in Chapter 7.

What is OLE DB?

OLE DB is Microsoft's newest method for accessing data in an extremely flexible manner. Within the UDA model, it operates at the system level, and is designed eventually to replace ODBC. However, it should be noted that at the present time, Microsoft actually has an OLE DB provider for ODBC, which allows you to use OLE DB to access any data source that has an ODBC driver, at the cost of some added overhead. Examples of databases still using ODBC drivers are SQL Server, Oracle and Sybase. (Note that SQL Server 6.5 does not have a native OLE DB provider, the OLE DB provider that exists for SQL Server is for version 7.0.)

When using the older technologies, such as DAO or ODBC, you were limited to data sources that are either SQL/relational based or which could be made to appear as SQL-based data, for example Excel spreadsheets. With OLE DB, however, there is no such limitation. You can write an OLE DB provider for any data source including hierarchical data.

> It should be noted that **hierarchical data** is data which is divided into chapters, each containing rowsets, which are arranged in a hierarchical fashion. By comparison with Explorer, each chapter can be likened to a folder and each rowset a file within the folder.

OLE DB consists of a set of approximately sixty COM interfaces, which define a unified means for accessing any data source. These interfaces essentially componentize the DBMS functionality. As a user, that is a consumer, you simply call methods on these interfaces as you would with any COM object.

We will look at OLE DB in three closely related ways:

❑   Consumers, Services and Providers

❑   The set of four main objects

❑   The set of COM interfaces

Design Goals of OLE DB

ODBC was designed to solve the problem of accessing various SQL data sources, while minimizing changes to the code in client applications that use these data sources. However, it has certain weaknesses. First of all, every data source must be shoehorned into the SQL model. This means that a SQL parser must be written even for data sources that don't use SQL. If a non-SQL source has to implement a SQL parser, this is a big performance hit.

OLE DB was designed with a number of goals in mind:

- ❑ Flexibility — OLE DB should be able to access a wider range of data sources than previous technologies
- ❑ Performance — the efficiency of data access over the Internet needed to be improved
- ❑ Reliability — Microsoft has released key OLE DB components as system components, thereby increasing exposure and allowing any problems to be quickly identified and rectified

Now let us now look at some of the ways OLE DB meets these goals. It is designed to allow any data source to be accessed as long as a provider exists for it. Potentially, any data source can be accessed.

OLE DB also handles hierarchical, or chaptered, rowsets, which are not supported by ODBC.

OLE DB also provides certain services that can be shared among providers, such as handling queries and cursors. This reduces the amount of additional work that has to be done in implementing a provider. Thus you can expose proprietary data sources (data not contained in a traditional database) to an application, as easily as you can normal data sources. By reducing the amount of code that needs to be implemented each time, we also increase reliability.

OLE DB and ADO were designed to operate in a *stateless* mode, which means that the client and server are able to break their connection between data access operations. Thus, as we'll see later when we discuss RDS (Remote Data Service) in Chapter 8, the client can perform operations on the data locally and only connect to the remote data source in order to retrieve data and return modified data.

OLE DB components have been shipped as part of more recent releases of the Windows operating system (Windows NT 4.0, Win98 and IE 4.0). They are fully integrated into the OS and don't have to be separately configured and maintained. This also means that the components can be extensively utilized by users of these systems, thus allowing the kinks of this new technology to be worked out.

Data access can be managed on a remote server. This centralizes the location where providers are installed, thus allowing the distribution and maintenance to be more easily controlled, which again increases the reliability of OLE DB.

Last but by no means least, there is no driver manager. The removal of this layer from OLE DB improves performance.

Thus, you can see that OLE DB has a number of advantages over the prior models. It is designed for performance and reliability both locally and over remote connections.

Consumers, Providers and Services

One of the easiest ways to look at OLE DB is in terms of how the different components interact. So, let's start by examining:

❑ Consumers

❑ Providers

❑ Services

An OLE DB provider is the component that implements the OLE DB interfaces for a specific data source, and exposes the data via these interfaces. An OLE DB consumer is any component that accesses data via the OLE DB interfaces. Service components, on the other hand, can act as both providers and consumers, transporting and processing data.

We'll look at these three components in more detail in the following sections. Firstly, in order to understand how these components interact, consider the following diagram:

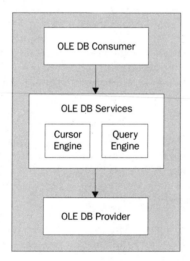

OLE DB Consumers

An **OLE DB consumer** is simply an application that requests and uses data from an OLE DB provider. Any client that accesses a data source via OLE DB, that is calls methods on OLE DB interfaces, is an OLE DB consumer. This definition can be broadened to include ADO, which, because it depends on OLE DB to access data, can also be considered a consumer. We'll be seeing more of OLE DB consumers in the next chapter.

OLE DB Providers

OLE DB providers serve the same purpose in OLE DB, as drivers do in ODBC. Essentially, they implement the set of interfaces that comprise OLE DB, but it is not necessary for a provider to implement *all* these interfaces. To be an OLE DB provider, an object must encapsulate access to the data and then expose it to other objects or applications.

They must implement a minimal amount of functionality, so that at the very least, a consumer can connect to a data source, retrieve data in a tabular form and step through it sequentially in one direction. This is no different to reading a text file into an application using such common C functionality as `fscanf()` or `fgets()`. The ability to implement only a minimal amount of functionality is a great advantage, as you do not have to include the overhead of functionality that you're not going to use.

However, when appropriate, OLE DB providers can implement additional functionality, which allows for more complex operations, such as the handling of SQL commands and bookmarks (placeholders which allow you to return a particular record or row in the rowset). We'll look at this in more depth later on in the chapter, when we discuss the OLE DB interfaces.

Available Providers

There are several OLE DB providers already available. Among them are the following:

- ❑ OLE DB provider for ODBC drivers
- ❑ OLE DB provider for Jet databases
- ❑ OLE DB provider for SQL Server
- ❑ OLE DB provider for Oracle

As we saw earlier, the OLE DB provider for ODBC drivers is used when accessing data from an existing source that requires an ODBC connection. With the large number of data sources still depending on ODBC, this particular provider is commonly used.

The OLE DB provider for Jet databases is designed to handle data from the following sources:

- ❑ Access files
- ❑ ISAM databases (FoxPro, Paradox, Btrieve etc.)

The OLE DB provider for SQL Server can only be used with version 7.0. For earlier versions of SQL Server, you have to use the OLE DB provider for ODBC drivers.

The OLE DB provider for Oracle supports Oracle 7.3.3 and above, including Oracle 8.0. This provider also offers support for Microsoft Transaction Server (MTS).

Other providers available at the time of writing include one for Active Directory Services (ADS) and one for index file system and web data.

OLE DB Service Components

Some OLE DB components encapsulate services that both provide *and* utilize data. Such components are known as **service components**. Typical examples of service components are:

- ❑ Query processor
- ❑ Cursor engine
- ❑ Synchronization component
- ❑ Shape component

A query processor will take a query and retrieve rowsets in the same way a normal consumer does. However, like a provider, it is able to return rowsets to the client.

A cursor engine provides the functionality that allows you to scroll through a set of data. Like the query processor, a cursor engine is an intermediary between the client application and the provider. It is able to select a rowset from the provider and supply it to the client application.

Synchronization allows you to refresh data in the rowset to take into account changes that might have been made by another user.

Finally, a shape component is geared towards hierarchical data — the SHAPE language, which is built into the ADO client cursor, allows you to create such hierarchical rowsets.

Recall that service components are COM objects that can be used by a number of data providers. The fact that OLE DB service components are separate objects means that, unlike with ODBC drivers, OLE DB providers don't need to implement query processors and cursor engines, but can call an existing query processor. This is extremely important in that it greatly reduces the amount of coding that needs to be done to get a provider written. Furthermore, there is less new code that has to be verified.

OLE DB Objects

In this section, we'll be examining OLE DB from the perspective of the OLE DB object model. We'll take a brief look at all the objects, but we'll focus in detail on the four major ones.

Data Sources, Sessions, Commands and Rowsets

In understanding how OLE DB works it is critical to understand it's four major objects:

- ❑ Data Sources
- ❑ Sessions
- ❑ Commands
- ❑ Rowsets

These four components interact with each other in order to allow the user to retrieve and modify data in any data source that has an OLE DB provider. The diagram below shows how these objects fit together:

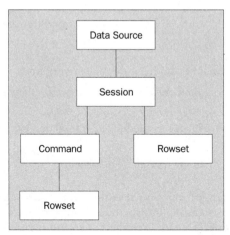

Note that there are other OLE DB objects, but we'll be focussing on just these four in this section.

Let's consider what happens in the simplest case of connecting to a database and retrieving some data.

Connecting to the Data Source

After choosing your OLE DB provider, which requires you to use an enumerator, the next step in connecting to a database is to log in. This is where the **data source** object comes in. Once the provider is selected, the data source object provides the connection information that is necessary to connect to the data source in question. To do this we use COM. As will all COM objects, every provider has a class ID, which is passed to the CoCreateInstance() function as a parameter which creates the data source object.

CoCreateInstance() is a COM function used to create a COM object — as you are unfamiliar with COM, you should have a look at one of the references mentioned earlier in the chapter.

The data source object also contains information on whatever permissions are needed for accessing the data. If the user has the appropriate permission, as provided by a login name and password if necessary, the data source object itself logs the user on. You provide authentication information to the data source object through its IDBProperties interface (we'll be looking at the OLE DB interfaces later on). Once this information is provided, you can use another interface of the data source object, IDBInitialize, to make the connection to the database. Then you create one or more session objects — each session acting as a separate transaction within the application. Session objects are critical as they are used to create the rowset and command objects that actually obtain the data.

The **session object** manages a particular interaction with the database supplying the query and retrieving the data. Furthermore, each session object comprises a single transaction, which is best defined as a single work unit within a provider.

To be defined as an atomic unit of work, it has to have what is commonly referred to as the ACID test. The acronym ACID stands for:

❑ Atomicity — that is, it cannot be divided into smaller work units

❑ Concurrency — where more than one transaction can occur at any one time

❑ Isolation — defined as the level of knowledge one transaction has about changes made by another

❑ Durability — changes made to the rowset are persistent

In addition, the session object can return information about the data source itself, which is commonly referred to as **metadata**, for example, information about the tables that make up the data source. It also supports specific interfaces for creating tables and indexes where applicable.

However, the most important tasks a session object has to do are open a rowset, access the session properties and return the data source object that created the session. Other tasks are optional: the ability to create command objects, manage local transactions manually, modify the database, and so on.

Retrieving Data

The **command object** is created by the session object and gives the user the ability to interact with the database using any language supported by the data source, including SQL commands, both DML and DDL (see Chapter 2) as well as non-SQL languages such as SHAPE. However, the command object is usually implemented by providers for SQL-based data sources and not implemented by simple data sources. When a command object executes a query, the resulting data is returned as a rowset object.

Data is retrieved and stored in the **rowset object**. There are quite a few properties that can be set on a rowset, such as properties that tell the rowset that there are bookmarks, what the isolation level of the rowset is and so on. Typically, they are set by creating a property object and adding the properties to it. This object is then passed to the rowset's Open() function.

A rowset can either be created by a session object or via a command object. The rowset object allows you to scroll through a set of data, update rows, delete rows and insert new rows. How much of this functionality is actually implemented depends upon what properties the database supports and what functionality the consumers will need. In the simplest of cases, the rowset object will allow you to scroll through the data in a forward direction only.

Accessors

One major part of OLE DB, which distinguishes it from other data access technologies, is the concept of accessors. An accessor describes how data is stored within the consumer. It consists of a set of bindings between columns in the rowset, or parameters, and details of how data is stored in a buffer in the consumer. Implementing the `IAccessor` interface is a requirement for both the rowset and command objects. Accessors, which are referenced by `HACCESSOR` handles, are created using the `IAccessor::CreateAccessor()` method.

Error, Transaction and Enumerator Objects

The data source, session, command and rowset are not the only OLE DB objects. There are three other objects that provide important functionality, but aren't directly connected to the model described above. These are:

- ❏ The error object
- ❏ The transaction object
- ❏ The enumerator object

The **error object** is probably the most important of the above objects. Like the command object, this is optional, that is, the error object is not required for OLE DB to work — unlike the data source, session and rowset objects. It supports extended error information. Each method associated with any OLE DB object will provide return codes and status information, which allows for a certain amount of error handling and diagnosis. As with any COM object, this information is contained within an `HRESULT`. However, for the programmer who wishes to provide a more meaningful message to their user if something goes wrong, the error object provides further information — a description of the error or, in certain situations, a SQL error message. Note that error objects can be associated with any of the other objects in the hierarchy — errors can occur at any point of the process.

Although the session object provides for a certain amount of transaction functionality, more advanced functionality can be obtained by creating a **transaction object**. This would be necessary when, for example, you want to be able to access different levels of a nested transaction. A nested transaction occurs when a database transaction object sets up a second inner transaction. Changes made within the inner transaction are completely invisible to the outer transaction until the inner transaction is committed. The inner transaction object must be released before the outer one can be released.

The **enumerator object** actually sits on top of the object hierarchy — it is used to search for available data sources, or even other enumerators. This object would be used when we don't have a known data source to which to connect. For example, suppose we wish to write an application that allows the user to choose a data source to connect to, you would create an enumerator object to provide a list of the available sources.

An Overview of the Data Access Process

Now we have looked at each of the OLE DB objects in turn, we can put this information together and see more clearly how OLE DB works, by looking at the sequence of events that take place when a typical consumer interacts with a database:

- ❑ First initialize COM by calling `CoInitialize()`
- ❑ Create the data source object by calling `CoCreateInstance()`
- ❑ Set the properties of the provider, that is create a property object
- ❑ Open a connection to the data source and create a session
- ❑ Create and initialize a rowset or command object
- ❑ Create a property object for the rowset/command and set the properties
- ❑ Open the rowset/command and execute the command
- ❑ Create an accessor
- ❑ Return the data from the rowset, binding it to the accessor
- ❑ Use the data from the rowset
- ❑ Release objects created
- ❑ Uninitialize COM

Alternatively, this can be demonstrated in the form of a diagram:

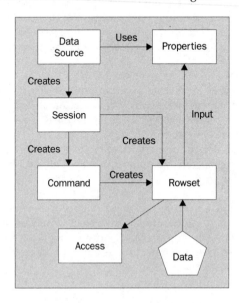

Thus you can see how OLE DB consumers actually use the COM objects described earlier to interact with the database.

The OLE DB Interfaces

We have just looked at a high level at the main objects in OLE DB. Now let us take a different perspective and focus at a lower level on the interfaces themselves. There are some sixty interfaces that are part of OLE DB. Only certain ones are mandatory and hence guaranteed to be available to a consumer of an OLE DB COM object. As with any COM object, you use the standard COM function `QueryInterface()` to determine what interfaces an object supports.

The interfaces' functionality is classified by Microsoft into five groups, according to the objects that implement that functionality:

- Data Source
- Session
- Command
- Rowset
- Transaction

Note that a number of the interfaces, such as ISupportError and IAccessor, span a number of functionalities and thus are supported by more than one object in the OLE DB model.

With such a large number of interfaces, it might appear on the surface that OLE DB can get rather unwieldy. However, in reality, you are only using a small set of interfaces at any given time. Furthermore, when creating a provider you only need implement the interfaces that are necessary. This again partitions the work that must be done.

Although there are around sixty COM interfaces comprising OLE DB, there are just sixteen interfaces that an OLE DB provider must implement, which supply the minimum level of functionality needed for OLE DB to operate. Remember that for an OLE DB provider, the minimal level of functionality it must support is the ability to create a rowset object, and retrieve the data through which it can scroll in a forward direction only.

Note that the term 'mandatory' in this context means that the interface is required when a particular OLE DB object is implemented. This is true of data source, session and rowset objects, which are required at all times. However, for optional objects such as command and transaction objects, their mandatory interfaces only come into play if these objects are created.

For an OLE DB provider, the implementation of the `IAccessor` interface is also mandatory.

Data Source Object Interfaces

Recall that the data source functionality is concerned with the overall connection between the OLE DB provider and the application using the data source. It is involved in essentially creating the connection to the data source and performing authentication. In order to do this, it sets the parameters of the connection (i.e. data source string, user ID, password), storing them in a property object.

There are ten interfaces involved with data source management — they are summarized in the table below:

Interface	Mandatory	Description
IDBCreateSession	Yes	Creates session object
IDBInitialize	Yes	Initializes properties of data source object
IDBProperties	Yes	Gets and sets properties
IPersist	Yes	Provides CLSID of an object that has persistent storage
IDBInfo		Provides information on keywords and literals the provider supports
IPersistFile		Loads and saves an object to disk
ISupportErrorInfo		Supplies information on whether object returns OLE automation error objects.
IConnectionPointContainer		Supports connection points
IDBAsynchStatus		Provides information about the status of asynchronous rowset generation or population
IDBDataSourceAdmin		Creates, destroys and modifies data sources

The necessity of the first three interfaces becomes obvious in light of our previous discussion of data sources and the steps involved in using OLE DB to access data. `IDBCreateSession` is the interface that actually contains the methods to create a session. As the session object is what is used for creating the rowset and command object, the `IDBCreateSession` is clearly mandatory. It creates a unit of work or transaction within the provider. Once a data source object is created, it is the `IDBInitialize` interface that initializes the data source object so it can be used, either opening the file or connecting to the database, depending on where the required data is. The properties for the data source are set with the `IDBProperties` interface, which includes methods such as `GetProperties()` and `SetProperties()`. This is what is used to set such critical things as a logon password.

The `IPersist` interface is important in that is the base interface for those interfaces that provide for storage and retrieval of objects. These are:

- ❑ `IPersistFile` — serializes to a file)
- ❑ `IPersistStorage` — serializes to a storage
- ❑ `IPersistStream` — serializes to a stream

`IPersist` contains one method, `GetClassID()`, which returns the class ID, or CLSID, of the object that is to be saved or retrieved. This method is thus called whenever any of these interfaces are used.

The Session Object Interfaces

Session objects are a key link in the chain between initializing a data source and actually returning data to the application in the form of rowsets. Thus, all OLE DB data providers must implement a session object.

Once the data source is connected via the data source interfaces, the session object interfaces are used to set up individual connections that are used as the basis of the other interfaces used to retrieve and modify data. There are twelve interfaces involved but only three are mandatory. The interfaces are shown in the table below:

Interface	Mandatory	Description
IGetDataSource	Yes	Returns information about the data source that created the session
IOpenRowset	Yes	Creates a new rowset
ISessionProperties	Yes	Gets and sets properties of session object
IDBCreateCommand		Creates a new command
IDBSchemaRowset		Provides advanced database schema information
IIndexDefinition		Creates and drops indexes
ISupportErrorInfo		Information on whether the object returns OLE automation error objects
ITableDefinition		Creates, drops and alters tables

Interface	Mandatory	Description
ITransaction		Aborts, commits and obtains information about transactions
ITransactionJoin		Provides information on whether a provider supports distributed transactions
ITransactionLocal		Starts, commits or aborts sessions on the local connection
ITransactionObject		Obtains a transaction at a given transaction level

The consumer creates a rowset object using the `IOpenRowset` interface, and since a rowset object is the means by which it obtains access to the data, this interface is clearly mandatory. A rowset populated by data from a table can be opened by calling `IOpenRowset::OpenRowset()` and specifying the table required.

`IGetDataSource` is also a key interface as it allows the session to return the data source that created it. You might want to use this in order to create another session to the same data source.

The consumer needs to be able to get and set the properties of a session object, hence `ISessionProperties` is a required interface.

The remaining nine non-mandatory interfaces are concerned with creating command and transaction objects, creating and modifying tables and indexes and providing information on a data source of unknown structure — the `IDBSchemaRowset` interface.

The Command Object Interfaces

The command object handles queries to the data source. Some of its interfaces are responsible for handling parameters to the queries and others deal with output resulting from them. There are also interfaces that provide information on the form in which the data is retrieved.

Implementing command functionality is not mandatory, as you can perform simple data access without it. In fact, simple data sources don't support any sort of query language at all. You do not need to implement command functionality in order to open a table and retrieve the data. However, if you want more sophisticated control of data retrieval — for example, the ability to use a SQL query — you must implement the command object. However, it is recommended that DBMS-based providers implement command functionality. If you do implement a command object, then six of the ten interfaces are required.

Interface	Mandatory	Description
IAccessor	Yes	Accessor management (creates, releases etc.)
ICommand	Yes	Executes command
IColumnsInfo	Yes	Exposes information about columns of rowsets or prepared command
ICommandProperties	Yes	Specifies the command properties, from the set of rowset properties
IConvertType	Yes	Provides information on type conversions
ICommandText	Yes	Gets and sets command text
IColumnsRowset		Complete information about the rowset — more detailed than IColumnsInfo
ICommandPrepare		Prepares and optimizes commands in advance of execution
ICommandWithParameters		Handles commands that have parameters
ISupportErrorInfo		Information on whether object returns OLE automation error objects

IAccessor is the interface that allows the columns returned to be mapped to variables. The consumer uses the IAccessor interface to determine how the retrieved data is stored in memory. It is an important interface and its implementation is thus mandatory, not only for command objects, but also on rowsets themselves, as we shall see shortly.

ICommand is the interface that handles the basic command functionality — the ability to Execute() and Cancel() commands. This interface also has a method GetDBSession() that allows the client to query the command object for a pointer to the session object that created it. One possible use for this method is to use the session object to create another command object.

IColumnsInfo is the most basic means of returning information about the columns involved in a rowset or command. Its methods can return information such as the number of columns, a column's name, its size and so on. This kind of information is usually required, so this is a mandatory interface. Just as we set properties for connections, we do the same for commands. This is why ICommandProperties is a required interface.

`IConvertType` is needed to return information on whether particular data type conversions are supported on items in a rowset or command. In particular, the interface supports a single member function `CanConvert()` that takes a 'from' type and 'to' type as parameters, returning information on whether or not this is a valid conversion for the data.

The client can get and set the text of the command to be executed using the `ICommandText` interface. Since all command objects are based upon a text command of some type, the `ICommandText` interface must be supported.

The non-mandatory interfaces include `IColumnsRowset`, `ICommandPrepare` and `ICommandWithParameters`. `IColumnsRowset` is implemented when detailed information beyond the level supported by `IColumnsInfo` is needed. `ICommandPrepare` is implemented when the data source supports prepared, that is compiled, commands. Finally, `ICommandWithParameters` is implemented, indeed must be implemented, if the provider supports parameters.

The Rowset Object Interfaces

The interfaces on the rowset object group manipulate the data itself. Recall that the rowset is an abstraction of the data that has been retrieved from the database. In this sense, it is similar to the recordset classes we saw in the last chapter in ODBC and DAO.

There are five mandatory interfaces that deal with rowsets, and thirteen optional interfaces as well. These interfaces are summarized below:

Interface	Mandatory	Description
IAccessor	Yes	Accessor management (creates, releases, etc.)
IRowset	Yes	The main interface supporting rowsets
IRowsetInfo	Yes	Returns information about a rowset
IColumnsInfo	Yes	Exposes information about columns of rowsets or prepared commands
IConvertType	Yes	Provides information on type conversions
IChapteredRowset		Manages chaptered (hierarchical) data
IRowsetChange		Updates, deletes and inserts rows into a rowset

Interface	Mandatory	Description
IRowsetFind		Searches for a row meeting given criteria within a rowset
IRowsetIdentity		Rowset identity — two handles pointing to the same row will always reflect the same data
IRowsetLocate		Fetches rows in a non-sequential manner
IRowsetRefresh		Retrieves current values for the rows in the rowset
IRowsetScroll		Fetches rows at approximate positions
IRowsetUpdate		Delays transmission of changes
IColumnsRowset		Completes information about the rowset — more detailed than IcolumnsInfo
IRowsetView		Creates and applying views
IConnectionPointContainer		Supports connection points
IDBAsynchStatus		Provides information about the status of asyncronous rowset generation or population
ISupportErrorInfo		Information on whether object returns OLE automation error objects

Rowsets have some similarities to commands, since they need to perform some similar tasks, for example, binding the columns of data returned to an accessor. Thus, three of its mandatory interfaces are the identical to what as we've already seen with command objects, namely:

❑ IAccessor

❑ IColumnsInfo

❑ IConvertType

This means that client code can be written to these abstract interfaces and be used with rowsets of commands interchangeably.

The most basic functionality of managing the rows and returning data from these rows is encapsulated in the methods of the `IRowset` interface. These methods include `GetNextRows()`, which fetches rows of data, and `GetData()`, which binds the values from the columns to member variables in the client program using the accessor.

`IRowsetInfo` provides elementary functionality, such as returning the properties set for the rowset. As with command objects, you create a property structure that is passed into the `OpenRowset()` function.

The `IRowset` interface supplies the minimum required functionality for a rowset object, which allows the client to step through the data sequentially, returning one or more rows at a time.

However, it does not allow for updating and deleting records or the ability to use bookmarks. These are achieved by implementing the non-mandatory interfaces. For example, `IRowsetChange` implements functions that modify data — adding, updating and deleting rows. `IRowsetLocate` implements bookmark functionality. More sophisticated providers — for example, those accessing enterprise databases such as SQL Server or Oracle — should implement most if not all of the optional interfaces.

The Transaction Object Interfaces

A transaction is simply a means of grouping a number of related commands on the database to avoid database inconsistency (as was discussed in Chapter 1). The transaction object interfaces allow us to control when changes are committed.

Like the command object, already described, transaction objects are non-mandatory. However should you need one, then three of the four interfaces are mandatory. The table below lists these four interfaces:

Interface	Mandatory	Description
ITransaction	Yes	Supports aborting or committing the transaction, and returning information about the transaction
IConnectionPointContainer	Yes	Supports connection points
ITransactionOptions	Yes	Gets and sets options for a transaction
ISupportErrorInfo		Supplies information on whether object returns OLE automation error objects.

The key mandatory interfaces involved with transactions are `ITransaction` and `IConnectionPointContainer`. Notice that while `IConnectionPointContainer` is optional for rowset support, its mandatory for transaction support.

The `ITransaction` interface includes the most basic of transaction functionality and is thus mandatory if the transaction object is being implemented. `ITransactionOptions` is an interface that allows one to set two main options for a transaction, the timeout and a textual description of the transaction.

Pros and Cons of OLE DB

OLE DB has several advantages over previous technologies. First, it can encompass non-relational data in a natural fashion. It can handle all sorts of data including proprietary data formats without the need to make them look like SQL/relational sources. ODBC can be used to access non-relational sources, like Excel, but has to force all data into a SQL format whether it is naturally in that format or not. In OLE DB, this forced conformation to SQL doesn't occur, improving efficiency.

Another very important aspect of OLE DB is the fact that it's built upon COM, thus gaining all the advantages that COM offers. There are several means by which OLE DB achieves this. For example, we've seen how the data provider is able to delegate the work of query engines and cursor engines to service components. This is an improvement over ODBC where all such functionality had to be implemented in every driver, whereas in OLE DB, only one query engine or cursor engine need be installed on the client.

OLE DB is also designed to work well for both client/server and web-based applications, where data is accessed over the Internet. Unlike older technologies, OLE DB reduces to a minimum the need to go across the network to the data source. Service components such as cursors live on the client and can process client requests without having to go back to the server each time. These components are platform dependent and have to be installed on each client desktop. On the Internet/server side is RDS (Remote Data Services). Here, we only connect to the data on the server when a call on the data is made. The overall outcome of this is reduced server traffic. (We will discuss RDS in Chapter 8.)

The main disadvantage of OLE DB is the fact that it can be cumbersome to use, and cannot be used directly by higher level languages such as Visual Basic and VBScript. In addition, for data sources requiring ODBC drivers, it does insert another layer between the application and the data. We need to do this because at present the number of OLE DB providers are limited but there are a great number of ODBC drivers available. The OLE DB provider for ODBC drivers is a way of resolving this issue until more OLE DB providers are available.

ADO and Templates

Microsoft has created some tools to make OLE DB easier to use, which include C++ template classes that encapsulate all the COM code, leaving the developer to focus on the specific problem at hand, and also ADO which allows higher level languages like Visual Basic to access the power and flexibility of OLE DB.

ActiveX Data Objects (ADO)

The position of ADO within the Universal Data Access model is shown below:

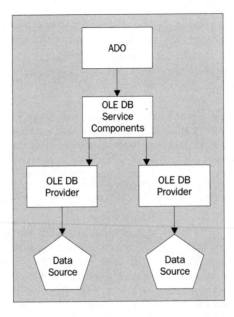

ADO is a high level set of automation objects that allow a programmer to access data via OLE DB, but without the detailed control that you get using the OLE DB interfaces directly. For example, less commonly used interfaces such as ITransactionJoin are not supported. ADO allows high level languages such as Visual Basic and ASP (Active Server Pages) to take advantage of OLE DB and use any OLE DB data sources directly. It is designed to adapt the functionality provided by any OLE DB data source, so the need to modify code when changing data sources is minimized.

Despite the neutrality of ADO in terms of data sources and its ease of use, a programmer can still access the OLE DB interfaces provided a language is used that can access COM through a vtable. However, ADO, with it's greater overhead, is slower than OLE DB.

We will talk in detail about ADO and how it relates to Visual C++ 6.0 later on in Chapter 7.

Templates

In Visual C++ 6.0, Microsoft has included template support for both OLE DB providers and consumers. To make things even easier, this is supported by the ATL Object Wizard, as we'll see in the next chapter. This wizard generates skeleton code for the object in question, thus saving the programmer much time and effort. However, the programmer must still implement any additional required functionality.

The OLE DB consumer wizard generates code that allows for basic access to the data source specified, including creating an accessor. The basic OLE DB consumer so created allows for forward scrolling of data.

The OLE DB provider wizard is particularly valuable as it creates a basic implementation of all the required interfaces. This allows the programmer to focus on implenting the interfaces and functionality they are concerned about.

Summary

This chapter has provided an overview of OLE DB. We have seen its place within Microsoft's Universal Data Access (UDA) model, and discussed the OLE DB architecture from several different angles. We have looked at providers, consumers and service components. OLE DB has a number of advantages over previous methods of data access in terms of flexibility, efficiency and reliability. Many of these advantages come from the fact that OLE DB is built upon COM.

While OLE DB is made up of many interfaces, there are two key factors that can make it easier for the programmer to use. First, you only need concern yourself with a few interfaces at any given time. Second, you would only include other interfaces if specific functionality is needed. Finally, Microsoft Visual C++ 6.0 supplies templates for both OLE DB providers and consumers, which provide all the basic code needed for simple applications.

Next, we will look at OLE DB in a practical way, by developing an example of an OLE DB consumer.

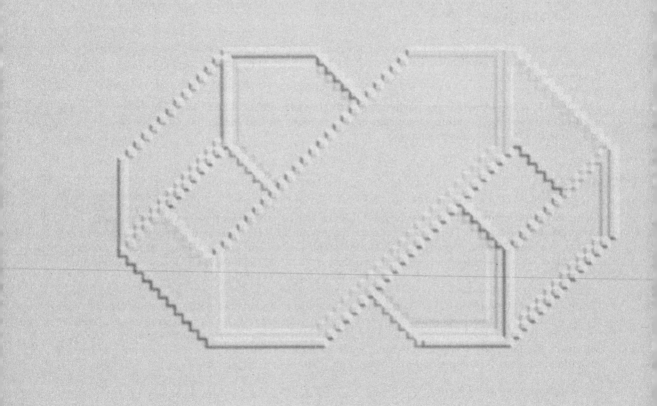

5

OLE DB Consumers

In this chapter, we'll be taking a more in depth look OLE DB consumers, and in particular, using the OLE DB consumer templates. After a brief run through the consumer template classes in Visual C++, we'll have a go at a practical example that uses them to access some data. First, we'll step through the code that the ATL Object Wizard generates, and see how much of the hard work is done for us, and then we'll add some new code to customize the application for our needs.

What is an OLE DB Consumer?

In the last chapter, we discussed OLE DB and the ideas behind it in some depth, and introduced the concept of OLE DB consumers. An OLE DB consumer is simply an application that uses OLE DB COM objects and the OLE DB provider in order to access data. An OLE DB consumer works by calling the methods on the OLE DB COM interfaces implemented by the OLE DB provider.

An OLE DB consumer can be an application (as our example will demonstrate) that uses an OLE DB provider to access its data, but this isn't the only definition. One can even define the ADO objects as OLE DB consumers, in that they use OLE DB objects to provide database services.

The OLE DB Consumer Templates

In this section, we'll be looking at the OLE DB Consumer Templates. These are an important addition to VC 6.0, and they make using OLE DB a much more straightforward process for the C++ programmer.

What are the Consumer Templates?

Directly implementing OLE DB consumers is hard work. As we saw in the last chapter, OLE DB objects can implement many interfaces. Thus, Microsoft saw a need to put a wrapper around OLE DB that would make using OLE DB objects easier, but without a full layer of code, such as ADO. Hence, Visual C++ 6.0 introduced the OLE DB consumer templates and the associated wizard. Instead of directly accessing OLE DB objects, one simply uses these wrapper classes, which are based on ATL classes, as well as related macros in order to take advantage of OLE DB functionality.

If you are unfamiliar with ATL please see Appendix B for a brief overview. You could also check out one of the ATL references listed in Appendix A.

The main thing that these wrapper classes do is to combine a number of OLE DB interfaces into one class. Yet, they do not require the overhead of ADO.

As we will see, these template classes can be mapped to similar functionality in ODBC and DAO. As with recordsets, the wizard actually generates the classes, which we can then incorporate into our application. Changes can be made to these classes to control how we access the data.

The OLE DB Consumer Classes

In this section, we'll take a quick look at the main consumer classes that implement the OLE DB interfaces. In particular, we'll be looking at:

- ❑ CDataSource
- ❑ CSession
- ❑ CTable
- ❑ CCommand
- ❑ Accessor classes
- ❑ CRowset

CDataSource

This is the wrapper class around the data source object specified by OLE DB. Its purpose is to connect to the database through an OLE DB provider — in effect, it represents a connection to the database. A CDataSource object takes input such as the location of the data source and the authentication information, which is needed to log on to the data source.

CSession

Each session object creates a single access session to the database. From this session, it is possible to create a rowset or command object and thus access the data in the database. We can also create tables and indexes though the session object. Sessions allow for transactions. Multiple sessions can be created for each data source — you might want do this when you need to separate transactions in the same application.

CTable and CCommand

CTable and CCommand are classes that allow us to access rowsets. CTable is specified as follows:

```
template <class TAccessor = CNoAccessor, class TRowset = CRowset >
class CTable : public CAccessorRowset <TAccessor, TRowset >
```

CCommand is specified as follows:

```
template <class TAccessor = CNoAccessor,
          class TRowset = CRowset,
          class TMultiple = CNoMultipleResults>
class CCommand :
        public CAccessorRowset<TAccessor, TRowset>,
        public CCommandBase,
        public TMultiple
```

The various classes parameterizing CTable and CComand are:

- ❑ TAccessor — an accessor class. The default is CNoAccessor. (We'll look at accessor classes a little later in this section).

- ❑ TRowset — a rowset class. The default is CRowset.

- ❑ TMultiple — this class can be either CMultipleResults if the class is to return multiple rowsets, or the default, CNoMultipleResults.

CTable is generally used for simple rowsets, where no parameters are specified and no multiple results are necessary. The OLE DB consumer wizard (part of the ATL object wizard) will allow you to specify either a command or a table object.

If one selects a command (an SQL select statement in the RDBMS world), then the CCommand class is used. This has the advantage of flexibility. Once you use the wizard to create a command based on one table, it can later be modified to handle a more complex query. This, as we will see later on in the chapter, is the means by which we'll create a command object using a query that includes more than one table.

Accessor Classes

In writing an OLE DB consumer application, one important task is creating the **accessor** that will be bound to the CCommand or CTable object. Recall from the last chapter that the accessor is the object that binds the data from the database to the member variables in the command or table object in the consumer application. Thus it determines how the data looks to the client application.

There are several types of accessor that one can choose from:

- ❑   CAccessor
- ❑   CDynamicAccessor
- ❑   CDynamicParameterAccessor
- ❑   CManualAccessor

Let's take a look at each of these in a bit more detail.

CAccessor

CAccessor is the simplest type of accessor, and is used when you already know the structure of the data to which you wish to bind. It is specified as follows:

```
template < class T > Class CAccessor : public T, CAccessorBase
```

CAccessorBase is the base class for all the accessor classes. It has two main functions — managing multiple accessors within a given rowset and handling binding of both columns and parameters. As we will see in our coded example later, T is the user class that defines the accessor.

This template class assumes that we know at compile time we know what the record set will look like. The COLUMN_ENTRY() macro is used to bind the columns retrieved to public variables. One can also include parameters (in a parameterized query, for example) using the PARAM_MAP() macro. We will see how these are used later on in the chapter.

Finally, there is the DEFINE_COMMAND() macro, where the SELECT statement determining the data retrieved is defined. If the rowset is to be based on a simple table, for example, then the SELECT statement will be SELECT * FROM [TableName]. CAccessor is the most efficient accessor class, since all the information is provided at compile time.

CDynamicAccessor

The second type of accessor is `CDynamicAccessor`. It is specified as follows:

```
class CDynamicAccessor : public CAccessorBase
```

This is the accessor you would use when you want to access data, but don't know the structure of that data at compile time. It has a method, `GetValue()`, which retrieves the data from the rowset, rather than binding public variables to each column.

CDynamicParameterAccessor

The third type of accessor is is `CDynamicParameterAccessor`. It is specified as follows:

```
class CDynamicParameterAccessor : public CDynamicAccessor
```

This accessor inherits from the `CDynamicAccessor` class, so has all of this functionality. The main difference is that, as the name implies, it incorporates support for parameters. The additional methods it supports are all associated with getting and setting parameter data (`GetParam()` and `SetParam()`), and obtaining information about the number and type of parameters. Note that it is slower than the dynamic accessor.

CManualAccessor

Finally, we have `CManualAccessor`. This is specified as:

```
class CManualAccessor : public CAccessorBase
```

This allows one to bind the columns explicitly at run time. Binding essentially allows the application to access data in the rowset's shared memory. This binding is done using the `CreateAccessor()` method to bind a buffer to hold the data, and `AddBindEntry()` to bind the type of data and part or all of the buffer specified in `CreateAccessor()` to the column. This class also has methods to handle parameters. The advantage here is that this accessor is that it is very fast. It is, however, more complex to code.

CRowset

A rowset is the object that a program uses to both retrieve and set data.

This class has functionality to traverse the database — to scroll forwards and backwards through the rows, and to move to the first and the last records. There are also methods to add rows (`ClearRecord()` and `Insert()`), delete rows (`Delete()`), update data in a row (`SetData()`), as well as other related functionality. Thus it is similar to the `CRecordset` in ODBC and CDaoRecordset in DAO (which we saw back in Chapter 3).

Creating an OLE DB Consumer Application

We've briefly discussed OLE DB consumers and looked at some key classes and templates. Now it's time to find out how to actually implement one. This sample application will present a simple form based interface that will allow you to:

- ❑ Scroll through a database table
- ❑ Add records
- ❑ Delete records
- ❑ Modify records

We'll be using the invoice database that we've used earlier in the book. You could try this out using any database for which you have the appropriate provider, or indeed, any database for which you have set up an ODBC connection. The example outlined below was based on the Access database used in previous examples.

We'll start by creating a standard MFC project as we've done before in previous examples — create a simple single document MFC application using a `CFormView`. Call the application `TestOLEDB`.

The easiest way to take advantage of an OLE DB provider is to use the OLE DB consumer wizard that comes with Visual C++ 6.0. This will add the appropriate template classes to our project based on what we select in the various steps of the wizard. These steps are outlined in the following section.

Inserting An ATL Object

The OLE DB consumer classes are ATL objects. Therefore, our first step is creating the appropriate ATL object, which we do using the ATL Object Wizard.

First, from the **Insert** menu, select **New ATL Object**. If you're using an MFC project this will bring up the following dialog:

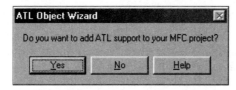

Select Yes and the ATL wizard dialog will appear. Click on Data Access:

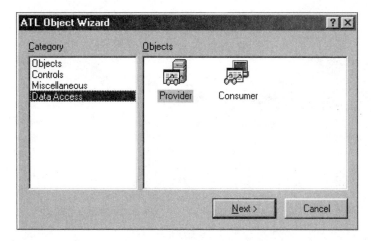

As you can see, we have two choices here — the provider templates and the consumer templates. Select Consumer and click on Next:

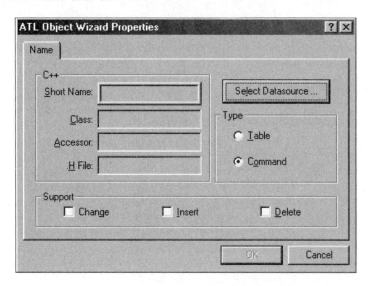

Now, you will now need to select the data source, and in order to do this, you need to select the provider you'll be using:

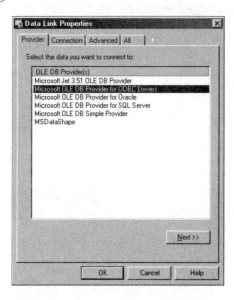

You should see a number of providers listed in this dialog. Some providers such as the OLE DB Simple Provider are experimental or sample providers.

Select the OLE DB provider for ODBC drivers and click on **Next**.

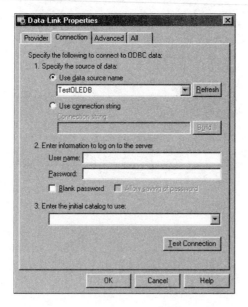

You can select from those data sources for which you have set up an ODBC connection. (Recall that this process was described in Chapter 3.) We select the connection we want, add the logon information and after testing the connection (click on Test Connection) click on OK.

The next dialog allows us to choose the table on which we wish to base the recordset. As with ODBC and DAO, the wizard assumes table access — if a different query is desired, then the generated code will have to be modified by hand.

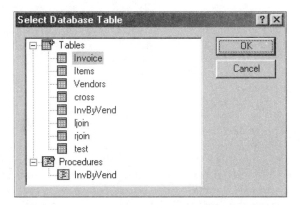

Here, you should choose the `Invoice` table and click on OK. We're back to the first dialog again, and the names of the classes that will be generated have been filled in:

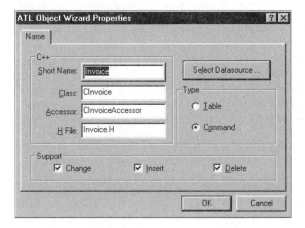

Note that you should also select Change, Insert and Delete here (these are not checked by default), as we will be updating, inserting and deleting records using this class.

Before we go on to add some code of our own, let's take some time to look at what the wizard has generated for us.

The Generated Classes

If you look in ClassView, you should find two new classes — CInvoice and CInvoiceAccessor. The definitions and implementations of these two classes are contained within one small file, Invoice.h. In this section, we'll examine this file, section by section.

```
class CInvoiceAccessor
{
public:
    LONG m_InvoiceID;
    LONG m_VendorID;
    LONG m_ItemID;
    LONG m_Units;

BEGIN_COLUMN_MAP(CInvoiceAccessor)
    COLUMN_ENTRY(1, m_InvoiceID)
    COLUMN_ENTRY(2, m_VendorID)
    COLUMN_ENTRY(3, m_ItemID)
    COLUMN_ENTRY(4, m_Units)
END_COLUMN_MAP()
```

The above code extract shows the start of the definition of the accessor class. This is the class that allows the data coming back from the database to be bound to variables that can be used. The COLUMN_ENTRY() macro is where the binding is defined — each member variable is mapped to a column from the invoice table.

Later, we'll need to change the COLUMN_ENTRY() for the invoice ID to support the fact it's an identity column. We will actually see how this comes into play in the view class when we want to update a row, or insert a new one.

Shown below is the rest of the definition of the CInvoiceAccessor class:

```
DEFINE_COMMAND(CInvoiceAccessor, _T(" \
    SELECT \
        InvoiceID, \
        VendorID, \
        ItemID, \
        Units  \
        FROM Invoice"))

    // You may wish to call this function if you are inserting a record and
    // wish to initialize all the fields, if you are not going to explicitly
    // set all of them.
    void ClearRecord()
    {
        memset(this, 0, sizeof(*this));
    }
};
```

The DEFINE_COMMAND() macro defines the SELECT statement, which in this case simply selects all the columns from the invoice table. This statement is generated automatically, because we chose to base our rowset on the invoice table. Notice how the columns of the SELECT statement map to the entries in the column map.

The rest of the header file contains the generated definition of the command class. This is interesting, because it is in this class where we can see the steps involved in connecting to the data source and opening a rowset.

```
class CInvoice : public CCommand<CAccessor<CInvoiceAccessor> >
{
public:
    HRESULT Open()
    {
        HRESULT         hr;

        hr = OpenDataSource();
        if (FAILED(hr))
            return hr;

        return OpenRowset();
    }
```

The Open() method of the command class calls OpenDataSource(), which is the method that actually sets the properties for the data source — we'll see this in a moment. The Open() method then calls OpenRowset(), which is also defined further down in the Invoice.h file. Note that CInvoice::Open() is called from the constructor of the document class and is subsequently closed in the destructor.

The OpenDataSource() method sets the properties and opens the data source:

```
    HRESULT OpenDataSource()
    {
        HRESULT        hr;
        CDataSource db;
        CDBPropSet    dbinit(DBPROPSET_DBINIT);

        dbinit.AddProperty(DBPROP_AUTH_PERSIST_SENSITIVE_AUTHINFO, false);
        dbinit.AddProperty(DBPROP_INIT_DATASOURCE, OLESTR("TestOLEDB"));
        dbinit.AddProperty(DBPROP_INIT_PROMPT, (short)4);
        dbinit.AddProperty(DBPROP_INIT_LCID, (long)2057);
        hr = db.Open(_T("MSDASQL"), &dbinit);
        if (FAILED(hr))
            return hr;

        return m_session.Open(db);
    }
```

CDataSource is the class that handles the data source. The properties that have been generated are as follows:

- ❑ DBPROP_AUTH_PERSIST_SENSITIVE_AUTHINFO says whether or not sensitive authentication information can be persisted (saved). In this case, false means it cannot.

- ❑ DBPROP_INIT_DATASOURCE is the data source we're going to use. In the listing above, this is TestOLEDB, which is an ODBC connection that has been set up for the sample database.

- ❑ DBPROP_INIT_PROMPT determines when you will be prompted for authentication information. Here, it has been set to 4, which is the constant for DBPROMPT_NOPROMPT, as we are not using authentication.

- ❑ DBPROP_INIT_LCID deals with location (local preference).

In the call to CDataSource::Open(), the name of the OLE DB provider being used is passed as one of the arguments. In this case, it is MSDASQL — the OLE DB provider for ODBC.

The OpenRowset() method sets the rowset properties and opens the rowset:

```
HRESULT OpenRowset()
{
    // Set properties for open1
    CDBPropSet    propset(DBPROPSET_ROWSET);
    propset.AddProperty(DBPROP_IRowsetChange, true);
    propset.AddProperty(DBPROP_UPDATABILITY, DBPROPVAL_UP_CHANGE |
                        DBPROPVAL_UP_INSERT | DBPROPVAL_UP_DELETE);

    return CCommand<CAccessor<CInvoiceAccessor> >::Open(m_session,
                                                    NULL, &propset);
}
```

This is where we're more likely to change things manually — we'll actually do this later on in the chapter, when we change some of the properties of the rowset. The first thing that's done here is setting the properties, which is achieved by calling CDBPropSet::AddProperty(). The properties that have been set for our rowset are:

- ❑ DBPROP_IRowsetChange — this is set to true, so the rowset is updateable

- ❑ DBPROP_UPDATABLITY — here, we can change, insert and delete rows, as we specified in the final dialog of the wizard creating the rowset

One important thing to note is that properties such as IRowsetChange and IRowsetLocate correspond to interfaces implemented by the provider.

The final line is where the rowset is opened. Since CCommand is a template that requires an accessor, we pass it a CAccessor. CAccessor is also a template class, and we parameterize it with the CInvoiceAccessor class defined earlier. The Open() method itself takes as arguments the property set we have just defined and the CSession (m_session) which was opened by the OpenDataSource() method shown above. Note that m_session is a member variable of the CInvoice class:

```
CSession m_session;
```

Considering all the functionality this file implements, its size is quite small. The secret is in the template classes, CCommand, CAccessor and so on.

To summarize, Invoice.h first implements the CInvoiceAccessor. This is where the public variables that hold the current record values are specified. Next, the COLUMN_MAP() macro maps the variables to the columns. The DEFINE_COMMAND() macro is where the SQL command itself is specified. Now, we have the necessary class to input as a parameter to CAccessor. Finally, in the CCommand based class CInvoice, the Open() method and associated OpenDataSource() and OpenRowset() methods are implemented. We can now use the CInvoice class to access the database as we did the CDaoRecordset based class and CRecordset based classes back in Chapter 3.

Remember that all the code that has been shown so far is generated code. We'll make some changes to this file later, when we actually use it in our simple application.

Modifying the Document and View Classes

Now, let's go back to the MFC code. We need to design the form, then modify the document and view classes to allow the user to add, delete, modify and traverse through the rows of data.

The main dialog form looks much the same as the ones we used for the examples in Chapter 3:

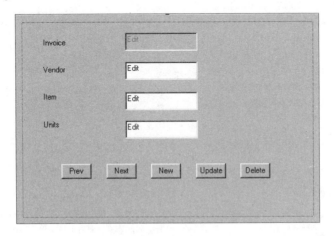

As before, you'll need to add variables corresponding to the edit controls, as well as handlers for the command buttons.

In this section, we'll be looking at the changes we'll need to make to the document and view classes in this application. The first step is to add a `CInvoice` object as a member variable to the document class:

```
// Attributes
public:
    CInvoice m_Invoice;
    bool m_bNoItems;
// Operations
```

Note that another variable, `m_bNoItems`, is also added here. This is to help us keep track of whether or not the rowset is empty.

We'll also need to include the header file for `CInvoice`:

```
#include "Invoice.h"
```

The constructor and destructor are similar to what we've seen in the ODBC example, but in this case we are using the OLE DB class:

```
CTestOLEDBDoc::CTestOLEDBDoc()
{
    if(m_Invoice.Open() == S_OK)
    {
        if(m_Invoice.MoveNext() != S_OK)
            m_bNoItems = true;
        else
            m_bNoItems = false;
    }
}
```

In the constructor, we open the database object. Since it starts at the beginning of a file, we know that if a `MoveNext()` operation fails, then there are no rows in the table. If this is the case, we set `m_bNoItems` to `true`; otherwise, we set it to `false`.

```
CTestOLEDBDoc::~CTestOLEDBDoc()
{
    m_Invoice.Close();
}
```

As you can see, the destructor simply closes the data source.

That's all the changes that need to be made to the document class, so let's go on to see what functionality needs to be added to the view class.

Firstly, you should add a new member variable to `CTestOLEDBView`, `m_bNew`, which is a Boolean variable used to keep track of whether or not we are in the process of adding a new record.

Here is the constructor for the view class:

```
CTestOLEDBView::CTestOLEDBView()
  : CFormView(CTestOLEDBView::IDD)
{
    //{{AFX_DATA_INIT(CTestOLEDBView)
    m_units = _T("");
    m_invoiceID = _T("");
    m_itemID = _T("");
    m_vendorID = _T("");
    //}}AFX_DATA_INIT
    m_bNew = false;
}
```

The main thing that goes on here is the initialization of the member variables corresponding to the edit controls on the form we created earlier. The only code that needs to be added is the line to initialize the Boolean member variable, m_bNew, which is set to `false`, since we are not creating a new record at this point.

> *The generated methods of the view class that have not been altered in the example will not be discussed here. The message map and data exchange functions were discussed in Chapter 3.*

Now let's examine the message handlers for the command buttons on the form. These are:

- ❑ `OnPrev()`
- ❑ `OnNext()`
- ❑ `OnNew()`
- ❑ `OnUpdateRec()`
- ❑ `OnDelete()`

OnNew() simply clears the form and sets the m-bNew variable, to indicate that a new record is being created. The code for this is exactly the same as that covered in Chapter 3 in the ODBC/DAO examples.

The `OnNext()` and `OnPrev()` are also similar to the earlier code we have seen, but not identical, so the code listings for these methods are included below:

```
void CTestOLEDBView::OnPrev()
{
    char tres[MAX_INVOICE];

    // Get pointer to invoice rowset
    CInvoice* pInvoice = &GetDocument()->m_Invoice;

    // move to the previous record, but if it's BOF move to the
    // first record
    if(pInvoice->MovePrev() != S_OK)
    {
```

```
            pInvoice->MoveFirst();
            MessageBox("At beginning of file","File Warning",MB_OK |
                                                MB_ICONINFORMATION);
    }

    // set the values on the form from the current record
    m_invoice = ltoa(pInvoice->m_InvoiceID,tres,10);
    m_item = ltoa(pInvoice->m_ItemID,tres,10);
    m_units = ltoa(pInvoice->m_Units,tres,10);
    m_vendor = ltoa(pInvoice->m_VendorID,tres,10);
    UpdateData(FALSE);
}

void CTestOLEDBView::OnNext()
{
    char tres[MAX_INVOICE];

    // Get pointer to invoice rowset
    CInvoice* pInvoice = &GetDocument()->m_Invoice;

    // move to the next record, but if it's EOF move to the
    // last record
    if(pInvoice->MoveNext() != S_OK)
    {
        MessageBox("At end of file","File Warning",MB_OK |
                                            MB_ICONINFORMATION);
        pInvoice->MoveLast();
    }

    // set the values on the form from the current record
    m_invoice = ltoa(pInvoice->m_InvoiceID,tres,10);
    m_item = ltoa(pInvoice->m_ItemID,tres,10);
    m_units = ltoa(pInvoice->m_Units,tres,10);
    m_vendor = ltoa(pInvoice->m_VendorID,tres,10);
    UpdateData(FALSE);
}
```

Note that you'll need to #define the constant MAX_INVOICE *at the top of* TestOLEDBView.cpp.

The handler for the **Update** button, OnUpdateRec(), is probably one of the more interesting functions. The implementation for this is shown below:

```
void CTestOLEDBView::OnUpdateRec()
{
   char strTmp[MAX_INVOICE];
   HRESULT hr;

   // Get pointer to doc object
   CTestOLEDBDoc* pDoc = GetDocument();

   // Get pointer to invoice rowset
   CInvoice* pInvoice = &pDoc->m_Invoice;

   // update the variables in the view class from the form
   UpdateData(TRUE);

   if(m_bNew)
   {
      pInvoice->ClearRecord();
   }

   // update the member variables of the reowset class
   pInvoice->m_InvoiceID_status = DBSTATUS_S_IGNORE;
   pInvoice->m_ItemID = atol(m_item);
   pInvoice->m_Units = atol(m_units);
   pInvoice->m_VendorID = atol(m_vendor);

   if(m_bNew)
   {
      // insert a new row if we are adding a new record
      hr = pInvoice->Insert();
      if(FAILED(hr))
         MessageBox("Failed Insert");
      else
         MessageBox("Successful Insert");

      // move to last record and set invoice ID in view class from rowset
      pInvoice->MoveLast();
      m_invoice = ltoa(pInvoice->m_InvoiceID,strTmp,10);

      // change bNoItems if the rowset was empty
      if(pDoc->m_bNoItems == true)
         pDoc->m_bNoItems = false;

      // update the data on the form and m_bNew
      UpdateData(false);
      m_bNew = false;
   }
   else
   {
      // update the data in the database
      hr = pInvoice->SetData();
      if(FAILED(hr))
         MessageBox("Failed Update");
      else
         MessageBox("Successful Update");
   }
}
```

There's quite a lot of code in this `OnUpdateRec()` method, so let's go through it in some detail. First, if we are creating a new record it calls `ClearRecord()` (created automatically by the wizard). This initializes the field data. It then sets the field values to those that have been filled in on the form. Note how we set the parameter `m_InvoiceID_status` to `DB_STATUS_S_IGNORE`. This is essential as it tells the system to not try to set the value. The reason is that in this case the database will do it automatically. We will see in the final version on the invoice rowset code how the class was modified to accommodate this.

If we're creating a new record we call the `InsertRow()` method on the rowset object and move to the last record. We can do this, since we know our record will be the last due to the ordering by invoice ID, which is an auto-increment or identity column. When we're at the last record (which is the new record) we retrieve the `invoiceID` and update that value on the form. If we are doing an update, then we call instead the `SetData()` method on the rowset.

Since it's a COM object, these methods all return an `HRESULT` that can be checked for success. (Note that you should check this using the `FAILED()` and `SUCEEDED()` macros). If it's successful insert or update, then a success message is presented to the user, otherwise a failure message is returned.

We'll look at the `OnDelete()` handler in the next section, but before we leave this one, we should look at the implementation of the `OnUpdate()` method, which we need to override. This is called when the data is updated, most importantly when the form is first initialized:

```
void CTestOLEDBView::OnUpdate(CView* pSender, LPARAM lHint, CObject* pHint)
{
    char strTmp[MAX_INVOICE];

    //we maintain a local variable of CTestOLEDBDoc class so we don't
    //have to worry about casting
    CTestOLEDBDoc* pDoc = GetDocument();

    if(pDoc->m_bNoItems)
        return;

    // Get pointer to invoice rowset
    CInvoice* pInvoice = &pDoc->m_Invoice;

    //we convert the long values returned to a char * and set it
    //to the associated variable
    pInvoice->MoveFirst();
    m_invoice = ltoa(pInvoice->m_InvoiceID,strTmp,10);
    m_item = ltoa(pInvoice->m_ItemID,strTmp,10);
    m_units = ltoa(pInvoice->m_Units,strTmp,10);
    m_vendor = ltoa(pInvoice->m_VendorID,strTmp,10);

    //update the screen- false indicates that the updated variables should
    //be passed to the form.
    UpdateData(FALSE);
}
```

This method simply sets the variables (corresponding to the fields on the form) with the data from the database. The function `UpdateData()` is called with the parameter set to `FALSE` to cause the form to be updated.

Adding Delete Functionality

We will now add some new functionality to our application — we're going to add a handler for the **Delete** button, OnDelete(). In this handler, we'll delete the current row in the rowset and move back to the first row.

The tricky part here is that the deleted row remains but is unavailable and produces an error when one moves to it. We can work around this problem by closing and reopening the rowset. While this is a little awkward, it does work:

```
void CTestOLEDBView::OnDelete()
{
    // maintain a local variable of CTestOLEDBDoc class
    int iRes;
    char tres[50];
    CTestOLEDBDoc* pDoc = GetDocument();

    // Get pointer to invoice rowset
    CInvoice* pInvoice = &pDoc->m_Invoice;

    iRes = MessageBox("Are you sure you want to delete the current record",
                "Delete",MB_ICONWARNING | MB_YESNO);

    if(iRes == IDNO)
        return;
    if(pInvoice->Delete() != S_OK)
        return;

    //close and reopen the database in order to clear the deleted rec
    pInvoice->Close();
    pInvoice->Open();

    if(pInvoice->MoveNext() != S_OK)
    {
        pDoc->m_bNoItems = true;
        m_invoice = "";
        m_item = "";
        m_units = "";
        m_vendor = "";
    }
    else
    {
        pDoc->m_bNoItems = false;
        m_invoice = ltoa(pInvoice->m_InvoiceID,tres,10);
        m_item = ltoa(pInvoice->m_ItemID,tres,10);
        m_units = ltoa(pInvoice->m_Units,tres,10);
        m_vendor = ltoa(pInvoice->m_VendorID,tres,10);
    }

    UpdateData(FALSE);
}
```

When the user presses the **Delete** button, we prompt them with a message box to ensure that they really want to follow this course of action. Note that in the `MessageBox()` function we use the constants `MB_ICONWARNING` and `MB_YESNO` to put a 'warning' icon in the message box and make the user respond **Yes** or **No**.

We then close and reopen the rowset, displaying the first record. If there are no records left, then the fields on the form are simply left blank for the user to fill in.

Changing the Rowset Classes

Finally, let's look at the changes we need to make to `Invoice.h`. Recall that in the handler for the Update button, we introduced a new variable for the primary key, `m_InvoiceID_status`:

```
class CdboinvoiceAccessor
{
public:
    LONG m_InvoiceID;
    LONG m_VendorID;
    LONG m_ItemID;
    LONG m_Units;
    ULONG m_InvoiceID_status;
```

This is the status variable for the `InvoiceID`, which was used in `OnUpdateRec()` to tell OLE DB to ignore the `InvoiceID` column, since the database handles setting this column. We also need to change the `COLUMN_MAP` entry for the invoice ID:

```
BEGIN_COLUMN_MAP(CInvoiceAccessor)
    COLUMN_ENTRY_STATUS(1, m_InvoiceID,m_InvoiceID_status)
    COLUMN_ENTRY(2, m_VendorID)
    COLUMN_ENTRY(3, m_ItemID)
    COLUMN_ENTRY(4, m_Units)
END_COLUMN_MAP()
```

The actual SQL `SELECT` function used has not changed. However, we will see how to change this in the next section when we do a more complex query.

The `Open()` method of the `CInvoice` class, which is used to open the command object does not need to be changed from the generated version. `OpenDataSource()`, on the other hand, requires one new line. This method is used to open the connection to the data source — we need to add a call to close the session before we open it:

```
    hr = db.Open(_T("MSDASQL"), &dbinit);
    if (FAILED(hr))
        return hr;
    m_session.Close(); //make sure the session pointer is released
                       //before opening it
    return m_session.Open(db);
}
```

Remember that `OpenRowset()` takes the open session object and opens a rowset so data can be accessed. The properties need to be set first, and currently, we just have those that we selected when creating the application using the wizard, that is, the abitlity to change the rowset by inserting new data, deleting data and updating existing data.

We can also add properties by hand into the code, however. One thing we might want to do is scroll backwards through the rowset as well as forwards — we can do this very easily by adding the `CANSCROLLBACKWARDS` property. Another handy property is `IMMOBILEROWS`, which indicates that newly added rows will always be added at the end of the rowset.

The following lines need to be added to the `OpenRowset()` method to give us these extra properties:

```
propset.AddProperty(DBPROP_CANSCROLLBACKWARDS,true);
propset.AddProperty(DBPROP_IMMOBILEROWS,true);
```

Once you have made all these changes, you should be ready to build and execute the example. You should see something like this:

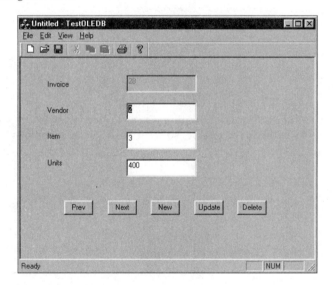

More Complex Queries

The rowset we've just created was reasonably simple — it was just based on the invoice table. The next step is to create a more complex query. In this case, we will create a rowset that performs a `SELECT` statement based on joining both the invoice and vendor tables.

The first step is using the wizard to create a rowset that uses one of the tables. You can use the same procedure as before, but this time, base the rowset on the vendors table. The resulting rowset contains the following accessor:

```
class CVendorsAccessor
{
public:
    LONG m_VendorID;
    TCHAR m_VendorName[51];

BEGIN_COLUMN_MAP(CVendorsAccessor)
    COLUMN_ENTRY(1, m_VendorID)
    COLUMN_ENTRY(2, m_VendorName)
END_COLUMN_MAP()

DEFINE_COMMAND(CVendorsAccessor, _T(" \
    SELECT \
        VendorID, \
        VendorName, \
        FROM Vendors"))

    // You may wish to call this function if you are inserting a record and
    // wish to initialize all the fields, if you are not going to explicitly
    // set all of them.
    void ClearRecord()
    {
        memset(this, 0, sizeof(*this));
    }
};
```

Now all we need to do is modify this accessor with the actual query we wish to use. We'll be selection three more fields from the invoice table, so we'll need to add member variables to handle them here:

```
    LONG m_VendorID;
    TCHAR m_VendorName[51];
    LONG m_InvoiceID;
    LONG m_ItemID;
    LONG m_Units;
```

We also add the corresponding entries in the column map.

```
BEGIN_COLUMN_MAP(CVendorsAccessor)
    COLUMN_ENTRY(1, m_VendorID)
    COLUMN_ENTRY(2, m_VendorName)
    COLUMN_ENTRY(3, m_InvoiceID)
    COLUMN_ENTRY(4, m_ItemID)
    COLUMN_ENTRY(5, m_Units)
END_COLUMN_MAP()
```

Finally we insert the new SELECT command under the DEFINE_COMMAND() macro:

```
DEFINE_COMMAND(CVendorsAccessor, _T(" \
    SELECT Vendors.VendorID, Vendors.VendorName, Invoice.InvoiceID,\
        Invoice.ItemID, Invoice.Units FROM \
        Vendors INNER JOIN Invoice ON \
        Invoice.VendorID=Vendors.VendorID"))
...
```

One tip here — the easiest way to do this is to use the query tool in your database to create and test the query and simply use cut and paste to install it in the define command macro. You can do it manually but that is more error prone. In Access, for example, the query looks like this:

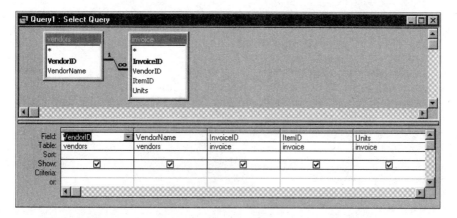

This query might then be used to create a simple report:

ID	Name	Invoice	Item	Units
1	Vendor 1	29	5	200
1	Vendor 1	32	2	40909
1	Vendor 1	44	2	3
1	Vendor 1	45	2	100
2	Vendor 2	28	3	400
2	Vendor 2	33	1	100
2	Vendor 2	37	2	5000
3	Vendor 3	35	4	133
3	Vendor 3	36	1	1000

Now let's look briefly at the code used to create the report. The first thing you'll need to do is to create a new class (using Class Wizard) derived from CView. Call this class CReport, as this will form the basis of our report. We'll need to add a method to this class, FillLines(), that will actually step through the recordset we've just created and extract the data. The prototype for this function is:

```
void FillLines();
```

We'll also need a couple of member variables to the CReport class:

```
int iLines;
CString* pstrText[MAXLINES]
```

MAXLINES is simply a constant that you'll need to #define at the top of CReport.h. This will be the maximum number of lines that can be output, so set it to some suitably large value, such as 2000.

We'll add a new menu (Action) with a menu item (Report) to allow the user to bring up the report shown above. Add a handler for this menu item, OnActionReport(), the implementation of which is shown below:

```
void CMainFrame::OnActionReport()
{
    CTestOLEDBDoc* pDoc = (CTestOLEDBDoc*)this->GetActiveDocument();
    CSingleDocTemplate pTTemplate(
        IDR_MAINFRAME,
        RUNTIME_CLASS(CTestOLEDBDoc),
        RUNTIME_CLASS(CMainFrame),       // main SDI frame window
        RUNTIME_CLASS(CReport));
    CFrameWnd* frame = pTTemplate.CreateNewFrame(pDoc, NULL);
    frame->InitialUpdateFrame(pDoc,true);
}
```

Here, we simply bring up a new window for our report. The data that will be displayed here is based on the same document class, CTestOLEDBDoc. Note that you'll need to add a new member variable to the document class of type CVendors, so that we can access the data from the query rowset.

Now let's look at the implementation of the view class that we've just created, CReport. The first function we'll look at is FillText(). This method fills a string array with the values from the database, which is then drawn to the screen in OnDraw():

```
void CReport::FillText()
{
    CString strTxt;
    CSize szTxt;
    char strTmp[10];
    iLines = 0;

    // get pointer to document class
    CTestOLEDBDoc* pDoc = (CTestOLEDBDoc*)this->GetDocument();

    // get pointer to query rowset
    CVendors* pVendors = &pDoc->m_Vendors;

    // open rowset
    if(pVendors->Open() == S_OK)
    {
        // step through records
        while(pVendors->MoveNext() == S_OK && iLines < MAXLINES)
        {
            pstrText[iLines] = new CString;
            *pstrText[iLines] = ltoa(pVendors->m_VendorID,
                                                (char*)&strTmp,10);

            *pstrText[iLines] += "\t";
            *pstrText[iLines] += pVendors->m_VendorName;
            *pstrText[iLines] += "\t\t";
            *pstrText[iLines] += ltoa(pVendors->m_InvoiceID,
                                                (char*)&strTmp,10);
            *pstrText[iLines] += "\t";
            *pstrText[iLines] += ltoa(pVendors->m_ItemID,
                                                (char*)&strTmp,10);

            *pstrText[iLines] += "\t";
            *pstrText[iLines] += ltoa(pVendors->m_Units,
                                                (char*)&strTmp,10);

            iLines++;
        }
        pVendors->Close();
    }
}
```

In this method, we simply open the recordset that's based on the query and step through the rows one by one. Note that we don't need to call `MoveFirst()` after opening the rowset and before starting this loop, because it is opened at BOF. The call to `MoveNext()` moves us to the first record in the rowset. Inside the loop, we write out the data from each row to a string, which will later be written to the report.

One important point about `FillText()` is that it must be called in `OnInitialUpdate()`, *not* the constructor, or the database access will not work since the document is not yet returned correctly.

So, the change to the OnInitialUpdate() method is as follows:

```
void CReport::OnInitialUpdate()
{
    CView::OnInitialUpdate();
    FillText();
}
```

As you can see, this simply calls FillText().

The final function we need to implement in the CReport class is OnDraw(). This is where we actually use the text we stored in FillText():

```
void CReport::OnDraw(CDC* pDC)
{
    CDocument* pDoc = GetDocument();
    CSize szTxt;
    szTxt= pDC->GetTextExtent("ABCDEFGHIJ");
    CString strHead="ID\tName\t\tInvoice\tItem\tUnits";
    pDC->TabbedTextOut(0,0,strHead,NULL,0,0);
    int i;
    for(i = 0; i < iLines; i++)
    {
        pDC->TabbedTextOut(0,(i+1)*(szTxt.cy + 5), *pstrText[i],NULL,0,0);
    }
}
```

First, we get a pointer to the document object. We then need to obtain information about the size of the text, which is where GetTextExtent() function comes in. This takes a string and returns a CSize object containing its height and width. We then set up the heading and output the string using TabbedTextOut(). As with the standard TextOut(), the first three parameters are the x coordinate, y coordinate and string.

We then output the strings we set up earlier, again we using TabbedTextOut(). The only difference is that we must put each record on a different line. We do this by putting the string at a location which is the height of the text + 5 (an arbitrary space) times the line number.

This concludes the changes we need to make, so now you can build the application and try this out for yourself.

Conclusion

In this chapter, we have covered a number of areas regarding OLE DB Consumers. We have seen what the different consumer template classes are and discussed briefly the functionality covered by the main classes.

We went on to look at a practical example using these classes, which we created using the ATL Object Wizard. Our application allowed the user to scroll through a rowset, add new records, update records and delete records. Along the way, we saw how to handle identity columns in rowsets, and how to change the SQL statement on which a rowset is based, in order to handle more complex queries.

You can now see how one works with the OLE DB consumer in a practical way. It is quite simple to create an application to perform basic operations on a table, as well as to access data in a more complex query scenario.

6

An OLE DB Consumer Example

Over the last few chapters, we have created examples of basic OLE DB, ODBC and DAO database applications using MFC. In this chapter we will utilize what we have learned so far to develop a more complex database example.

In order to demonstrate OLE DB in a practical setting we will create a simple *Training Log* application. This example covers the development of a database application for the users of a gym. We will lay aside, for the time being, our Access 'Invoice' data source, and we will use instead a SQL Server database called 'Weights'. This database will hold information about the users themselves, the exercises they do and general information that allows them to track their workout.

The sample program created in this chapter will allow the user to modify and browse all the tables in this database. There will be facilities to allow the addition of new users, as well as information about their exercises as they progress.

We'll begin this chapter by looking at the problem domain and seeing what tables we'll need, and what general functionality will be required from the application. This will be followed by a discussion of the structure of the database — how the tables are laid out and what the relationships are between them.

As in the last chapter, we'll be using MFC to develop the application with the help of the ATL object wizard to create the OLE DB consumer classes we'll be using to access the SQL Server database. Once these classes have been created, we'll see what changes need to be made to the document class that will contain them and how the various views are created that will allow the user to access the data.

Finally, we will also deal with some of the practical issues in developing a real application, including source control, installing the application, and multi-user aspects.

Designing the Training Log Application

Before creating the database and the application, it is important to first understand the problem domain. When one goes to the gym there are two types of exercises:

- ❑ Resistance training — lifting weights and so on
- ❑ Aerobic training — using the treadmill, exercise bike, taking an aerobic class, etc

Typically, when a person joins a gym, they will be provided with a card to track their progress. The card of course is limited. You can only track a very limited number of workouts due to space considerations, so what you end up with is a series of cards which become progressively hard to manage. Thus, a database would be useful for tracking workouts in the long run.

What we need to think about is what sort of information we're going to want to store in the database, and how we want to view it. Clearly, we'll need information on the users of the gym, their full names, and also their measurements and how they change over a period of time. It would be a good idea to keep a table of different exercises, a description of them, whether they fall into the category of resistance training or aerobic training, whether or not they can be done at home, and so forth. We'd also like to create some log tables, so that users of the gym can keep track of what exercise they did when.

The purpose of this application will be to maintain records of the users of a gym and the exercises they do. It will allow the users to keep a log of their workouts over a period of time and therefore monitor their progress. Users will need to be able to step through the records to view the data, and also add new information when required.

So, now that we know what we're after, let's look at the design and lay out of the database.

The Weights Database

In this section, we'll be looking in more detail at the design and creation of the weights database for the training log application. Since it will ultimately be a multi-user application, we will use an SQL Server database. It will be created using SQL Server and its purpose is to manage the data from the training sessions — both aerobic and resistance training — of the various users of the gym.

It will consist of six tables, namely:

- ❑ Exercises
- ❑ Users
- ❑ Comment
- ❑ Measurement
- ❑ AerobicLog
- ❑ ResistanceLog

These tables and the relationships between them are shown in the figure below:

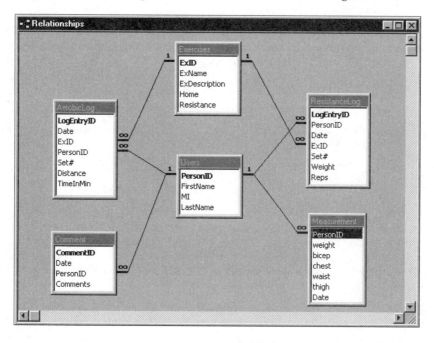

Note that although this is a SQL Server database, the screenshot above is taken using Access, in order that the layout of the tables and the relationships between them might be displayed.

Let's look at each of these tables in a bit more detail.

Exercises

The `Exercises` table maintains a list of the various exercises one might do during a workout. The first field in this table, `ExID`, is a unique ID, which will be the primary key — this is assigned as an `IDENTITY` counter, set initially to 1 and which is incremented by 1 for each new record. The other fields are the name of the exercise together with a brief description, whether the exercise can be performed at home (as opposed to the gym) and whether it is classed as a resistance training exercise (as opposed to an aerobic one).

Note that we are going to use a `CLUSTERED` index on the primary key field, which, as you may remember from Chapter 1, means that the table will be physically ordered based on the primary key `ExID`.

Users

This table contains the list of the clients registering their exercise program. The table will consist of the individual's full name: first name, last name and, if appropriate, the middle initial. The first field, though, will be a user ID, which will be the primary key. Again, we'll create a clustered index on the primary key.

Comment

The purpose of the `Comments` table is to allow the user to store comments on how his or her routine went on any given day. This table will consist of a primary key, `CommentID`, with a clustered index, the `PersonID` (a foreign key linked it to the `User` table), the date and the comments themselves.

Measurement

The `Measurement` table stores the client's statistics for a given session. It consists of the user ID, once again a foreign key linked to the `User` table, the date, and information on the user's weight, and waist, biceps, chest and thigh measurements, in inches. By storing measurement information with the date, it allows users to monitor any changes in their statistics over time. Note that there is no primary key in this table.

AerobicLog

Information about the client's aerobic workout is stored in the `AerobicLog` table. It will consist of a unique ID and the user ID (the primary and foreign keys respectively), the date, the number of the set, time taken to complete the exercise (in minutes) and distance (in miles) where appropriate. Note that a 'set' is a group of repetitions of a given exercise. For example, if one is doing a bench press, lifting the bar up and bringing it back down a number of times in a row would be a set. Each time one raises and lowers the bar would be a rep (or repetition).

The `AerobicLog` table contains the information that a user would enter about their aerobic exercises. Note that in this table we specify the primary key as usual, but we have set two `FOREIGN KEY`s as well:

❏　PersonID from the User table

❏　ExID from the Exercises table

In addition to the clustered index on the primary key, we'll be creating a non-clustered index on the PersonID field. This allows searching and sorting on PersonID in a more efficient manner, and will also help performance with joins involving the PersonID field.

ResistanceLog

Finally, the ResistanceLog table is used to store information about the client's resistance workout. As with the AerobicLog table, it will contain a unique ID (the primary key), the PersonID (the foreign key which links it to the user table), the date and the set number. In addition, there will be an exercise ID (a second foreign key linking this table to the exercises table), the reps and the client's weight.

Again, we have a non-clustered index on the PersonID field, in addition to the clustered index on the primary key.

Thus we have a basic table structure where we can maintain the information we need about our workout. While there is obviously some relationship between distance and time, reps and weight and a person's measurements, they are not functional relationships and therefore we can say this database is at least in **third normal form** as each attribute column in the tables describes the primary key. For a fuller explanation of the third normal form (3NF) see Chapter 1.

Creating the Database

If you want a quick and easy method of creating this database yourself, you can use the script, SQLscript.txt, which is included with the code to download from the Wrox Press web site. The steps you need to follow to create the database are outlined below:

❏　Bring up SQL enterprise manager

❏　Select the server you're using from the list

❏　Create a new empty database called weights

❏　Click on Tool/SQL Query tool

❏　Copy the text from the script and pass it into the query tool

❏　In the query tool, click on execute

This will create the database and the tables, which you can then fill with some initial data from the file `weights.dat`, also supplied with the code download. To do this, you need to:

❑ Copy the weights.dat file to your root directory

❑ Right-click on the database and select **Backup/Restore,** and then the **Restore** tab

❑ Click From Device and then Add Device — point to the `.dat` file

Finally, select the device and click **Restore Now**

The User Interface

While we'll be using the ATL Object wizard to create the data access classes, the UI itself will be written using MFC, as all our examples have been. Once completed, the application will display data on users, exercises and exercise logs of users. In fact, we'll have a different view (form) corresponding to each of the tables discussed above, so that it's data may be displayed to the user of the application. We'll just look at a few of these here to get a feel for how the application is going to work.

The screenshot below shows what the exercise form will look like:

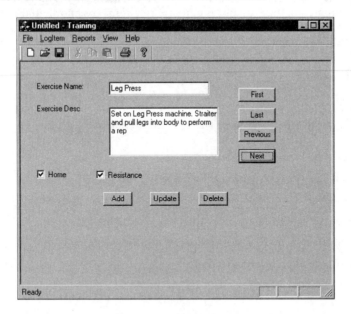

As you can see this is similar to the form views we have created for our previous examples. However, you'll notice that this form has a few more features than the ones we've created in previous examples.

In the form shown above, there are First and Last buttons to jump straight to the first or last record, there are two check boxes, Home and Resistance, and there are two new items on the menu bar, LogItem and Reports. The LogItem menu will allow us to switch between various forms displaying different data, and Reports lets us bring up a report for a particular user, which can be selected from a simple dialog box, as shown below:

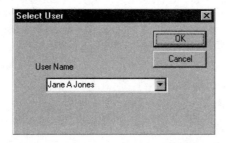

When a particular user is selected, a report will be displayed, like this:

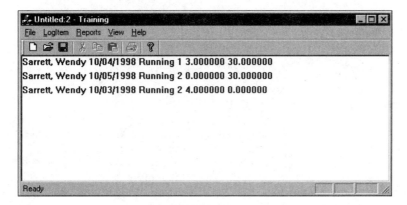

The report shows data that is gathered from three different tables, so we'll need to create a rowset class that's based on a query joining these tables.

Creating the Training Log MFC Application

Now we should turn our attention to creating the MFC application that will enable us to access the data from the weights database. To create the main application, we'll use the same techniques as we've used previously. As before, you should create a blank SDI MFC application using the AppWizard, basing the view class on CFormView. This will form one of the views of the data — the rest will have to be added later. Call the application Training.

To access the data, we'll be using the OLE DB classes and templates, which were introduced in the last chapter. The OLE DB database class will be contained in the document class, so remember not to set any database support in the AppWizard.

So, the basic structure of the application will take the form of one document class containing the rowset objects as members, and several different view classes that can all access the data from the same document. We'll have a form to display the data from each of the tables, and also a report showing data selected from multiple tables.

As you can see, this project is going to be much more complex than any example we have seen before. Each form will have edit boxes to display each field of the corresponding table, and will contain buttons for traversing the rowset — Next, Prev, First and Last, an Add button to insert a record, and also Delete and Update buttons. Some forms will contain additional features, which we'll see as we develop each view class.

We'll begin by looking at the creation of the OLE DB classes used to access the data, and then go on to see what changes need to be made to the MFC code. The document class is fairly straightforward, but there is more complexity in creating a view class for each of the rowsets we wish to display. At the end of this section, we'll see how to create a report based on a query that joins three of the tables.

Creating Data Access Classes

For a SQL Server 6.5 database, you'll need to set up an ODBC connection, so that you can use the OLE DB provider for ODBC. The data access classes are generated using the ATL Object Wizard. The steps are outlined below, but if you're unclear how to do this, you can go back to the last chapter where the process is discussed in more detail.

Select the Consumer object from the Wizard, and then the datasource. You'll be prompted to choose a provider, and then the database, and then a table from the database (for the first class, select dbo.Users). You can leave the class and file names as the defaults, but don't forget to check the three Support boxes: Change, Insert and Delete to enable manipulation of the rowset. When you finally click OK, you should have two new classes in the project, CdboUsers and CdboUsersAccessor, which are defined in the file dboUsers.h.

Now, this process needs to be repeated for each of the tables, so by the end you should have all of the following classes in addition to those just created:

- ❑ CdboExercises and CdboExercisesAccessor
- ❑ CdboComment and CdboCommentAccessor
- ❑ CdboMeasurement and CdboMeasurementAccessor
- ❑ CdboResistanceLog and CdboResistanceLogAccessor
- ❑ CdboAerobicLog and CdboAerobicLogAccessor

These are the classes that will be used to access the data in the various tables. As in previous examples, the rest of the application will access the data through the document class, in this case, CTrainingDoc.

The generated code defining the above classes will not be discussed in detail here, as this was covered in the last chapter. We will however, take a quick look at the changes that need to be made.

The Users Classes

The header file `dboUsers.h` contains two classes `CdboUserAccessor` as well as `CdboUser`:

```
class CdboUsersAccessor
{
public:
    LONG m_PersonID;
    TCHAR m_FirstName[21];
    TCHAR m_MI[2];
    TCHAR m_LastName[21];

    //This parameter holds the status of personID
    //which is an identity (or counter) column
    ULONG m_user_status;
```

Note that a new variable has been added here to deal with identity column (primary key) of the users table. Later, we set this variable to `DB_STATUS_S_IGNORE` to tell the system not to set this value, as it will be set by the database.

The column map will also need to be updated to take account of this change:

```
BEGIN_COLUMN_MAP(CdboUsersAccessor)
    COLUMN_ENTRY_STATUS(1, m_PersonID, m_user_status)
    COLUMN_ENTRY(2, m_FirstName)
    COLUMN_ENTRY(3, m_MI)
    COLUMN_ENTRY(4, m_LastName)
END_COLUMN_MAP()
```

That's all the changes that need to be made to the accessor class for the Users table. Let's just have a quick look at `CdboUsers`, and see what changes are necessary.

In the `CdboUsers::OpenDataSource()` method, we need to add a line of code to close the session before opening it — we saw this in the last chapter. Without this change, closing and reopening the rowset will cause the program to crash.

In terms of properties, those generated for the data source (in the `CdboUsers::OpenDataSource()` method) are fine. We will, however, add a couple of new properties to the rowset:

```
HRESULT OpenRowset()
{
    // Set properties for open
    CDBPropSet propset(DBPROPSET_ROWSET);
    propset.AddProperty(DBPROP_IRowsetChange, true);
    propset.AddProperty(DBPROP_UPDATABILITY, DBPROPVAL_UP_CHANGE |
                               DBPROPVAL_UP_INSERT | DBPROPVAL_UP_DELETE);
    propset.AddProperty(DBPROP_CANSCROLLBACKWARDS, true);
    propset.AddProperty(DBPROP_REMOVEDELETED, true);

    return CCommand<CAccessor<CdboUsersAccessor> >::Open(m_session, NULL,
                                                             &propset);
}
```

The CANSCROLLBACKWARDS property allows us to scroll backwards through the rowset, and the REMOVEDELETED property effectively removes a deleted row, so that errors don't occur while browsing.

A Note on Foreign Keys

We need to spend a little time discussing the slightly more complex case of a table with foreign keys. We take advantage of these, for example, in the AerobicLog table. Here, two foreign keys are defined from the Exercises and User tables. Note that while referential integrity allows the mapping of the ExID field in the exercise table to the ExID field in the AerobicLog table, we would like the values of ExID limited to rows in the Exercises table where the exercise is *aerobic*, that is not include those which are resistance.

This can be enforced by constraints in the database, but for now we will enforce this programatically, as we define the CdboExercises class (see the next section). What we are going to introduce here is a parameterized query. To do this we put question marks where the parameters go and then create a parameter map where we map the parameters to variables. Recall that we used a parameterized query in the ODBC example, back in Chapter 3.

The Exercises Classes

First let's look at `CdboExercisesAccessor`. The complete listing for this class is shown below:

```cpp
class CdboExercisesAccessor
{
public:
    LONG m_ExID;
    TCHAR m_ExName[21];
    TCHAR m_ExDescription[256];
    VARIANT_BOOL m_Home;
    VARIANT_BOOL m_Resistance;
    //This paramater holds the status of the exercise ID.
    ULONG m_exid_status;

    //these hold the parameter for the parameterized query
    //that his classes is based upon
    VARIANT_BOOL m_Res1;
    VARIANT_BOOL m_Res2;

BEGIN_COLUMN_MAP(CdboExercisesAccessor)
    COLUMN_ENTRY_STATUS(1, m_ExID,m_exid_status)
    COLUMN_ENTRY(2, m_ExName)
    COLUMN_ENTRY(3, m_ExDescription)
    COLUMN_ENTRY_TYPE(4, DBTYPE_BOOL, m_Home)
    COLUMN_ENTRY_TYPE(5, DBTYPE_BOOL, m_Resistance)
END_COLUMN_MAP()

BEGIN_PARAM_MAP(CdboExercisesAccessor)
    COLUMN_ENTRY(1, m_Res1)
    COLUMN_ENTRY(2, m_Res2)
END_PARAM_MAP()

DEFINE_COMMAND(CdboExercisesAccessor, _T(" \
    SELECT \
        ExID, \
        ExName, \
        ExDescription, \
        Home, \
        Resistance \
            FROM dbo.Exercises WHERE Resistance = ? OR Resistance = ?"))

    // You may wish to call this function if you are inserting a record and wish to
    // initialize all the fields, if you are not going to explicitly set all of them
    void ClearRecord()
    {
        memset(this, 0, sizeof(*this));
    }
};
```

Note that, as before, we need to add a status variable for the primary key, and change the column map accordingly. Note that we also have to define the two variables we will use to hold the parameters for the parameterized query. In order to use them, they have to be defined in a parameter map, which is added just after the column map.

The parameter map maps the Boolean variables m_Res1 and m_Res2 defined above with the parameters in the query — basically it says that the first parameter in the query (the first ?) is bound to m_Res1, and the second to m_Res2.

This becomes clear when you look at the query itself — note that the last line of the SQL statement has been changed to make this a parameterized query. Now we include the query itself in the code. Notice the WHERE clause, where Resistance has the value m_Res1 or m_Res2. Since the Resistance parameter is a Boolean variable, we can use this clause to get:

- ❑ All the records in the exercise class (by setting m_Res1 equal to 1 and m_Res2 equal to 0 or vice-versa)
- ❑ Just the resistance exercises (by setting both m_Res1 and m_Res2 equal to 1)
- ❑ Just the non-resistance aerobic exercises (by setting both m_Res1 equal to 0).

The CdboExercises class is also defined in dboExercises.h. The only changes that need to be made here are to add the CANSCROLLBACKWARDS and REMOVEDELETED properties to the rowset before it is opened, and to close the session before it is opened (in OpenDataSource()).

Definition of the Remaining Rowset Classes

We complete this section by defining the remaining classes which are used to access the data. These are:

- ❑ CdboComment and CdboCommentAccessor
- ❑ CdboMeasurement and CdboMeasurementAccessor
- ❑ CdboAerobicLog and CdboAerobicLogAccessor
- ❑ CdboResistanceLog and CdboResistanceLogAccessor

Most of the changes that need to be made here, we have seen already. For the rowsets with primary keys, we need to add a status variable to the accessor class and alter the column map accordingly. This applies to all of the above accessors apart from CdboMeasurementAccessor.

The other neccessary changes are in `OpenDataSource()`, where a line needs to be added to close the session prior to opening it, and to `OpenRowset()`, where the `CANSCROLLBACKWARDS` and `REMOVEDELETED` properties should be added.

Implementing the Document Class

One of the most important classes in the application is the document class. As in all the previous examples, we employ just one `CTrainingDoc` object to maintain all the data in the application. More specifically, this is where all the rowset objects are maintained.

The rowset objects are actually opened in their respective view classes as and when required, but they are all closed in the document object. The advantage of this is that we don't have lots of rowset objects open, if they are never required. On the other hand, closing them all in the document means we are not constantly opening and closing rowsets as a user moves between views.

Later on, we'll create a rowset that is simply used for reporting — this will simply be opened when it's required for the creation of the report and closed afterwards. Other rowsets with parameters are open and closed when used, as the parameters are reset at that time.

In order to keep track of whether or not the rowsets are open, we maintain a parameter for each in the document class to indicate its status — whether it's open or closed, empty and so on.

The document class is defined as follows. It is found in `TrainingDoc.h`:

```
class CTrainingDoc : public CDocument
{
protected: // create from serialization only
    CTrainingDoc();
    DECLARE_DYNCREATE(CTrainingDoc)

// Attributes
public:
    //These are the command objects for exercise and user
    CdboExercises dbEx;
    CdboUsers dbUser;

    //another implementation of these DB objects for using in a combo box
    CdboUsers dbUserLst;
    CdboExercises dbExLst; //one for the user list, the other for exercises

    //these hold the command objects for the measument and comment tables,
    //resistance log, aerobics log and reporting of aerobic workouts
    CdboMeasurement dbMeas;  //measument table
    CdboComment dbComment;  // comment table
    CdboResistanceLog dbResLog;  //resistance log table
    CdboAerobicLog dbAeroLog;    //aerobic log table
    CdboAerobicPerson dbAeroPRep;  //aerobic workout for a person
```

```
//these are the variables that hold the status of the rowsets
short iNoUser;
short iNoEx;
short iNoUserLst;
short iNoExLst;
short iNoMeas;
short iNoComm;
short iNoRes;
short iNoAero;

int iPID; //used by the report dialog to hold the user ID selected
```

Notice that we maintain all the command objects in this class. This makes it easy to access the data from wherever in the program that is necessary. The series of short variables shown above are the parameters used maintain the status of the rowsets. They can have one of four values:

❑ DBEMPTY — the database can be opened but it is empty

❑ DBOPEN — the database is open and has data

❑ DBERROR — the database does not open properly

❑ DBCLOSED — the database has not been opened

These are defined in the DBClasses.h file as they are used in many files:

```
#ifndef DBSTATUS
#define DBSTATUS
#define DBOPEN 1
#define DBEMPTY 0
#define DBERROR -1
#define DBCLOSED -99
#endif
```

The implementation of the document class is found in TrainingDoc.cpp. The code for the class constructor and destructor are shown below.

```
// CTrainingDoc construction/destruction

CTrainingDoc::CTrainingDoc()
{
    iNoEx = DBCLOSED;
    iNoUser = DBCLOSED;
    iNoUserLst = DBCLOSED;
    iNoExLst = DBCLOSED;
    iNoMeas = DBCLOSED;
    iNoComm = DBCLOSED;
    iNoRes = DBCLOSED;
    iNoAero = DBCLOSED;
}
```

In the constructor we simply initialize the parameter holding the database status to DBCLOSED. The data connections will be opened in the view classes. However, to avoid constant opening and closing we will close the data sources in the destructor:

```
CTrainingDoc::~CTrainingDoc()
{
   dbEx.Close();
   dbUser.Close();
   dbExLst.Close();
   dbUserLst.Close();
   dbMeas.Close();
   dbComment.Close();
   dbResLog.Close();
   dbAeroLog.Close();
}
```

Developing the User Interface

In order to see the data accessed by the data access classes, we define a series of view classes, one for each of the tables. Here, we will open the rowset and implement handlers on the command buttons on each form that allow the user to scroll through the rowsets, add and delete records and so on.

The first such class we will develop will display the data for the User table. It is called CUserView and is derived from CFormView.

The CUserView Class

The CUserView class is the class that contains the code behind the form where we manage the user table. This form permits one to browse the rowset, add rows, delete rows and update rows. The layout of the form itself is shown below:

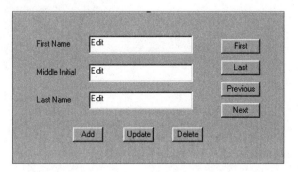

Using ClassWizard, you should define the variables that correspond to controls on the form, as well as adding handlers for the buttons.

Note that you should call the handler for the **Update** *button* OnUpdateRec(), *rather than* OnUpdate(), *as we'll be overriding the inherited* OnUpdate() *method later.*

An OLE DB Consumer Example

The Class Header

The class is declared as follows:

```cpp
// UserView.h : header file

#ifndef __AFXEXT_H__
#include <afxext.h>
#endif

class CUserView : public CFormView
{
protected:
    CUserView();          // protected constructor used by dynamic creation
    DECLARE_DYNCREATE(CUserView)

public:
    //{{AFX_DATA(CUserView)
    enum { IDD = IDD_USERS };
    CString m_firstname;
    CString m_lastname;
    CString m_mi;
    //}}AFX_DATA

// Attributes
public:

// Operations
public:
    CTrainingDoc* GetDocument();

// Overrides
    // ClassWizard generated virtual function overrides
    //{{AFX_VIRTUAL(CUserView)
    public:
    virtual void OnInitialUpdate();
    protected:
    virtual void DoDataExchange(CDataExchange* pDX);   // DDX/DDV support
    virtual void OnUpdate(CView* pSender, LPARAM lHint, CObject* pHint);
    //}}AFX_VIRTUAL

// Implementation
protected:
    virtual ~CUserView();
    bool m_bNew;

#ifdef _DEBUG
    virtual void AssertValid() const;
    virtual void Dump(CDumpContext& dc) const;
#endif
```

```
      // Generated message map functions
      //{{AFX_MSG(CUserView)
      afx_msg void OnAdd();
      afx_msg void OnDelete();
      afx_msg void OnFirst();
      afx_msg void OnLast();
      afx_msg void OnUpdateRec();
      afx_msg void OnNext();
      afx_msg void OnPrev();
      //}}AFX_MSG

      DECLARE_MESSAGE_MAP()
   };
```

This is pretty similar to what we've seen in Chapter 3. The highlighted sections show the variables and handlers that have been added using ClassWizard to handle the controls on the form. Also highlighted are two inherited functions that we need to override — `OnInitialUpdate()` and `OnUpdate()`.

Note that we also need to implement `GetDocument()`, which is used to return a pointer to the document associated with the view. You can simply cut-and-paste the implementation for this from the view class generated with the application — `CTrainingView`.

Finally, we need another member variable, `m_bNew`, to tell the `OnUpdateRec()` handler whether we're updating the record or creating a new one. It is `false` by default, but set to true when the user clicks on **Add**.

Construction

The implementation of the constructor is shown below:

```
CUserView::CUserView()
   : CFormView(CUserView::IDD)
{
   //{{AFX_DATA_INIT(CUserView)
   m_firstname = _T("");
   m_mi = _T("");
   m_lastname = _T("");
   //}}AFX_DATA_INIT
   m_bNew = false;
}
```

The only addition here is the initialization of the `m_bNew` member variable to `false`.

Data Exchange and Validation

As we've seen before, the `DoDateExchange()` function is where data is passed between the form and the `CUserView` class:

```
void CUserView::DoDataExchange(CDataExchange* pDX)
{
    CFormView::DoDataExchange(pDX);
    //{{AFX_DATA_MAP(CUserView)
    DDX_Text(pDX, IDC_FIRSTNAME, m_firstname);
    DDV_MaxChars(pDX, m_firstname, 20);
    DDX_Text(pDX, IDC_LASTNAME, m_lastname);
    DDV_MaxChars(pDX, m_lastname, 20);
    DDX_Text(pDX, IDC_MI, m_mi);
    DDV_MaxChars(pDX, m_mi, 1);
    //}}AFX_DATA_MAP
}
```

Note the use of the `DDV_MaxChars()` macro to limit the number of characters that the field can accept. We limit the size of the input based on how large the field is in the database.

Initialization

Let's take a look now at the `OnInitialUpdate()` method that is called when the view is first attached to the document. Here we handle the initial formatting of the screen when it's initialized. The function gets a pointer to the parent frame, repositioning the elements (`ReCalcLayout()`) and resizing the frame window (`ResizeParentToFit()`).

In addition, it is in `OnInitialUpdate()` where we open the data source used in the view if it isn't already open. The status of the rowset object can be checked via the `iNoUser` variable in the document object. Recall that this is initialized as `DBCLOSED`. If the source is successfully opened, then we change the variable `iNoUser DBOPEN` to indicate this fact.

The full listing for `OnInitialUpdate()` is shown below:

```
void CUserView::OnInitialUpdate()
{
    CTrainingDoc *pDoc = GetDocument();
    if(pDoc->iNoUser == DBCLOSED)
    {
        if(pDoc->dbUser.Open() == S_OK)
        {
            if(pDoc->dbUser.MoveNext() != S_OK)
                pDoc->iNoUser = DBEMPTY;
            else
                pDoc->iNoUser = DBOPEN;
        }
        else
        {
            pDoc->iNoUser = DBERROR;
            AfxMessageBox("Can't open Rowset");
        }
    }
}
```

```
    CFormView::OnInitialUpdate();
    GetParentFrame()->RecalcLayout();
    ResizeParentToFit();
}
```

Note how we can also use the `iNoUser` variable to indicate an empty rowset, or the fact that an error has occurred.

The related method, `OnUpdate()`, is called by the framework when the window is initially created, or any other time the document's view is changed:

```
void CUserView::OnUpdate(CView* pSender, LPARAM lHint, CObject* pHint)
{
    CTrainingDoc *pDoc = GetDocument();

    //if iNoUser is true it means that the rowset failed to open
    //correctly
    if(pDoc->iNoUser == DBOPEN)
    {
        m_lastname = pDoc->dbUser.m_LastName;
        m_firstname = pDoc->dbUser.m_FirstName;
        m_mi = pDoc->dbUser.m_MI;
    }
    else
    {
        m_lastname = "";
        m_firstname = "";
        m_mi = "";
    }
    UpdateData(FALSE);
}
```

In this method, we simply check that the rowset is open, and then update the variables corresponding to the fields on the form.

Adding Functionality for the Buttons

Now we implement our own message handlers. Versions of these functions will be included in all the view classes, so they will only be presented in full for the `CUserView` class. We'll just look at these in the other classes, where the implementation differs.

The first of these is `OnAdd()`. The purpose of this function is to clear the form and set `m_bNew` to `true` so that the `OnUpdateRec()` function will treat the input as a new record:

```
// add a new record, reset m_bNew for the UpdateRec fucntion
void CUserView::OnAdd()
{
    m_firstname = "";
    m_lastname = "";
    m_mi = "";
    UpdateData(FALSE);
    m_bNew = true;
}
```

Next, we have the `OnDelete()` function:

```
void CUserView::OnDelete()
{
    HRESULT hr;
    CTrainingDoc *pDoc = GetDocument();
    CString strMsg = "Are you sure you want to delete ";
    strMsg = strMsg + pDoc->dbUser.m_LastName;
    int iRes = MessageBox(strMsg,"Delete?", MB_YESNO);
    if(iRes == IDYES)
    {
        hr = pDoc->dbUser.Delete();
        if(FAILED(hr))
        {
            AfxMessageBox("Cannot delete record - it is used in a related table");
            return;
        }
        hr = pDoc->dbUser.MoveFirst();
        if(SUCCEEDED(hr))
        {
            m_lastname = pDoc->dbUser.m_LastName;
            m_firstname = pDoc->dbUser.m_FirstName;
            m_mi = pDoc->dbUser.m_MI;
        }
        else
        {
            pDoc->iNoUser = DBEMPTY;
            m_lastname = "";
            m_firstname = "";
            m_mi ="";
        }

        UpdateData(FALSE);
    }
}
```

If the deletion is successful, it moves to the first record and updates the form with that record's data. If it fails, it returns an error to the user.

This is important because we established foreign key constraints among many of the tables. What this means is that if a value is used as a foreign key in a different table, it cannot be deleted.

If the record deleted leaves the table empty (we determine this by the result of the `MoveFirst()`), then after deleting the record, we set `iNoUser` to `DBEMPTY`, so that methods like `Update()` know there are no valid records and clear the form.

Note that you have to be careful about the return codes. For example, in this case you can use the `FAILED()` macro to test the result of the delete call. However, we will see in the `MovePrev()`/`MoveNext()` calls it's not necessary the case. These calls can return an HRESULT greater than 0 if they fail. This makes the macro inappropriate in this case because it considers a negative HRESULT as failed and an HRESULT greater than or equal to 0 as a success.

As its name suggests, the OnFirst() function selects and displays the very first record in the rowset.:

```
void CUserView::OnFirst()
{
    CTrainingDoc* pDoc = GetDocument();
    HRESULT hr = pDoc->dbUser.MoveFirst()

    if(hr == S_OK)
    {
        m_lastname = pDoc->dbUser.m_LastName;
        m_firstname = pDoc->dbUser.m_FirstName;
        m_mi = pDoc->dbUser.m_MI;
    }
    else
    {
        pDoc->iNoUser = DBEMPTY;
        m_lastname = "";
        m_firstname = "";
        m_mi ="";
    }
    UpdateData(FALSE);
}
```

This is the first of the functions used to browse the rowset. If this method succeeds, we fill the form with the data returned from the first record. If it fails we clear the form and set iNoUser to DBEMPTY.

The related function OnLast() is shown below:

```
void CUserView::OnLast()
{
    CTrainingDoc *pDoc = GetDocument();
    HRESULT hr = pDoc->dbUser.MoveLast();
    if(SUCCEEDED(hr))
    {
        m_lastname = pDoc->dbUser.m_LastName;
        m_firstname = pDoc->dbUser.m_FirstName;
        m_mi = pDoc->dbUser.m_MI;
    }
    else
    {
        AfxMessageBox("Last Record has been deleted");
        m_lastname = "";
        m_firstname = "";
        m_mi ="";
    }
    UpdateData(FALSE);
}
```

One important lesson to learn here is how to deal with deleted records. Normally, when a record is deleted, it is marked as deleted but not removed from the rowset. The outcome of this is that problems occur when browsing the rowset. In the last chapter, we got around this by closing and reopening the rowset, but a better method is to use the DBPROP_REMOVEDELETED parameter in the rowset, which does what it says — removes the deleted row from the rowset so errors do not occur while browsing.

Now we come onto the `OnUpdateRec()` function. This is the function that will either add a new record or update the current record, depending on the value of m_bNew. New records are added to the end of the rowset. The implementation is as follows:

```
// Updates the current record or creates a new record
void CUserView::OnUpdateRec()
{
    HRESULT hr;
    CTrainingDoc* pDoc = GetDocument();

    UpdateData(true);
    if(m_bNew)
    {
        pDoc->dbUser.ClearRecord();
    }
    //ignore the ID row since the database will take care of it
    pDoc->dbUser.m_user_status = DBSTATUS_S_IGNORE;
    strcpy (pDoc->dbUser.m_FirstName, m_firstname.GetBuffer(21));
    strcpy(pDoc ->dbUser.m_LastName, m_lastname.GetBuffer(21));
    strcpy(pDoc ->dbUser.m_MI, m_mi.GetBuffer(2));

    //if m_bNew is true then insert a new record, otherwise update the
    //current record
    if(m_bNew)
    {
        hr = pDoc->dbUser.Insert();
        if(FAILED(hr))
        {
            MessageBox("Failed Insert");
            m_bNew = false;
            return;
        }
        else
            MessageBox("Successful Insert");
        m_bNew = false;
        pDoc->iNoUser = DBOPEN;
        pDoc->dbUser.MoveLast(); //since ID would make new rec last
    }
    else
    {
        hr = pDoc->dbUser.SetData();
        if(FAILED(hr))
            MessageBox("Failed Update");
        else
            MessageBox("Successful Update");
    }
    UpdateData(FALSE);
}
```

We know the new record is the last record because the rowset is ordered by its clustered index, UserID. Since UserID is an IDENTITY column, the new record will be assigned a value for UserID that is the next increment after the most recently assigned value. This value will therefore be greater than all the other values in UserID.

Note as well, if a new record is successfully inserted, we set iNoUser to DBOPEN as we know that there is data in the table and the rowset is open.

SetData(), is equivalent to the Update() function of other data access technologies. This is the call to update the current data.

Another important thing to point out is that dbUser.m_user_status is set to DBSTATUS_S_IGNORE. This is necessary or the system will expect you to provide a value for m_PersonID. However, since this is an IDENTITY column we let the database table provide this. Therefore, we must tell the system to ignore this column.

The next two message handlers, OnNext() and OnPrev(), are very similar. Like the functions we included in our previous projects, they allow stepwise movement through the rowset — forwards and back:

```
void CUserView::OnNext()
{
    HRESULT hr;
    CTrainingDoc* pDoc = GetDocument();

    hr = pDoc->dbUser.MoveNext();
    if(hr != S_OK)
    {
        //if the value returned indicates the end of the rowset
        //move to the last record
        if(hr == DB_S_ENDOFROWSET || hr == DB_E_BADSTARTPOSITION)
        {
            MessageBox("Last Row", "File warning", MB_OK | MB_ICONWARNING);
            hr = pDoc->dbUser.MoveLast();
            if(hr != S_OK)
                return;
        }
        else //otherwise there another kind of error - return a warning and
        {    //get out
            MessageBox("Error in file", "File Warning", MB_OK | MB_ICONSTOP);
            return;
        }
    }

    m_lastname = pDoc->dbUser.m_LastName;
    m_firstname = pDoc->dbUser.m_FirstName;
    m_mi = pDoc->dbUser.m_MI;

    UpdateData(FALSE);
}
```

If the move fails, we check first to see if the return value is either DB_S_ENDOFROWSET or DB_E_BADSTARTPOSITION, which inform us that we have reached either end of the rowset. If such an error is returned, a message box is displayed to the user and the last record is displayed.

Note that these error values are defined in oledberr.h, and you should add a #include for this file to StdAfx.h. These values are defined in hexadecimal. One trick here that you might already be familiar with — if you do get an error value returned to an HRESULT it will be returned as a decimal (usually negative), Microsoft's built-in calculator allows you to convert from decimal to hex and you can then check oledberr.h (or any other ole error include file) to see what the error means.

Now here's `OnPrev()`:

```
void CUserView::OnPrev()
{
    HRESULT hr;
    CTrainingDoc *pDoc = GetDocument();
    hr = pDoc->dbUser.MovePrev();
    while(hr != S_OK)
    {
        if(hr == DB_S_ENDOFROWSET || hr == DB_E_BADSTARTPOSITION)
        {
            MessageBox("First Row", "File warning", MB_OK | MB_ICONWARNING);
            hr = pDoc->dbUser.MoveFirst();
            if(hr != S_OK)
                return;
        }
        else
        {
            MessageBox("Error in file", "File Warning", MB_OK |
                                              MB_ICONSTOP);
            return;
        }
    }
    m_lastname = pDoc->dbUser.m_LastName;
    m_firstname = pDoc->dbUser.m_FirstName;
    m_mi = pDoc->dbUser.m_MI;

    UpdateData(FALSE);
}
```

Including Files

Because we need to include all the database classes in many places, it would be a lot more straightforward to have them all together in one file. You can add them to `DBClasses.h`, which already contains the definitions of the status parameters.

This include file essentially is a set of `#include`s with all the rowset class `.h` files:

```
#include "dboExercises.h"
#include "dboUser1.h"
#include "dboMeasurment.h"
#include "dboComment.h"
#include "dboResistanceLog.H"
#include "dboAerobicLog.h"
#include "dboAerobicPerson.h"
```

```
#ifndef DBSTATUS
#define DBOPEN   1
#define DBEMPTY  0
#define DBERROR -1
#define DBCLOSED -99
#endif
```

You can then add this file as a `#include` for any of the other files that require the definitions of the rowset classes.

The AerobicLog View Class

The next view class we will develop is that for the `Aerobics Log`. This class will be substantially different from the `CUserClass`, the reason being that the `AerobicLog` table contains foreign keys.

While the view class for a table without foreign keys only needs to access its own table, we now need to include data from the table supplying the foreign key as well.

Here, we use the `Exercises` table to fill a dropdown list box with the available aerobic exercises. We also use the `User` table to fill a dropdown list box with the users in the database.

Let's now look at the view class. We've already seen the full implementation of the `CUserView` class, so we'll just look at selected methods of the `CAeroLog` view class, defined in `AeroLog.cpp`.

The following screenshot shows what the form should look like:

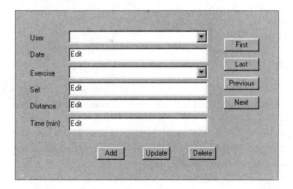

As before, you should add the appropriate member variables to the view class corresponding to the edit and combo boxes on the form, as well as handlers for the seven buttons.

Referential Integrity

You might be wondering why we have drop-down list boxes in the above form, rather than simple edit boxes. Well, the reason for using these for the user and exercise is to limit the choices for these values. In the case of user, it is simply enforcing the foreign key of user ID. We need to make it impossible for someone to fill in a record for the `AerobicLog` table that includes a user who is not defined in the `Users` table.

In the case of the `Exercises` table, things are a bit more complex. We are not only enforcing the foreign key, but also limiting the list to those exercises that are aerobic. We simply won't include non-aerobic exercises in the drop-down list.

Changes to the Header

We'll also be adding some helper functions this time, so you should add the prototypes for these to the header file:

```
void RefreshName();
void RefreshEx();
int GetUsrID(int iID);
int GetExID(int iID);
void SetFormData();
```

Note that again, we have a Boolean variable, m_bNew, which is initialized to `false` in the constructor. We'll be using this in all the view classes created.

The `RefreshName()` and `RefreshEx()` functions will be used to populate the lists in the combo boxes with the data on users and exercises. As you might expect from their names, `GetUsrID()` and `GetExID()` retrieve the ID's for the selected user and exercise respectively.

In this class, updating this form will be more complex, so we'll have a `SetFormData()` function that simply updates the form data.

Initialization

The `OnInitialUpdate()` method of the `CAeroLog` class is very similar to that for the `CUserView` class. Recall that we simply checked the status of the rowset class, and opened it if necessary. The only difference here is that we have two rowset classes to open — not only the `dbAeroLog` object, but also the `dbUsrLst` object, which is used to populate the drop down list for the users. Note that the `dbExLst` object, used to fill the drop-down list for the exercises, is opened in the `RefeshEx()` function, which we'll see later.

The purpose of the virtual method `OnUpdate()` is to call this function. These functions are all implemented in `AeroLog.cpp`:

```
//When we update the form we simply se the form data
void CAeroLog::OnUpdate(CView* pSender, LPARAM lHint, CObject* pHint)
{
    SetFormData();
}
```

Command Button Handlers

The `OnUpdateRec()` function is very different from what we have seen before. It's purpose, however, is exactly the same as for `CUserView` — it either updates the current record value or inserts a new record, depending on the value of m_bNew.

What is interesting here is how the Date field is handled. We have to parse the value of m_date, validate the values for day, month and year before we pass them to the database's date parameter. While the date is one field in the database, the corresponding variable is in the form of a struct in the C++ code, where we have to pass the day, month and year separately.

Note that we set pDoc->iNoAero to DBOPEN on an insert since, if we have successfully added a record, we know the rowset is open and has at least one record.

```
//This will either update the current row or insert a new row,
// depending on the value of m_bNew
void CAeroLog::OnUpdateRec()
{
    CTrainingDoc* pDoc = GetDocument();
    int month;
    int day;
    int year;
    UpdateData(true);

    //we parse the m_date value into mm, dd, yyyy and validate the values
    month = atoi(m_date.Left(2));
    if(month < 1 || month > 12)
    {
        MessageBox("Invalid date...date should be in the form
                                                \"mm/dd/yyyy\"");
        return;
    }
    year = atoi(m_date.Right(4));
    if(year < 1990 || year > 9999)
    {
        MessageBox("Invalid date...date should be in the form
                            \"mm/dd/yyyy\" year must be > 1990");
        return;
    }
    day = atoi(m_date.Mid(3,2));
    switch(month) {
    case 9:
    case 4:
    case 6:
    case 11:
        if(day < 1 || day > 30)
        {
            MessageBox("April, June, September and November only have 30 days");
            return;
        }
        break;
    case 2:
        {
            int iMaxDay;
            if(year % 4 != 0)
                iMaxDay = 28;
            else
                iMaxDay = 29;
            if(day < 1 || day > iMaxDay)
            {
```

```
            MessageBox("February only has 28 or 29 days");
            return;
        }
    }
break;
default:
    if(day < 1 || day > 31)
    {
        MessageBox("Day must be 1-31");
        return;
    }
break;
}
pDoc->dbAeroLog.ClearRecord();
pDoc->dbAeroLog.m_logid_status = DBSTATUS_S_IGNORE;

//here we create a time object based on the values we parsed from m_date
CTime dTemp(year,month,day,0,0,0);
pDoc->dbAeroLog.m_Date.day = day;
pDoc->dbAeroLog.m_Date.month = month;
pDoc->dbAeroLog.m_Date.year = year;

pDoc->dbAeroLog.m_Date.hour = 0;
pDoc->dbAeroLog.m_Date.minute = 0;
pDoc->dbAeroLog.m_Date.second = 0;
pDoc->dbAeroLog.m_PersonID = m_user.GetItemData(m_user.GetCurSel());
pDoc->dbAeroLog.m_ExID = m_exercise.GetItemData(m_exercise.GetCurSel());
pDoc->dbAeroLog.m_Distance = atof(this->m_distance);
pDoc->dbAeroLog.m_Set = atoi(this->m_set);
pDoc->dbAeroLog.m_TimeInMin = atof(this->m_time);
if(m_bNew == true)
{
    HRESULT hr2 = pDoc->dbAeroLog.Insert();
    if(FAILED(hr2))
    {
        AfxMessageBox("Error on Insert");
        m_bNew = false;
        return;
    }
    else
    {
        AfxMessageBox("Successful Insert");
        pDoc->dbAeroLog.MoveLast();
    }
    m_bNew = false;
    pDoc->iNoAero = DBOPEN;
}
else
{
    if(pDoc->dbAeroLog.SetData() != S_OK)
        AfxMessageBox("Error On Update");
    else
        AfxMessageBox("Successful Update");
}
UpdateData(false);
}
```

The OnAdd() function is also different. It will clear the form as we've seen previously, enabling data to be entered. The difference however, is that it calls the RefreshName() and RefreshEx() functions. These functions, that we will see later, clear and fill the two list boxes.

```
void CAeroLog::OnAdd()
{
    CTrainingDoc* pDoc = GetDocument();
    pDoc->dbUserLst.Close();
    pDoc->dbUserLst.Open();
    RefreshName();
    RefreshEx();
    m_distance ="";
    m_set ="";
    m_time = "";
    m_date = "";
    m_bNew = true;
    UpdateData(FALSE);
}
```

Note that we close and reopen the rowset that contains the list of users. This assures that the data in the rowset is current. RefreshEx() does this within the function itself. The reason for this is that it uses parameters. While the parameters are retained in the parameter variables in the rowset, they can be changed. These parameters have been set before calling RefreshEx(). Closing and reopening the rowset assures the values returned to the rowset are current. Hence, it's easier to set the parameters and reopen the rowset.

Note that the variables that are instances of rowsets, such as dbUserLst, are declared in the document class.

The OnPrev() and OnNext() functions are basically the same as that for the CUserView class, so they won't be shown here. There are only two differences:

- ❑ Instead of using the dbUser member of the document class, we are using the dbAeroLog member
- ❑ Rather than set update the data on the form at the end of the function, we simply call SetFormData()

The OnDelete() function is also very similar to that for the CUserView class:

```
void CAeroLog::OnDelete()
{
    HRESULT hr;
    CTrainingDoc* pDoc = GetDocument();
    int res = MessageBox("Are you sure you want to delete this record",
                                            "Delete?", MB_YESNO);

    if(res == IDYES)
    {
```

```
        if(pDoc->dbAeroLog.Delete() != S_OK)
        {
            AfxMessageBox("Cannot delete record - it is used in a related table");
            return;
        }

        hr = pDoc->dbAeroLog.MoveFirst();
        if(FAILED(hr))
        {
            pDoc->iNoAero = DBEMPTY;
        }
        SetFormData();
    }
}
```

If the call to `MoveFirst()` fails after the record has been deleted, then we know that the rowset must be empty, so we set the status variable, `iNoAero`, to `DBEMPTY`. Finally, there is a call to `SetFormData()`, which will deal with the empty rowset scenario itself if necessary. We'll see the implementation for this function later on.

Shown below are the implementations for the `OnFirst()` and `OnLast()` handlers:

```
void CAeroLog::OnFirst()
{
    CTrainingDoc* pDoc = GetDocument();
    HRESULT hr = pDoc->dbAeroLog.MoveFirst();
    if(FAILED(hr))
        return;
    else
        SetFormData();
}

void CAeroLog::OnLast()
{
    CTrainingDoc *pDoc = GetDocument();
    CTrainingDoc *pDoc = GetDocument();
    HRESULT hr = pDoc->dbAeroLog.MoveLast();
    if(FAILED(hr))
    {
        AfxMessageBox("Last Record has been deleted,moving to previous record");
        hr = pDoc->dbAeroLog.MovePrev();
        if(hr != S_OK)
        {
            AfxMessageBox("Unsuccessful Move");
            return;
        }
        else
            SetFormData();

    }
    else
        SetFormData();
}
```

Helper Functions

Now we turn to some more brand new functionality. First, the `RefreshName()` function, whose purpose is to fill out the combo box specified by `m_user`. Remember that this is important, because we don't want a record added with an unknown user. The implementation for this function is shown below:

```
void CAeroLog::RefreshName()
{
   int iRes;
   CTrainingDoc* pDoc = GetDocument();
   CString strItem;

   HRESULT hr = pDoc->dbUserLst.MoveFirst();
   m_user.ResetContent();
   while(hr == S_OK)
   {
      strItem = pDoc->dbUserLst.m_FirstName;
      strItem += " ";
      strItem += pDoc->dbUserLst.m_MI;
      strItem += " ";
      strItem += pDoc->dbUserLst.m_LastName;
      iRes = m_user.AddString(strItem.GetBuffer(128));

      //we set the item's data to the userID of the user
      //who's name we have just entered
      m_user.SetItemData(iRes,pDoc->dbUserLst.m_PersonID);
      hr = pDoc->dbUserLst.MoveNext();
   }
   m_user.SetCurSel(0);
}
```

We start by clearing the box (by calling `ResetContent()`) and then fill it line by line, stepping through the values from the `User` table in the database. After the combo box is filled, `SetCurSel(0)` sets the combo box (or dropdown list) to the first item in the list (Index 0).

The related function, `RefreshEx()`, fills out the `Exercise` combo box. Since the data source filling the list box is based on a parameterized query, we need to set the parameters so that we only select aerobic exercises and then reopen the rowset:

```
void CAeroLog::RefreshEx()
{
   int iRes;
   CTrainingDoc* pDoc = GetDocument();
   CString strItem;
   pDoc->dbExLst.m_Res1 = 0;
   pDoc->dbExLst.m_Res2 = 0;
   pDoc->dbExLst.Close();
   pDoc->dbExLst.Open();
```

```
    HRESULT hr = pDoc->dbExLst.MoveFirst();
    m_exercise.ResetContent();
    while(hr == S_OK)
    {
        strItem = pDoc->dbExLst.m_ExName;
        iRes = m_exercise.AddString(strItem.GetBuffer(20));
        m_exercise.SetItemData(iRes,pDoc->dbExLst.m_ExID);
        hr = pDoc->dbExLst.MoveNext();
    }
    m_exercise.SetCurSel(0);
}
```

The next function GetUsrID() steps through the entries in the user combo box until the user ID stored in the item data (by SetItemData()) matches the user ID passed into the function.

```
int CAeroLog::GetUsrID(int iID)
{
    int i;

    for(i = 0; i < m_user.GetCount(); i++)
    {
        if(iID == (int) m_user.GetItemData(i))
            break;
    }
    if(i < m_user.GetCount())
        return i;
    else
        return -1;
}
```

You'll see how this function is used later, when we look at the code for the SetFormData() function. SetFormData() also uses the GetExID() function, which is the equivalent function to get the Exercise index. This is very similar to the function shown above:

```
int CAeroLog::GetExID(int iID)
{
    int i;

    for(i = 0; i < m_exercise.GetCount(); i++)
    {
        if(iID == (int)m_exercise.GetItemData(i))
            break;
    }
    if(i < m_exercise.GetCount())
        return i;
    else
        return -1;

}
```

Finally, we come to the SetFormData() function, which fills out the form view with the data from the current record:

```
void CAeroLog::SetFormData()
{
    int res;          //holds result variable
    char strTmp[10];  //holds temporary string when we convert float to str
    int dec;          //returns dec when convert float to str
    int sign;    //returns sign when convert float to sign
    char *strTmpF, *strBuff, *strStTmp; //temporary string variable
    int i;  //index variable

    strTmpF = new char(20);
    strStTmp = strTmpF;
    *strTmpF = '\0';

    CTrainingDoc* pDoc = GetDocument();

    if(m_user.GetCount() == 0)
    {
        RefreshName();
        RefreshEx();
    }

    //if the rowset is empty get out
    if(pDoc->iNoAero == DBEMPTY)
    {
    this->m_distance = "";
    this->m_date = "";
    this->m_set = "";
    this->m_time = "";
    UpdateData(FALSE);
    return;
    }

    //if month isn't initialized, get out
    if(pDoc->dbAeroLog.m_Date.month > 12)
    {
        UpdateData(FALSE);
        return;
    }

    //we create a CTime object from the data object returned from the
    //database.
    CTime dTemp(pDoc->dbAeroLog.m_Date.year,pDoc->dbAeroLog.m_Date.month,
                pDoc->dbAeroLog.m_Date.day,pDoc->dbAeroLog.m_Date.hour,
            pDoc->dbAeroLog.m_Date.minute,pDoc->dbAeroLog.m_Date.second);

    //we format the CTime object to a mm/dd/yyyy string
    m_date = dTemp.Format("%m/%d/%Y");

    //initialize the variable for combo box selection to -1
    res = -1;

    //if GetCount is 0 the combo box has not been filled
    res = GetUsrID(pDoc->dbAeroLog.m_PersonID);

    //set the user dropdown list to the current user.
    m_user.SetCurSel(res);
```

```
res = GetExID(pDoc->dbAeroLog.m_ExID);
m_exercise.SetCurSel(res);

//here we convert the floating point value m_TimeInMin to a string
strBuff = _fcvt(pDoc->dbAeroLog.m_TimeInMin,2,&dec, &sign);

if(sign)
   m_time = "0";
else
{
   //fill the buffer with digits before the decimal point
   for(i=0; i < dec; i++)
      *strTmpF++ = *strBuff++;
   if(dec < 1)
      *strTmpF++ = '0';
   //attach the decimal point
   *strTmpF++ = '.';
   *strTmpF++ ='\0';

   //set the pointer strTmpF back to the start of the string
   strTmpF = strStTmp;

   //attach the rest of the buffer
   lstrcat(strTmpF,strBuff);

   m_time = strTmpF;
}

m_set = itoa(pDoc->dbAeroLog.m_Set,strTmp,10);

//we do the same thing for the distance
*strTmpF = '\0';
strBuff = _fcvt(pDoc->dbAeroLog.m_Distance, 2,&dec,&sign);

if(sign)
   m_distance = "0";
else
{
   for(i=0; i < dec; i++)
      *strTmpF++ = *strBuff++;

   if(dec < 1)
      *strTmpF++ = '0';
   *strTmpF++ = '.';
   *strTmpF++ = '\0';

   // set the pointer strTmpF back to the start of the string
   strTmpF = strStTmp;

   lstrcat(strTmpF,strBuff);

   m_distance = strTmpF;
}
UpdateData(FALSE);
}
```

As you can see, this is a relatively complex function, a lot of which is devoted to setting the output for m_date variables. We need to take the date data returned from the data source and convert it to a CTime object, arranged in dd/mm/yyyy format.

In the remainder of the function, floating point data from the m_Distance and m_TimeInMin variables are converted to string format. This is achieved by filling a string buffer with the digits up to the decimal point, concatenating the decimal point itself and finally appending the remaining digits.

Note also this is where the two methods GetUsrID() and GetExID() are called.

The Remaining View Classes

We have created classes to display the User and AerobicLog tables. We will now discuss the remaining view classes that will display the contents of the other tables.

The CCommentView Class

Like all the view classes in this project, the CCommentView class is derived from CFormView. The dialog box should look like the following screenshot:

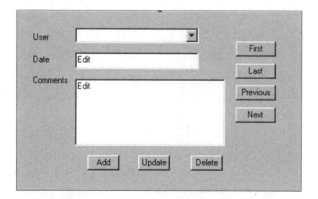

Note that we create one combo box and two edit boxes and we define seven message handlers for the seven buttons. Note that the drop-down list box for the users serves the same purpose as described above — we do not want to enter inconsistent data in the database by allowing a comment to be entered about a user who is not yet defined in the users table.

For the implementation of this list box, we have two helper functions, RefreshName() and GetUsrID(), which are the same as those used in CAeroLog.

An OLE DB Consumer Example

Initialization

The `OnUpdate()` function is exactly like that for the last class — in it, we simply call `SetFormData()` to update the form. Similarly, the implementation for OnInitialUpdate() is very similar — this is used to open the rowsets for the user list (for the drop-down list box) and the comments.

Button Handlers

The basic functionality of the button handlers is the same as we have seen already — the only change in most of these being the name of the member variable from the document class that holds the rowset object. In this case, it is `dbComment`. Remember, in `OnDelete()`, we need to set the status variable, `iNoComm`, to DBEMPTY if the last row in the rowset has been removed. Changes to the `OnUpdateRec()` function should be made to reflect the fact that we're updating the fields in the `Comment` table rather than the `AerobicLog` table. Finally, note that in `OnAdd()`, we call `RefreshName()`, but not `RefreshEx()`, as there is no list box for the exercises on this form.

Updating the Form

The `SetFormData()` function is simpler than that presented previously, and the implementation is shown below:

```
void CommentView::SetFormData()
{
    int i, res;
    CTrainingDoc* pDoc = GetDocument();

    if(pDoc->iNoComm == DBEMPTY)
    {
        this->m_comment = "";
        this->m_date = "";
        UpdateData(FALSE);
        return;
    }


    CTime dTemp(pDoc->dbComment.m_Date.year,pDoc->dbComment.m_Date.month,
                pDoc->dbComment.m_Date.day,pDoc->dbComment.m_Date.hour,
            pDoc->dbComment.m_Date.minute,pDoc->dbComment.m_Date.second);

    m_comment = pDoc->dbComment.m_Comments;
    m_date = dTemp.Format("%m/%d/%Y");
    res = -1;

    //if GetCount is 0 the combo box has not been filled
    if(m_user.GetCount() == 0)
        RefreshName();
```

```
for(i = 0; i < m_user.GetCount(); i++)
{
    if(m_user.GetItemData(i) == (DWORD)pDoc->dbComment.m_PersonID)
        res = i;
}
m_user.SetCurSel(res);
UpdateData(FALSE);
}
```

In this case, we only have three form items, the user drop-down list, the comment text and the date. The drop-down list and date are handled as we saw in the previous view. We still have to parse the data value as we did before. The comment is simply a string that can be directly passed to the variable corresponding to the edit box on the form.

The CMeasurementView Class

The dialog box for the CMeasureView class should look like the following screenshot:

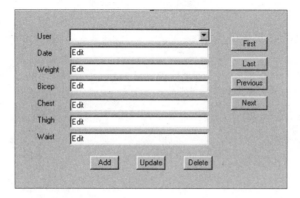

This time, we create one combo box, six edit boxes and we define seven message handlers for the seven buttons. Again, we're using the combo box to select the user, so we'll be using the helper functions RefreshName() and GetUsrID() in this class.

The code for OnInitialUpdate() and the button handlers is essentially the same — with the appropriate changes made for the Measurement table and fields in that table.

The implementation for the SetFormData() method of this class is shown below:

```
void CMeasure::SetFormData()
{
    int i, res;
    char strTmp[10];
    CTrainingDoc* pDoc = GetDocument();

    //if the rowset is empty get out.
    if(pDoc->iNoMeas == DBEMPTY)
    {
```

```
    this->m_bicep = "";
    this->m_chest = "";
    this->m_date = "";
    this->m_thigh = "";
    this->m_waist = "";
    this->m_weight = "";
    UpdateData(FALSE);
    return;
}

CTime dTemp(pDoc->dbMeas.m_Date.year,pDoc->dbMeas.m_Date.month,
                pDoc->dbMeas.m_Date.day,pDoc->dbMeas.m_Date.hour,
            pDoc->dbMeas.m_Date.minute,pDoc->dbMeas.m_Date.second);

m_bicep = itoa(pDoc->dbMeas.m_bicep,strTmp,10);
m_chest = itoa(pDoc->dbMeas.m_chest,strTmp,10);
m_date = dTemp.Format("%m/%d/%Y");
m_thigh = itoa(pDoc->dbMeas.m_thigh,strTmp,10);
m_waist = itoa(pDoc->dbMeas.m_waist,strTmp,10);
m_weight = itoa(pDoc->dbMeas.m_weight,strTmp,10);
res = -1;

//if GetCount is 0 the combo box has not been filled
if(m_user.GetCount() == 0)
    RefreshName();

for(i = 0; i < m_user.GetCount(); i++)
{
    if(m_user.GetItemData(i) == (DWORD)pDoc->dbMeas.m_PersonID)
        res = i;
}
m_user.SetCurSel(res);
UpdateData(FALSE);
}
```

The CResLogView Class

The dialog box displaying the data for the `ResistanceLog` table should look like the following screenshot:

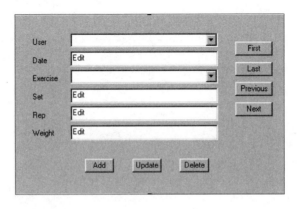

Note that this is very similar to the `Aerobics Log` view created earlier. There are two combo boxes, four edit boxes and the same seven buttons. Again, we won't go through all the code here, because much of it is very similar to what we have seen already.

As with `CAeroLog`, we have combo boxes for the selection of both the user and the exercise, so we'll be using the helper functions `RefreshName()`, `RefreshEx()`, `GetUsrID()` and `GetExID()`.

The implementation of this class can be found in `ResLogView.cpp`. Again, the details of the handlers for the command buttons won't be covered here — the basic functionality is the same.

Note that again, the helper function `SetFormData()` is used to refresh the data on the form.

The CTrainingView Class

The form for the `CTrainingView` class is used to display the data from the Exercise table. It is shown below:

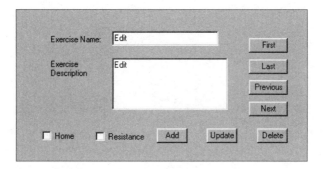

This is a little different from the previous form views, as we include two check boxes – **Home** and **Resistance**. We'll have a quick look at the implementation of this class to see how these are handled. On the other hand, the implementation is reasonably simple, as there are no drop-down list boxes on this form, so we don't need any helper functions to refresh the lists.

This implementation can be found in `TrainingView.cpp`. In the `OnAdd()` handler, the check boxes are simply left unchecked, and the edit boxes on the form filled with NULL strings:

```
void CTrainingView::OnAdd()
{
    m_home.SetCheck(0);
    m_resistance.SetCheck(0);
    m_exdesc="";
    m_exname="";
    UpdateData(FALSE);
    m_bNew = true;
}
```

The other button handlers are again similar to the implementations we have already seen, the main difference is in the way the check boxes are handled. Here is the implementation for `OnPrev()`:

```
void CTrainingView::OnPrev()
{
    HRESULT hr;
    CTrainingDoc *pDoc = GetDocument();
    hr = pDoc->dbEx.MovePrev();
    if(hr != S_OK)
    {
        if(hr == DB_S_ENDOFROWSET || hr == DB_E_BADSTARTPOSITION)
        {
            MessageBox("First Row", "File warning", MB_OK | MB_ICONWARNING);
            hr = pDoc->dbEx.MoveFirst();
            if(hr != S_OK)
                return;
        }
        else
        {
            MessageBox("Error in file", "File Warning", MB_OK | MB_ICONSTOP);
            return;
        }
    }

    if(pDoc->dbEx.m_Home)
        m_home.SetCheck(1);
    else
        m_home.SetCheck(0);
    if(pDoc->dbEx.m_Resistance)
        m_resistance.SetCheck(1);
    else
        m_resistance.SetCheck(0);
    m_exdesc = pDoc->dbEx.m_ExDescription;
    m_exname = pDoc->dbEx.m_ExName;
    UpdateData(FALSE);
}
```

Note how we simply check the values in the Home and Resistance fields of the record, and set the check boxes appropriately. The other command button handlers form a similar pattern to this.

Shown below is the handler for the **Update** button, `OnUpdateRec()`:

```
void CTrainingView::OnUpdateRec()
{
    HRESULT hr;
    CTrainingDoc* pDoc = GetDocument();

    UpdateData(TRUE);
    if(m_bNew)
        pDoc->dbEx.ClearRecord();

    pDoc->dbEx.m_exid_status = DBSTATUS_S_IGNORE;
    strcpy(pDoc->dbEx.m_ExDescription,(char *)m_exdesc.GetBuffer(255));
    strcpy(pDoc->dbEx.m_ExName,(char *)m_exname.GetBuffer(21));
```

```
if(m_home.GetCheck() == 1)
    pDoc->dbEx.m_Home = true;
else
    pDoc->dbEx.m_Home = false;

if(m_resistance.GetCheck() == 1)
    pDoc->dbEx.m_Resistance = true;
else
    pDoc->dbEx.m_Resistance = false;

if(m_bNew)
{
    hr = pDoc->dbEx.Insert();
    if(FAILED(hr))
    {
        MessageBox("Failed Insert");
        return;
    }
    else
        MessageBox("Successful Insert");
    m_bNew = false;
    pDoc->iNoEx = DBOPEN;
    pDoc->dbEx.MoveLast();
}
else
{
    hr = pDoc->dbEx.SetData();
    if(FAILED(hr))
        MessageBox("Failed Update");
    else
        MessageBox("Successful Update");
}
UpdateData(FALSE);
}
```

As you can see, there is much similarity between these view classes. If you want to see the code for each individual class in more detail, you can download the code from the Wrox web site to find the full implementation.

Once the view classes have all been implemented — all we have to worry about are the changes to the CMainFrame class that allow the user to switch between these different views. Let's take a look at that now.

Modifying the CMainFrame Class

The two classes ubiquitous to all the tables are the CMainFrame and CTrainingDoc classes. CTrainingDoc manages all the data and CMainFrame controls the process of switching between the views set up for each table.

The way this is achieved is by creating a menu called LogItem, that will have several menu items that allow the user to select the view they wish to see. The menu is shown below:

An OLE DB Consumer Example

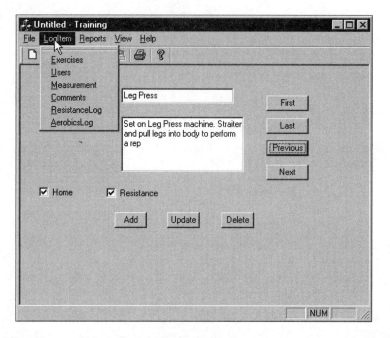

Using ClassWizard, we add handlers for each of the above menu items, and use the implementation of these functions to control the switching between views. The handler for the **AerobicLog** menu item, `OnLogItemAerobicLog()`:

```
void CMainFrame::OnLogitemAerobicLog()
{
    CRuntimeClass* pNewView;
    CView* pCurrView = this->GetActiveView();

    pNewView = RUNTIME_CLASS(CAeroLog);
    CCreateContext cContext;

    cContext.m_pNewViewClass = pNewView;
    cContext.m_pCurrentDoc = GetActiveDocument();

    CView* pView = STATIC_DOWNCAST(CView, CreateView(&cContext));

    if(pView != NULL)
    {
        pView->ShowWindow(SW_SHOW);
        pView->OnInitialUpdate();
        SetActiveView(pView,TRUE);
        this->RecalcLayout();
        pCurrView->DestroyWindow();
    }
}
```

The role of this function is to select the form displaying the data for the AerobicLog table. This is done by creating a CAeroLog object and setting it as the new view. CRuntimeClass is a basic MFC class that allows one to get information about a CObject at runtime. CCreateContext is involved with providing information to the framework in creating a window.

The handlers for the other five items on the LogItem menu are basically the same as the code shown above. The only difference for each function is in the line where pNewView is set — the appropriate view class should be used here.

> *Note that you should delete the blocks of code added to the top of CTrainingApp::InitInstance() that were added by the wizard on the addition of each new view class. If these remain, the program doesn't know which view to open on initialization. Remember that we saw this back in Chapter 3.*

Now you should be ready to build and run the code! Make sure you can switch between the views, and step through the records. Try adding some new data and check that your database is being updated.

Before we leave this example altogether, let's add one final piece of functionality. We'll create a report that displays some of the exercise history of a selected user.

Creating the Report

We'll take a look at how we select the data on which the report is based in a moment, but first, let's see how we go about bringing up the report. We can do this by adding another menu, **Reports**, with a single menu item, **Reports by Person**. The handler for this, OnReportsByPerson(), is shown below:

```
void CMainFrame::OnReportsByPerson()
{
    CRepDlg dlg;
    int iPSel;
    dlg.pDoc = (CTrainingDoc *)this->GetActiveDocument();
    dlg.DoModal();
    iPSel = dlg.iUser;
    CTrainingDoc *pDocTmp = (CTrainingDoc *)this->GetActiveDocument();
    pDocTmp->iPID = iPSel;
    CSingleDocTemplate pTTemplate(
        IDR_MAINFRAME,
        RUNTIME_CLASS(CTrainingDoc),
        RUNTIME_CLASS(CMainFrame),         // main SDI frame window
        RUNTIME_CLASS(CReport));
    CFrameWnd* frame=pTTemplate.CreateNewFrame(dlg.pDoc, NULL);
    frame->InitialUpdateFrame(dlg.pDoc,true);
}
```

Unlike the form view classes, this function actually creates a new frame window. It first displays a dialog box to get the name of the person who's record we want to see. The dialog has a drop-down list of user names from which the chosen user can be selected. We'll look at this dialog next. The PersonID of the selected user is stored in a member variable of the document class, so that the report view, CReport, can use it. We will see the report view in a minute.

Note that we also store a pointer to the document class in the dialog class — this is important, as it's through the document class that the dialog access its data to obtain the list of users.

Selecting the User

When selecting the user whose report you wish to display, the following dialog box is displayed:

Create a new dialog box, and a class for it (using ClassWizard) derived from CDialog and called CReportDialog. The dialog box is very simple, with only a single drop-down list box displaying a list of the possible users.

There are two member variables that need to be added to CReportDialog:

❑ iUser — to store the PersonID of the selected user

❑ pDoc — to store a pointer to the document object

Remember that the pDoc member is set in the OnReportsByPerson() function of CMainFrame.

We also have a method, RefreshName(), that is used to populate the drop-down list box with data from the Users table. As well as implementing this method, we need to add the handlers OnOK() and OnInitDialog().

OnOK() is called when the **OK** button is clicked on the dialog box. The implementation for this returns the PersonID for the user that was selected.

```
void CRepDlg::OnOK()
{
    UpdateData();
    iUser = m_user.GetItemData(m_user.GetCurSel());
    CDialog::OnOK();
}
```

Note that the default MFC OnOK() method simply closes the dialog window.

The OnInitDialog() method is executed when the dialog is initalized:

```
BOOL CRepDlg::OnInitDialog()
{
    CDialog::OnInitDialog();
    RefreshName();
    return TRUE;
}
```

This function calls a slightly different version of RefreshName():

```
void CRepDlg::RefreshName()
{
    int iRes;
    CString strItem;
    HRESULT hr = pDoc->dbUserLst.MoveFirst();
    m_user.ResetContent();
    while(hr == S_OK)
    {
        strItem = pDoc->dbUserLst.m_FirstName;
        strItem += " ";
        strItem += pDoc->dbUserLst.m_MI;
        strItem += " ";
        strItem += pDoc->dbUserLst.m_LastName;
        iRes = m_user.AddString(strItem);
        m_user.SetItemData(iRes,pDoc->dbUserLst.m_PersonID);
        hr = pDoc->dbUserLst.MoveNext();
    }
    m_user.SetCurSel(0);
}
```

Here, we simply clear the combo box and then step through the data in the dbUserLst rowset and add each name to the list.

Creating the Rowset

Another important aspect of this program is how we report our data — how we display complete records in a report format. The key aspect of reporting, for the purposes of OLE DB, is that while the query is more complex, the rowset itself does not need more than the simplest properties.

Let's illustrate this by creating a new rowset class — CdboAerobicPerson. This can be created just like the earlier rowset classes, except that this time, because we are simply displaying the data on the form, we don't need to add the insert, update and delete properties. We'll be basing the rowset on a query, but you can initially just create a rowset based on the AerobicLog table, and then alter the SQL statement that is executed in the command object.

Shown below is an extract of the file dboAerobicPerson.h, with the additional variables highlighted:

```
class CdboAerobicPersonAccessor
{
public:
    LONG m_LogEntryID;
    DBTIMESTAMP m_Date;
    LONG m_ExID;
    LONG m_PersonID;
    LONG m_Set;
    double m_Distance;
    double m_TimeInMin;
    LONG m_Res1;
    TCHAR m_ExName[21];
    TCHAR m_FirstName[21];
    TCHAR m_MI[2];
    TCHAR m_LastName[21];
```

Notice that we need to define quite a few variables. That's because our query will return several data fields. The reason for this is we not only have to return the values in the aerobic log table, but also have to return the names corresponding to the `PersonID` and `ExID`. These variables are mapped to the columns returned from the query:

```
BEGIN_COLUMN_MAP(CdboAerobicPersonAccessor)
    COLUMN_ENTRY(1, m_LogEntryID)
    COLUMN_ENTRY(2, m_Date)
    COLUMN_ENTRY(3, m_ExID)
    COLUMN_ENTRY(4, m_PersonID)
    COLUMN_ENTRY(5, m_Set)
    COLUMN_ENTRY(6, m_Distance)
    COLUMN_ENTRY(7, m_TimeInMin)
    COLUMN_ENTRY(8, m_ExName)
    COLUMN_ENTRY(9, m_FirstName)
    COLUMN_ENTRY(10, m_MI)
    COLUMN_ENTRY(11, m_LastName)
END_COLUMN_MAP()
```

We have a parameter defined in our query. We thus have to map it to the `m_Res` variable defined above. As we've seen before, the parameter map is where we do this.

```
BEGIN_PARAM_MAP(CdboAerobicPersonAccessor)
    COLUMN_ENTRY(1, m_Res)
END_PARAM_MAP()
```

This query is going to be much more complex than the one we saw earlier in the chapter. We need to join the `AerobicLog` table to those tables from which the foreign keys come, that is, `User` and `Exercises`. This is the only way we can then print the names on our report, rather than simply the IDs.

When we click on the report menu item, we first get a dialog box asking the client to choose the user whose information we would like to see. It is that user's ID that is passed into the query in the form of the parameter mapped above.

```
//This is the query we use for the report
DEFINE_COMMAND(CdboAerobicPAccessor, _T(" \
   SELECT \
      LogEntryID, \
      Date, \
      dbo.AerobicLog.ExID, \
      dbo.AerobicLog.PersonID, \
      Set#, \
      Distance, \
      TimeInMin, \
      ExName, \
      FirstName, \
      MI, \
      LastName \
      FROM dbo.AerobicLog INNER JOIN dbo.User \
         ON dbo.AerobicLog.PersonID = dbo.User.PersonID \
         INNER JOIN dbo.Exercises ON dbo.AerobicLog.ExID = dbo.Exercises.ExID \
         WHERE dbo.AerobicLog.PersonID=?"))
```

The `CdboAerobicPerson` class is similar to other classes we've defined derived from `CCommand`.
The one main difference is that we don't set any properties in `OpenRowset()` as we did in the case
of the other rowsets, where we were modifying and browsing data. The `Open()` and
`OpenDataSource()` methods are identical to what we have already presented for the `CdboUser`
class.

Here is the `OpenRowset()` method:

```
HRESULT OpenRowset()
{
   return CCommand<CAccessor<CdboAerobicPAccessor> >::Open(m_session);
}

CSession m_session;
};
```

The Report View Class

Let us now look at the report view itself. It is defined in a new class `CReport`, derived from
`CScrollView`. In this class, we open the rowset and fill an array of string buffers with the values
returned from the database. We then use the buffer, which is a variable in the view class, to draw
the report.

To start with, we add a member functions and variables:

```
void FillText();
int iLines;
CString *pstrText[MAXLINES];

CString FloatToCString(double dVal);
```

`FillText()` creates the string buffers using the data from the rowset, represented by the `CdboAerobicPerson` object. We'll also need the member variable, `iLines`, to store the number of lines in the report, and an array of pointers to `CStrings`, `pstrText[]`, which points to the strings holding the text. Finally, we'll have a helper function, `FloatToCString()` to convert floating point variables to `CStrings`.

`FillText()` is called from `OnInitialUpdate()`:

```
void CReport::OnInitialUpdate()
{
    CScrollView::OnInitialUpdate();

    CSize sizeTotal;
    sizeTotal.cx = sizeTotal.cy = 100;
    SetScrollSizes(MM_TEXT, sizeTotal);

    FillText();
}
```

The `FillText()` function is shown below.

```
void CReport::FillText()
{
    CString strTxt;
    CSize szTxt;
    char strTmp[10];
    iLines = 0;
    CTrainingDoc* pDoc = GetDocument();

    pDoc->dbAeroPRep.m_Res1 = pDoc->iPID;   //set the parameter
    if(pDoc->dbAeroPRep.Open() == S_OK)
    {
        while(pDoc->dbAeroPRep.MoveNext() == S_OK && iLines < MAXLINES)
        {
            pstrText[iLines] = new CString;
            CTime dTemp(pDoc->dbComment.m_Date.year,
                    pDoc->dbComment.m_Date.month, pDoc->dbComment.m_Date.day,
                    pDoc->dbComment.m_Date.hour, pDoc->dbComment.m_Date.minute,
                                        pDoc->dbComment.m_Date.second);
            *pstrText[iLines] = pDoc->dbAeroPRep.m_LastName;
            *pstrText[iLines] += ", ";
            *pstrText[iLines] += pDoc->dbAeroPRep.m_FirstName;
            *pstrText[iLines] += " ";
            *pstrText[iLines] += dTemp.Format("%m/%d/%Y");
            *pstrText[iLines] += " ";
            *pstrText[iLines] += pDoc->dbAeroPRep.m_ExName;
            *pstrText[iLines] += " ";
            *pstrText[iLines] += itoa(pDoc->dbAeroPRep.m_Set, &strTmp,10);
            *pstrText[iLines] += " ";
            *pstrText[iLines] +=
                            FloatToCString(pDoc->dbAeroPRep.m_Distance);
            *pstrText[iLines] += " ";
            *pstrText[iLines] +=
                            FloatToCString(pDoc->dbAeroPRep.m_TimeInMin);
```

```
            iLines++;
        }
        pDoc->dbAeroPRep.Close();
    }
}
```

Note that it is very similar to a function we came across in Chapter 5. In this function, we take advantage of CString's overridden += operator to fill each row.

Note the complex transformation of the data stored in m_Date in order to include it in the string. Note also that we have to change a floating point number to a CString in order to append the data stored in m_TimeInMin and m_Distance to the string.

We define a function FloatToCString() to achieve this:

```
CString CReport::FloatToCString(double dVal)
{
    int dec,sign;
    char *strTmpF, *strBuff, *strStTmp;

    CString res;
    int i;

    strTmpF = new char(20);
    strStTmp = strTmpF;
    *strTmpF = '\0';

    strBuff = _fcvt(dVal,2,&dec, &sign);

    if(sign)
        res = "0";
    else
    {
        for(i=0; i < dec; i++)
            *strTmpF++ = *strBuff++;
        if(dec < 1)
            *strTmpF++ = '0';
        *strTmpF++ = '.';
        *strTmpF++ ='\0';

        //want the result pointing to the start
        strTmpF = strStTmp;

        lstrcat(strTmpF,strBuff);
        res = strTmpF;
    }
    return res;
}
```

And finally, we come to the virtual function OnDraw() which is where we actually supply text to the report view window. Notice that we do no database access here —we simply write out a predefined buffer.

```
void CReport::OnDraw(CDC* pDC)
{
    CSize szTxt;
    szTxt= pDC->GetTextExtent("ABCDEFGHIJ");
    for(int i = 0; i < iLines; i++)
    {
        pDC->TextOut(0,i*(szTxt.cy + 5), *pstrText[i]);
    }
}
```

These are all the change we need to make to the CReport class. You should now have a fully functioning training log application. Try building and running the code. You should be able to produce a report that looks something like this:

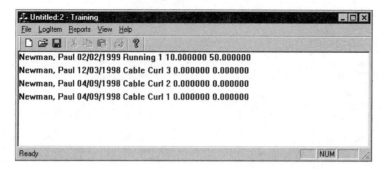

Further Issues

The application we have built up so far has been fairly simple. For a professional application, there are many other issues we would need to think about, including:

- ❏ Installation
- ❏ Source control
- ❏ Transactions
- ❏ Security

In this section, there will be a brief discussion of some of these issues that you would need to deal with in a real-life application.

Installation Issues

In a professional application, the first thing your users would see would be the installation program. Visual Studio 6.0 comes with a limited version of Installshield, a well-known and commonly used installation program. This is a big advance over the setup program, which came with older versions of C++. For many installation needs this should be just fine. However, if your installation needs go beyond the scope of this program, you can easily move up to the full professional version of Installshield.

In creating your installation there are a number of issues that need to be addressed. First, one has to be aware of not just the files that you created (executables, DLLs etc.), but also Microsoft's redistributable files that need to be included. In the case of our sample application, we need would need to think about ODBC drivers, the OLE DB components and the OLE DB provider for ODBC drivers. Not only does the correct version of these components need to be installed in the correct places, but COM objects such as OLE DB components and providers need to be registered. Finally, ODBC connections need to be set up. Fortunately Microsoft Data Access Components 2.0 contains redistributable components that can be used. These are files provided by Microsoft that you can provide with your application. This handles the installation and registration of the components, although ODBC links still have to be programmatically established.

In addition to concerns about code components, another issue is the database itself. How one goes about installing the database is dependent upon the database being used. If you are using a desktop database such as Access, you can include a version of the database being used by the system. For a more sophisticated database such as SQL Server, you essentially include a SQL script that will create the database and insert any initial data into it. The installation program must then call a command line program associated with the database, to execute the script.

Another possibility is to write a function contained within a DLL to read the script and make database calls. This avoids the complications involved with executing programs from an install script, for example not being able to get error messages back to the script.

Source Control

While our training log application is essentially a one person job, many applications are done by teams. In this case, there are issues of what is known as change control. This involves such things as avoiding two programmers trying to modify the same file at same time and stepping on each other's changes. Thus, one important aspect of dealing with a major project is source control.

Source control allows one to "check out" source code and lock it, thus preventing anyone other than yourself from changing it until you're done. When you have finished making your changes, you can then "check in" (put your new version back into source control) the code and unlock it, once again allowing others to change it. The changes you have made are recorded by the source code control system so you can go back to any version of the files at any time.

In fact, in many cases you will check out most of the code without locking it from other users and only lock those files which you will need to change. This allows others to simultaneously lock and modify other files in the project. It is good practice to verify that your changes were actually incorporated into source control. You can do this by checking a read-only copy of the files you have just checked in. Then, rebuild the project from scratch. If the changes appear in the executable, then you know they were properly incorporated. Furthermore, this verifies that your changes are compatible with any that others might have made in terms of actually building the application. Obviously only testing will verify that you did not break something at runtime.

The enterprise version of Visual Studio comes with Visual SourceSafe, Microsoft's solution for source control. As you can imagine, using source control is *essential* in a multi-developer project to prevent two developers changing the same file at the same time. However, even if you're a single developer it can be extremely valuable. Not only does it provide a backup of your files, but it also allows you to retrieve previous versions, should you make changes and later decide you need to back out.

Visual SourceSafe is linked to Visual C++ as it can be accessed via the Visual C++ menu. However, it has a whole interface of it's own:

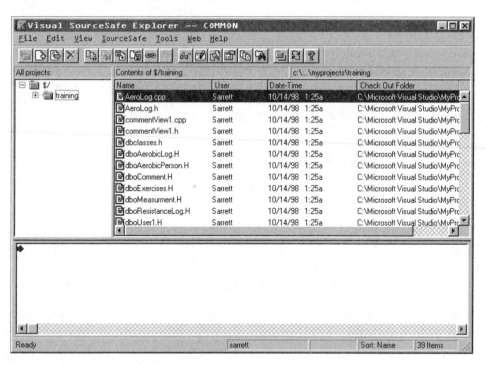

As you can see, it has a fairly standard Windows UI. The projects are on the left, listed in tree format. On the right are the project's individual files. You can use this interface as an alternative to going directly from the Visual C++ Project submenu.

Transactions

An important issue in database applications is transactions, which were introduced in Chapter 1. Now let's look briefly at how they are supported in OLE DB. When a transaction is begun, it tells the database that the changes called for by the following action queries should not actually be made to the database until the transaction is completed, or in the language of databases, committed.

Transactions are supported by OLE DB with the following three functions:

- ❑   StartTransaction()
- ❑   Commit()
- ❑   Abort()

These are part of the ITransactionLocal interface. In the consumer classes, this is supported by the CSession class.

These functions can be called from the rowset objects. Suppose in our example, we wished to implement a transaction in the AeroLog view. We could this with the following code:

```
pDoc->dbAeroLog.m_session.StartTransaction();

//add code to modify the database

pDoc->dbAeroLog.m_session.Commit();
```

Any change to the database that is specified between StartTransaction() and Commit() calls would not be permanently stored in the database until the Commit() is called. If something goes wrong for some reason and we don't wish to complete the transaction, then we simply call the Abort() function. This effectively which cancels any changes that we've made to the data within the transaction.

Multi-User Issues and Security

With a single user application, database access is easy. We don't have to worry about more than one individual manipulating the database at one time. The example developed in this chapter used SQL Server 6.5, which is inherently a multi-user application. When there are many users, we have to be concerned with record locking and related matters. For example, we should test how the application will behave if two users attempt to update data at the same time. Such a situation is handled by record locking, which in OLE DB, we can achieve by setting various properties when opening the rowsets.

Security

Another issue to consider is database security. OLE DB provides for this, as we can set user IDs and passwords by setting initialization parameters in the `OpenDataSource()` function.

For example, you might add the following lines of code to the `CdboAerobicLog` rowset class:

```
dbinit.AddProperty(DBPROP_AUTH_PASSWORD, OLESTR(""));
dbinit.AddProperty(DBPROP_AUTH_USERID, OLESTR("sa"));
```

Here, we can set the user ID and the password. We could pass these parameters in, but in the above example, the user ID and password are hard coded. It essentially is giving the application full access (at the System Administration level) to the SQL server database. In an application that wishes to provide for user login, one could obtain the user ID and password via a login screen and pass them into the application as variables.

There is another level of security that applies when accessing the database itself. This is specified in the properties passed when opening the data source. The particular property involved is `DBPROP_INIT_MODE`, which can take on several values. The ones that apply in the multi-user context are the `DBMODE_SHARE` values. We can specify:

- ❑ `DBMODE_SHARE_DENY_READ` — other users cannot read the database
- ❑ `DBMODE_SHARE_DENY_WRITE` — other users cannot write to the database
- ❑ `DBMODE_SHARE_DENY_NONE` — all users can access the database
- ❑ `DBMODE_SHARE_EXCLUSIVE` — you are opening the database exclusively, in that no one else can access the database until you close it

Visibility

A related issue is visibility. You can control which changes made by others can be viewed. This depends upon the value of several rowset properties. You can enable or disable visibility of inserts, updates and deletes made outside the rowset by specifying the `DBPROP_OTHERINSERT` and `DBPROP_OTHERUPDATEDELETE` properties. You can do the same for visibility of changes made within the rowset by specifying the `DBPROP_OWNINSERT`, `DBPROP_OWNUPDATEDELETE` properties.

These properties are summarized below

- ❑ DBPROP_OWNUPDATEDELETE –The consumer of a rowset can see the updates/deletes they perform.
- ❑ DBPROP_OTHERUPDATEDELETE – The consumer of a rowset can see changes others have made to the data in a rowset.
- ❑ DBPROP_OWNINSERT – The consumer of a rowset can see the insert's they perform
- ❑ DBPROP_OTHERINSERT – The consumer of a rowset can see inserts other users make

Summary

In this chapter, we have tracked the development of a simple training log application that allows clients at a gym to record and monitor their workouts. In the process of this, we have seen how to incorporate OLE DB consumer classes from several different tables into one application. We saw how to create different views for each of the tables, and how the user can switch easily between them.

When dealing with the views of the aerobic logs and resistance logs, we saw how to constrain the addition of new records to the database programmatically, to ensure the maintenance of referential integrity. In addition, we saw how to use parameterized queries to limit the data displayed to just the relevant records.

The creation of a report displaying information on a particular user's exercise history demonstrated the use of a more complex query, which involve joining three tables.

Finally, we looked at some of the more complex problems that would have to be dealt with in the creation of a real-life professional application, including installation and source control issues.

The most important thing you should get from this chapter, however, is some specific techniques you can use to access and manage data via OLE DB.

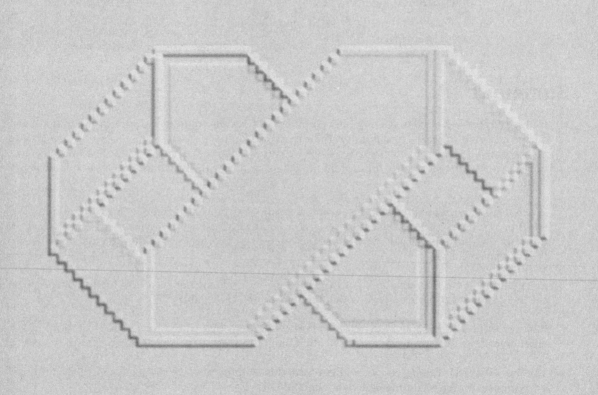

Introduction to ADO

As we have seen over the last couple of chapters, OLE DB is supported in a relatively straightforward manner using consumer templates in method in Visual C++. However, the need to work with the very large number of COM interfaces can still make things a bit confusing for the developer. Furthermore, OLE DB cannot be used directly from such popular development tools as Visual Basic. Thus a simpler means of taking advantage of OLE DB had to be developed — this was the motivation behind ADO.

OLE DB is an effective means of accessing a varied number of data sources. However, Microsoft's ADO (ActiveX Data Objects) provides a user-oriented method of data access, which parallels Visual Basic or ODBC recordsets. For this reason, we will discuss it here.

This chapter has the following objectives:

- ❑ Describe the ADO architecture
- ❑ Explain ADO objects
- ❑ Discuss how to access data using ADO
- ❑ Demonstrate ADO using a worked example

Why Active Data Objects?

In the previous chapters we have discussed the basics of OLE DB and used it to access and manipulate a data source. We have created a simple OLE DB consumer and went on to develop a more complex application in the training log example. We have seen that there are a large number of OLE DB interfaces, and programming more than the simplest of applications can become very complicated, requiring in-depth knowledge of C++ class templates. And there is the additional problem that OLE DB providers cannot be accessed using Visual Basic and scripting languages, such as JavaScript.

Microsoft's solution to these problems was to insert a layer in between OLE DB and the client which enables indirect access to OLE DB providers in any programming language. This layer is ADO — which stands for **ActiveX Data Objects**.

The use of ADO has spread quickly and is extensively used in Active Server Page (ASP) programming, one of Microsoft's key new Web technologies. For efficiency purposes, one usually writes an object in a compiled language to do the actual data access. ASP does not use ADO directly, rather these objects are then called by ASP.

ADO is also being targeted as the primary data access technology for Visual Basic programmers. Note that in this case, OLE DB is still the primary data access layer, but ADO is the layer that allows the VB programs to use OLE DB.

Like OLE DB, ADO is a COM-based technology allowing fast access to any type of data source. As with OLE DB, it is a consistent programming interface across data sources (although some data sources may implement optional functions and others may not).

> *One thing to be aware of when using ADO is that it is geared mainly for Visual Basic. This can be annoying, as the documentation itself is geared towards Visual Basic. Microsoft does supply a set of header files and `.idl` files for using ADO with Visual C++. This chapter should present good jumping off point for ADO, but if you need more information on ADO, you should check out ADO 2.0 Programmer's Reference (see Appendix A). You can also find out more information from the Microsoft Web site: www.microsoft.com/data/ado., where you can download several technical articles on ADO.*

You can download the latest version of ADO from the Microsoft website. It also comes with Visual Studio 6.0. The ADO DLL's are also installed along with applications such as Internet Explorer. The key DLL is `MSADO15.DLL`, which is found in `Program Files\Common Files\System\ADO`. (Note, Microsoft did not rename the DLL to MSADO20.DLL as one might expect...it is still MSADO15.DLL.)

The ADO Architecture

ADO consists of seven basic objects:

- Connection
- Recordset
- Command
- Error
- Field
- Property
- Parameter

Note that the last four objects in the above list are collection objects. While these are very similar to DAO objects (discussed in Chapter 3), the way they are interrelated is not. One of the design incentives of ADO was to avoid the complex hierarchy of DAO, which means that ADO code is far more efficient.

The ADO object model is illustrated in the diagram below:

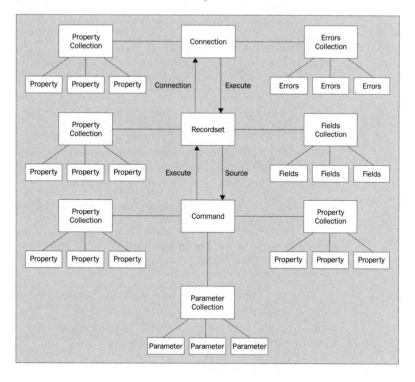

Now we will examine each object in the ADO model in depth, starting with the higher level objects.

Higher Level Objects: Connection, Recordset and Command

In this section we present the details of the three main objects within ADO, namely **connection**, **recordset** and **command**. Each has its own set of properties and methods, which are covered in turn.

The Connection Object

The connection object provides a wrapper around both OLE DB data source and session COM objects. Its primary functions are to supply the means of accessing the data source itself, and manage the resulting session.

It is similar to the environment variable HENV in ODBC — there is one HENV in each ODBC application and it contains information that is global to the application, such as connection handles. The ADO connection object is also similar to the MFC CDatabase class object, in that you can control transactions and open and close ODBC connections. A connection object can also be used to set a range of parameters for the data source connection as we shall see shortly.

The properties supported by the Connection object are summarized in the table below:

Property	Description
Attributes	Tells the connection object whether commits and aborts will be "retaining", that is start a new transaction when a commit or abort occurs.
CommandTimeout	Indicates the number of seconds the system will wait for a command to execute.
ConnectionString	A text string, written in a specific format in order to specify to the data source the parameters necessary to create a connection. This is similar to what we saw in ODBC.
ConnectionTimeout	Determines how long the system will wait when attempting a connection before it will time out.
CursorLocation	Determines which library will be used to support cursor functionality. (Recall that cursors are the means by which one moves back and forth in a recordset.)
DefaultDatabase	A string that holds the name of the default database for the connection object. If no default database is specified, it may be necessary to include this name in any subsequent query. Note that this property is not available when creating client side connection.

Property	Description
IsolationLevel	Indicates what visibility one transaction has on the changes in another transaction. In other words, if there are multiple transactions occurring, this shows how isolated are they from each other.
Mode	Indicates the read/write permissions for the connection.
Provider	Supplies the name of the OLE DB provider involved in the connection. Note that this property can also be set in the connection string, though you should not set it in both places as the results can be indeterminate.
State	Describes whether the connection is open or closed. Its two values are adStateOpen and adStateClosed.
Version	Returns a string that indicates the version of ADO being used.

Attributes

The connection object attributes are a read/write long value. They are the sum of zero or more of the following values, the default being zero:

- ❑ adXactCommitRetaining — starts a new transaction once a CommitTrans has been completed. This is known as a 'retaining commit'.

- ❑ AdXactAbortRetaining — starts a new transaction once a RollbackTrans has been completed. This is known as a 'retaining abort'.

A CommitTrans() is a connection object method that saves changes to a transaction before closing the transaction. A RollbackTrans() is a similar method which does not save changes before closing. We'll see the methods of the connection object at the end of this section.

ConnectionString

ConnectionString is a text string, written in a specific format in order to specify to the data source the parameters necessary to create a connection. This is the same string used by ODBC. The value may be overridden by the string passed as the parameter in the connection object's Open() method.

Once a connection is open, ConnectionString is set to *read-only* — it's purpose being only to provide the information to open a particular connection. The string has the following form:

```
<argument>=<value>;<argument>=<value>;... ;<argument>=<value>
```

The argument can be any of the following:

- ❑ Provider — the name of the OLE DB provider.
- ❑ Data Source — the name of the data source. It can be the name of a file, database, or ODBC connection, depending on the provider.
- ❑ User ID — the login ID for the data source.
- ❑ Password — the login password for the data source.
- ❑ File Name — for predefined connection information saved in a file. Note that the format of the file is provider specific.
- ❑ Remote Provider — the name of the provider for a client side connection.
- ❑ Remote Server — the name of the server for a client side connection.

The arguments need not be specified in this order. Note that you cannot specify both *Provider* and *File Name* as arguments, as the information stored in the file would determine which provider is loaded.

An example of a connection string is the following:

```
"driver={sql server};server=ziggy;Database=testsml;UID=sa;PWD=;"
```

In this case, "driver " is referring to the SQL Server driver for ODBC. The OLE DB provider for ODBC does not need to specified specifically in the connection string, as this is the default provider.

CursorLocation

This parameter determines which library will be used to support cursor functionality. (Recall that cursors are the means by which one moves back and forth in a recordset.) The CursorLocation property can have one of the following two values:

- ❑ adUseClient — The cursor library is provided on the client side. This is important because the client side cursor libraries sometimes support functionality not available on the server side.
- ❑ adUseServer — The cursor functionality is provided by the server. While it is more closely related to the data source, and as a result may permit some additional flexibility, it may not support all the features of a client side cursor library. However, there maybe greater ability to see changes that have been made by others. This is the default value.

There is another value for this property, adUseClientBatch, which is the older name for adUseClient, but it is only supported for backward capability. adUseNone indicates that no cursor services are used, but again, this is supported for backward compatibility.

IsolationLevel

This property indicates what visibility one transaction has on the changes in another transaction. In other words, if there are multiple transactions occurring, the Isolation property is used to indicate how isolated they are from each other.

This becomes important when we are dealing with multiple users of the same database. Note that this value must be `adXactUnspecified` if used in a client side connection. Not all data sources necessarily support every level. Therefore, if the selected level isn't supported it treats it as though it's the next level of isolation. There are nine possible values:

❑ `adXactUnspecified` — the provider is unable to determine what the isolation level is

❑ `adXactChaos` — if a transaction has a higher level of isolation, you cannot overwrite its pending transactions

❑ `adXactBrowse/adXactReadUncommitted` — uncommitted changes in other transactions can be viewed

❑ `adXactCursorStability/adXactReadCommitted` — only committed changes in another transaction can be viewed

❑ `adXactRepeatableRead` — changes in other transactions are not visible, unless you requery the recordset

❑ `adXactIsolated/adXactSerializable` — transactions are isolated — this is the highest level of isolation

Mode

When reading or writing to a file, this property indicates the read/write permissions for the connection. This is mainly applicable to desktop databases. By default these permissions are not set. The possible values are:

❑ `adModeUnknown` — permissions are not set, or are indeterminate

❑ `adModeRead` — read-only permission

❑ `adModeWrite` — write-only permission

❑ `adModeReadWrite` — read and write permission

❑ `adModeShareDenyRead` — connections with read permission cannot be opened

❑ `adModeShareDenyWrite` —connections with write permission cannot be opened

❑ `adModeShareExclusive` — prevents a connection from being opened

❑ `adModeShareDenyNone` — prevents a connections from being opened with any set permissions

Methods

The important methods of the connection are described in the table below:

Method	Description
BeginTrans()	Starts a transaction. It must be completed with either a CommitTrans() or RollbackTrans().
CommitTrans()	Completes a transaction by saving the changes.
Open()	Opens a connection object.
RollbackTrans()	Completes a transaction by canceling the changes.

The Recordset Object

The **recordset object** provides a wrapper around the OLE DB rowset object, and as with the previous data access methods, the recordset represents the data retrieved from the data source. At any one time, it maintains the position of the current record. If you are not using a command object it also provides a means of retrieving the data. In addition, recordsets provide for batch updating of data. That is, one can make a number of changes, but transmit all those changes to the database at once. The advantage of this, of course, is that it minimizes traffic over the connection.

Cursor Types

Moving between the records of a recordset can be achieved by using cursors. There are four different types of cursor defined for an ADO recordset object. The cursor type is set either before opening the recordset, or passed as a parameter to the recordset's Open() method.

There are four types of cursor:

- ❑ Dynamic
- ❑ Keyset
- ❑ Static
- ❑ Forward-only

The **dynamic cursor** allows you to see an immediately updated view when another user changes the data that is included in your recordset. In other words, whenever you scroll to a record, you know it is a current record. Furthermore, added and deleted records are reflected in the recordset. The dynamic cursor also allows for forward and backward movement though the recordset, and if the OLE DB provider behind ADO supports bookmarks, then they are also supported by the dynamic cursor.

The second type of cursor is the **keyset cursor**. This operates in a similar way to a dynamic cursor, the main difference being that you can only see the changes made by other users to existing records, not additions or deletion. Access will be prevented to records that another user has deleted.

The third type of cursor is a **static cursor**, which gives you a snapshot of the data. It parallels the snapshot in the ODBC model. While you can move freely back and forth though the data, as you can with a dynamic or keyset cursor, any changes made by other users are invisible to you. Static cursors do allow you to update the recordset, and you will see the changes you make reflected in the recordset.

The fourth and last type of cursor is a **forward-only cursor**, which, as its name implies, only allows one-way movement though the recordset. However, like the dynamic cursor, it does allow you to view updated records. The advantage of the forward only cursor is that performance is enhanced when one only wants to scroll in one direction.

Performance Issues

One interesting fact is that when writing a web-based application using ADO, you can specify local caching of the recordset (on the client) in order to enhance performance. The way this is done is to use the ADOR object when opening the recordset. The only limitation of this technique is that cursor must be a static cursor. Hence, no changes to the data by other users will be visible to the user.

Before we examine the recordset object properties, there are two important performance issues that you need to be aware of. The first has to do with **batch updates**. Our previous examples have assumed that changes to recordsets are immediately transmitted to the data source. However, by calling the UpdateBatch() method, you can cache these changes and transmit them to the database at one time. This is a much more efficient way of carrying out multiple updates. Note, however, that batch updates are not supported by all OLE DB providers.

The second issue concerns managing connections. If a connection string, rather than a connection object, is passed as a parameter to the recordset object's Open() method, it will not use any previously existing connection object, but rather create its own. Furthermore, the handle to the connection object will not be saved, thus preventing additional recordsets from sharing the connection. Thus, when the next recordset is created, a new connection will need to be created as well. This leads to additional resources being needed to support multiple connection objects, rather than sharing one. Consequently, when there are multiple recordset objects being created, it is better to create a connection object first and use that throughout. As with batch updates, the ability to pass a connection string to the recordset's Open() method is not supported by all OLE DB providers.

Introduction to ADO

Properties

Now we will look at the properties of the recordset object:

Properties	Description
AbsolutePage	Returns the page in which the current record resides. A page is defined as a group of records whose size is equal to PageSize (defined later in the table).
AbsolutePosition	Returns the numeric position of the current record.
ActiveConnection	Can hold either a string representing a connection object or a connection object itself.
BOF	BOF is set to true if the record pointer is at the beginning of the file and false otherwise.
Bookmark	A VARIANT that identifies the current record. It can be set and returned at any time. However, not all OLE DB providers support this feature.
CacheSize	Controls caching in the recordset, so it is important for performance reasons. It is a long value that specifies how many records are cached.
CursorLocation	This is exactly the same as that for the connection object, and can have the same two values — adUseClient and adUseServer.
CursorType	Specifies the cursor type. The four types have already been described.
EditMode	This set of EditModeEnum values specify the edit state of the Recordset object. The three values are the following: adEditNone — the object is not in edit mode. adEditInProgress — the object is in edit mode but the data has not been saved. adEditAdd — the object is in the process of adding a new record but the data is not yet saved.
EOF	Set to true is the record pointer is at the end of the file and false otherwise.

Properties	Description
Filter	A VARIANT value that holds filtering criteria. This can be either be specified as one would an SQL WHERE clause or it can be an array of bookmarks. Alternatively, it can be one of the FilterGroupEnum values as specified: adFilterNone — remove all filtering adFilterPendingRecords — in batch update, allows the viewing of records to be updated AdFilterAffectedRecords – view records affected by the most recent Delete(), Resync(), UpdateBatch() and CancelBatch() commands. adFilterFetchedRecords – view records stored in the cache
LockType	Maintains any lock that has been placed on the recordset whilst updating. This prevents the indeterminate result of two users attempting to update the database at once. These values are part of the LockTypeEnum value. By default data cannot be altered: adLockReadOnly — no data can be changed by others during editing. adLockPessimistic — records are usually locked by the provider immediately upon editing. This is to protect the edit process and is known as pessimistic locking. adLockOptimistic — records are only locked when update is called. This is known as optimistic locking. adLockBatchOptimistic — optimistic updating for batch mode.
MarshallOptions	When using a client-side recordset, this property determines which modified records are sent back to the server, which can affect performance. By default all rows are returned to the server (adMarshalAll). Alternatively, this value can be set to adMarshalModifiedOnly. In this case, only rows that have been modified are sent back.
MaxRecords	Maintains the maximum number of records that will be returned from the data source when a query is executed. By default, it is unlimited and has the value zero.

Properties	Description
PageCount	Returns the number of pages of data contained within the recordset. Incomplete pages still count as a page for the purposes of PageCount. Note that this property is not supported by all providers.
PageSize	Determines the number of records that makes up a page. By default it is 10. This can be useful if your users are going to be viewing a fixed number of records at one time.
RecordCount	Returns the number of records in the recordset. If it is indeterminate a value of –1 is returned. Note that unless the provider supports approximate positioning, all records need to be retrieved for an accurate count.
Source	Can be set with either a string value or command object reference. It holds the specification of the source of the recordset, such as a SQL statement or table name. Note that only string values are returned for this property. Furthermore, it is read-only for an open recordset.
State	Verifies whether the recordset is open or closed. Hence, there are two possible values — adStateClosed and adStateOpen. If the recordset is performing an asynchronous method, then there are three other states it can have in combination with open and closed — adStateConnecting, adStateExecuting and adStateFetching.
Status	Holds the status of the current record where bulk operations such as batch update are concerned. It represents the sum of one or more values of RecordStatusEnum as specified in the ADO documentation.

The critical methods are summarized in the following table:

Method	Description
AddNew()	Prepares the recordset to accept a new record.
Close()	Closes the Recordset.
Delete()	Deletes either a single record or groups of records. In immediate mode the records are immediately deleted. However in batch mode they are not deleted until UpdateBatch() is called.
MoveFirst()	Move to the first record in the recordset.
MoveLast()	Move to the last record in the recordset.
MoveNext()	Move to the next in the recordset.
MovePrevious()	Move to the previous record in the recordset.
Open()	Opens the recordset object and creates the cursor that represents the data in the data source.
Update()	Saves any changes to the current record.
Edit()	Prepares recordset for updating data

The Command Object

The command object forms a wrapper around the OLE DB command object. However, implementation of an ADO command object is optional by a provider, as not all data sources support a query language.

In the case of a SQL-based data source, the command object represents the SQL statements. In the case of a non-SQL data source, it represents whatever data manipulation and data definition commands are specified for that particular source.

The command object also has the ability to accept different command types, including table names and stored procedures. It also allows for persistent queries, whereby the client can run a query more than once without having to specify it each time. In some objects there is support for parameterized queries. That is, one can define queries that contain parameters which are passed into the query at runtime. (We've already seen this in our ODBC and OLE DB examples.) If this is the case, you can use parameter objects to manage parameters to the commands.

The properties supported by the command object are described in the table below:

Parameter	Description
ActiveConnection	Maintains the definition of the connection object as a text string. It must be set before executing a command. By default it is NULL.
CommandText	Holds a SQL statement, if the provider is a SQL based data source, or it can be any statement that can be recognized by the data provider. For example, if you're working with a spreadsheet, it might be row and column coordinates. If there is an open connection, and the Prepared property is set to true, then the CommandText statement will store the compiled version of the query on the provider itself. This process is known as preparing the query.
CommandTimeout	Indicates the number of seconds the system will wait for a command to execute. By default, this value is 30 seconds.
CommandType	Defines the type of command object. It tells the system how to handle the command string passed into the object. It can take one of four values specified by the CommandTypeEnum constants. The possible values are: adCmdText — takes the form of a text string adCmdTable — takes the form of a table name adCmdStoredProc — takes the form of a stored procedure adCmdUnknown — type is unknown, the default value
Prepared	Can be set to either true or false. If it is true, the command text will be compiled and stored on the provider. Since compilation takes place, the first access may be slightly slower. However, subsequent accesses will be faster. This is important because the greater speed of subsequent access is the value of prepared commands.
State	See above

The key method for the command object is the Execute() method, which executes the actual command text.

The Support Objects: Errors, Fields, Properties and Parameters

Errors

When errors occur during ADO operations, it is helpful to save information about the errors in order to determine the application's next action, and/or for debugging purposes. This is where the error object comes in.

Typically, the error object is stored in an errors collection associated with the connection object. The errors covered by error objects come from the OLE DB provider, not ADO itself. ADO errors, since they are closer to the application, are handled by the application's error handling as any other application error would be.

The properties are in the following table:

Property	Type	Description
Number	long	The value of the error in the form of a long integer constant.
Source	string	The object that raised the error. It could be in the form of the object's name or programID. In ADODB calls, it is in the form of ADODB.ObjectName.
Description	string	Textual description of the error. Very useful in creating error messages for the user.
HelpFile	string	If the error has an associated help file, the fully qualified path to the help file is stored here.
HelpContext	long	If the error has an associated help topic, it is stored here. In the parlance of windows help files, it is the context ID of the error information.
SQLState	string	The five character error code returned by the provider when there is an error. These codes must follow the ANSI SQL standard.
NativeError	long	This is the error code produced by the database itself.

Fields

A field object maintains information about columns retrieved from the data source. The type of information it maintains is the name of the field, its type and size, and, if applicable, data precision.

The field objects themselves are part of a collection that is associated with the recordset object. All providers may not implement all the functionality of the field object.

The properties associated with fields are the shown in the table below:

Property	Description
ActualSize	A return-only long value that provides the actual length of the field's value. If this value cannot be determined it returns adUnknown.
Attributes	A read-only value that is any or more than one of the members of FieldAttributeEnum. There are 10 such values the values of which are specified in the ADO documentation
DefinedSize	A long read-only value that specifies the size of the field as defined. While the ActualSize is based of the data within the field, the DefinedSize is based on the size of the field as specified regardless of the size of the data.
Name	Holds the name of the object.
NumericScale	A byte value that indicates how many decimal places a numeric value is to be resolved.
OriginalValue	A VARIANT that returns the value that was in a specified field before any changes were made to it.
Precision	A byte value specifying the total number of digits to be used in representing a numeric value.
Type	Returns one of a number of members of the DataTypeEnum type as specified in the ADO documentation.
UnderlyingValue	A VARIANT that returns the current value that is visible to your transaction. Unlike OriginalValue, it may reflect changes that have been made by other transactions.
Value	Can be used to set or return data. Unlike OriginalValue and UnderlyingValue it is read/write.

Note that there are also two methods associated with the field object, AppendChunk() and GetChunk().

Properties

Property objects maintain information about the data source's capabilities. Properties are maintained by all the main objects.

Unlike the properties built into objects in ADO, the number of types of properties in a property collection is dynamic and dependant upon the specific provider. In effect, we can change the properties of the properties in a property collection. That is, we can change the name, type and attributes (indicating one or more characteristic of the property object). That's in addition to the value, which one can change in either a property object or a built in property.

There are four static properties associated with the property object:

❑ Attributes

❑ Name

❑ Type

❑ Value

These are the same as we saw with the field object.

Parameter

A parameter collection is associated with a command object. The traditional SQL example would be a query of the form:

```
"SELECT * from EMPLOYEES where dept = '?'"
```

In this case the '?' would be associated with a parameter, which is substituted at runtime. Each parameter object in a collection has associated with it a name, value, type and attributes, as well as several other properties. It is the parameter object that allows the command object to support parameterized queries, such as the one above.

The properties are the same as the ones we've seen above. However, there are two new ones, Attributes and Direction:

Property	Description.
Attributes	A read/write value that is any one or multiple members of `ParameterAttributesEnum`:
	`adParamSigned` – The parameter allows signed values (default)
	`adParamNullable` – The parameter allows null values
	`adParamLong` – The parameter allows long binary data
Direction	Specifies what kind of parameter is being specified — input, output, etc. It is similar to the specification used in IDL when defining a function. It returns or sets one of the members of `ParameterDirectionEnum`:
	`adParamInput` – an input value (the default.)
	`adParamOutput` – an output value
	`adParamInputOutput` – an input/output value
	`adParamReturnValue` – a return value

Using ADO in C++

So far we have looked at the various methods and properties of the different objects that comprise ADO. Let's turn our attention now to some more practical aspects of using ADO in C++.

In this section, the various methods that can be used to incorporate ADO into a C++ application will be discussed. There is a bit more work to be done by the programmer here, because there aren't any wizards to help us this time.

Finally, we'll look at some code to see how ADO actually works in a practical example.

Getting Started

Microsoft encourages users of C++ to use OLE DB by making life easier for them with the OLE DB provider and consumer templates that we discussed earlier. However, we will see ADO can be an easier way to access data, while still gaining many of the advantages of OLE DB over prior access methods. There are various ways of making ADO accessible from your Visual C++ application, and that's what we'll be looking at in this section.

While ADO does put another layer between your program and OLE DB, the performance hit will likely not be a factor for a typical application, depending on what you are doing. However, for a high performance application, the hit will be significant and it would be better to use the OLE DB consumers discussed in previous chapters.

We will now look at the various methods of using ADO, namely, using:

- ❑ MFC OLE
- ❑ #import
- ❑ The OLE SDK

Finally, a worked example using the latter of these three methods will be presented.

As with the rest of the code in this book, the sample can be downloaded from the Wrox Press web site.

An Aside on BSTRs and VARIANTs

Before we develop our example application, we need to take a quick look at BSTRs and VARIANTs. Since ADO is geared towards users of high-level languages like Visual Basic, we have to be aware of these two data types. When we come to use the OLE SDK, we will need to deal with them directly.

As we will see later, the OLE SDK consists of two .h that one can use to make ADO access easier in C++.

A BSTR is a pointer to a string containing wide (16-bit) characters. Due to the way the string is constructed, a BSTR cannot be assigned to a character array in the normal way. If we are using MFC in our application, we have to call the CString::AllocSysString() function to return the string as a BSTR. Otherwise, you will need to convert strings to BSTRs manually. In particular, Microsoft provides a number of functions, such as SysAllocStringByteLen() and SysAllocStringLen() that allow you to provide a string and the length of the string and return a BSTR.

A VARIANT is a structure which includes a union of a large number of different data types — integer, floating point and variable types, as well as pointers. Its purpose is to emulate the Variant type in Visual Basic. In MFC, the COleVariant class puts a wrapper around the VARIANT structure, which makes it easier to work with.

Another option that is more efficient (as it is directly supported by the compiler) is the _variant_t class. Variants are used by Visual Basic to allow one to store values of different types in the same variable. COleVariant makes it easier to work with variants, as no type conversions are necessary and one has access to methods such as one for type conversions. _variant_t is similar, but is compiler supported.

The MFC OLE Method

In contrasting the various methods of using ADO, the first one we will discuss is the MFC OLE method. This method of using ADO uses MFC. Basically, you can use the ClassWizard in to generate a wrapper class for the ADO functions.

You do this by adding a new class, selected from a type library. You need to find Msado15.DLL, which will probably be in `C:\Program Files\Common Files\System\ado`:

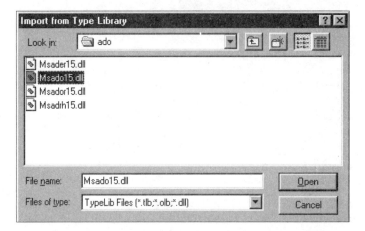

In the Confirm Classes dialog, you'll generally need to select all the classes listed.

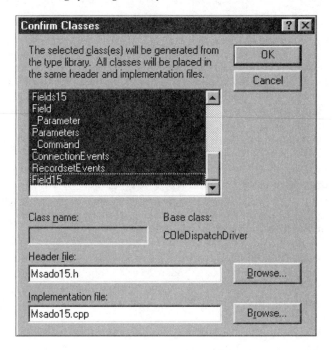

The will generate two files for you:

- ❑ `Msado15.h`
- ❑ `Msado15.cpp`

These contain all the wrapper classes which we can be used in implementing an ADO application via this method.

> Note that this can be done with any COM DLL that has a type library compiled in as a resource or type library itself.

The `Msado15.h` file that is created by this method essentially has class definitions of all the specified ADO classes, and the matching `Msado15.cpp` file provides the implementation of them. However, since the true implementation of the ADO object is in the DLL, all the methods simply invoke helper functions. An example of such a function is as follows:

```
void _Command15::SetActiveConnection(const VARIANT& newValue)
{
    static BYTE parms[] = VTS_VARIANT;
    InvokeHelper(0x60030000, DISPATCH_PROPERTYPUT, VT_EMPTY, NULL, parms,
                                                      &newValue);
}
```

We can then use these classes as we would any other class. This does have the advantage of hiding some of the complexity of COM from the programmer. Furthermore, it also hides BSTRs from the user, although it doesn't hide VARIANTs.

However, the functions do not return HRESULTs, which is a disadvantage in terms of error handling. Another problem is that the code uses some enumerated types that are not included, so this has to be done manually in your code. These enumerated types include `PropertyAttributeEnum`, `DataTypeEnum`, `ParameterDirectionEnum` and `CommandTypeEnum`.

The #import Method

This method has the big advantage of simplicity relative to other methods of accessing ADO in C++. It allows one to use the ADO objects in a very similar manner in Visual C++ as they would in Visual Basic.

The ADO DLL, msado15.dll contains all the ADO classes that we need. You can then import these into you code with the following line:

```
#import "C:\Program Files\Common Files\System\ado\msado15.dll" no_namespace
```

What this does is to read the type library informatiom from the file and generate the wrapper classes for you.

The term `no_namespace` means that the namespace that defines the contents of this item in the type library file will not be generated. This namespace contains the primary header items, and its purpose is to avoid name collisions.

Another major advantage of the `#import` method is that it hides VARIANTs and BSTRs, replacing them with `_variant_t` and `_bstr_t` which are much easier to work with, and are recognized by the Visual C++ compiler as keywords.

There are two issues you should bear in mind when using this method however. First, if an HRESULT returns an error code, an exception is raised. This can be an advantage as you can simply substitute exception handling for testing output values. Thus, you can use C++ exception handling techniques (i.e. try and catch blocks).

The second point is that default values for method parameters are not provided and "optional" parameters often have to be included.

Because of its big advantage of simplicity, the #import method is considered an excellent way to implement ADO in a Visual C++ application.

A Practical Example – using the OLE SDK

We will focus on a third method of linking to and using ADO, by utilizing the OLE SDK. It is very commonly used and avoids the error handling issues of MFC OLE, where HRESULTs are not returned.

However, it does use MFC for the user interface and to do conversions to and from BSTRs and VARIANTs. It is not quite as easy to use as the #import method, but it does allow more direct access to error handling via HRESULTs.

Creating the Application

The example we'll be developing in this section is similar to earlier ones using ODBC, DAO and later OLE DB. Again, it will be based on the invoice database, with the same user interface as these earlier examples.

So, all you need to do to get going is create an MFC project using AppWizard, basing the view class on CFormView. The ADO recordset class will have to be added manually, as the class wizard does not specifically support ADO. Let's take a look at this class now.

The ADO Recordset Class

We'll call the class CTestADORec, and implement the whole thing in one header file, TestADORec.h. In this class we'll have member variables corresponding to the fields of the invoice table (on which the form is based) and pointers to some ADO classes, namely ADORecordset, ADOFields and ADOField.

Note that you'll need to #include two header files:

```
#include <adoid.h>
#include <adoint.h>
```

These two files are included in Visual C++ in order to allow access to the ADO objects. This is where such objects as ADORecordset and ADOFields are defined, as are the related methods.

Here is the start of the class definition, where the member variables are defined that will be used in creating the recordset:

```
class CTestADORec
{
public:
    ADORecordset* MyRecordset;    // A pointer to an ADO Recordset object
    ADOFields* flds;              // A pointer to a collection of fields
    ADOField* fld;                // A pointer to an individual field
    LONG m_invoiceID;             // Variables to contain the data
    LONG m_vendorID;
    LONG m_itemID;
    LONG m_units;
```

The CTestADORec class will contain three member functions:

❑ Open() — opens the recordset

❑ GetData() — retrieve data from the recordset

❑ PutData() — set data in the recordset

The first of these is shown below:

```
HRESULT Open()
{
    HRESULT hr;
    CString strTmp;
    CString strCmd ( "invoice" );

    //you need to convert the connection string to ADO format
    strTmp.Format( "DRIVER={Microsoft Access Driver (*.mdb)};"
                                "DBQ=C:\\My Documents\\testsm.MDB;"
                                "DefaultDir=;"
                                "UID=admin;PWD=;" );

    hr = CoCreateInstance(CLSID_CADORecordset,
                          NULL,
                          CLSCTX_INPROC_SERVER,
                          IID_IADORecordset,
                          (LPVOID*) &MyRecordset);


    if(SUCCEEDED(hr))
    {
        COleVariant v1 = strTmp;
        COleVariant v2 = strCmd;
        hr = MyRecordset->Open(v2, v1, adOpenKeyset, adLockOptimistic, adCmdTable);

    }
    return hr;
}
```

This is the function that opens the recordset. First we declare two CString objects — one to hold the connection string and one to hold the name of the table on which the recordset itself will be based, that is, the invoice table.

In order to define the connection string, we need to get it into the right format for ADO. Recall that we discussed this earlier in the chapter. The string used in this example is:

```
strTmp.Format( "DRIVER={Microsoft Access Driver (*.mdb)};"
                        "DBQ=C:\\My Documents\\testsm.MDB;"
                        "DefaultDir=;"
                        "UID=admin;PWD=;" );
```

As the default provider used in this case is the OLE DB provider for ODBC, the "driver" specified above is the ODBC driver for Access. Note that, as in DAO, we give the path name for the database.

If, for example, you wished to access a SQL Server database, you could use the following syntax:

```
//you need to convert the connection string to ADO format
strTmp.Format( "driver={sql server};"
                        "server=ziggy;"
                        "Database=testsm1;UID=sa;PWD=;");
```

Using the above connection string would connect you to the testsm database on the server, ziggy. Clearly, you would need to change these to match your own set up.

We use the COM function, CoCreateInstance(), to create the recordset object.

```
hr = CoCreateInstance(CLSID_CADORecordset,
                      NULL,
                      CLSCTX_INPROC_SERVER,
                      IID_IADORecordset,
                      (LPVOID*) &MyRecordset);
```

If this object is successfully created, then we open the recordset:

```
if(SUCCEEDED(hr))
    {
    COleVariant v1 = strTmp;
    COleVariant v2 = strCmd;
    hr = MyRecordset->Open(v2, v1, adOpenKeyset, adLockOptimistic, adCmdTable);
    }
```

Note that the adOpenKeyset constant has been included, as a dynamic cursor is being created. This parameter is similar to a dynamic cursor, but changes made to the data by others can be viewed. For the purpose of this example, however, it doesn't make that much difference, but if we were writing a multi-user application, the issue of visibility of changes would have to be carefully considered.

The parameter adCmdTable means that we are opening a table (as opposed to a query) and adLockOptimistic means that a record will only be locked when it's going to be updated. The other choice would be pessimistic locking where records are locked upon editing.

The next method, GetData(), is called by the view class to current record and the values of each of the fields from the recordset object:

```
HRESULT GetData()
{
    HRESULT hr;
    COleVariant vTmp;

    // get the fields of the current record;
    hr = MyRecordset->get_Fields (&flds);

    // get the value of each of the fields
    if(hr == S_OK)
    hr = flds->get_Item(COleVariant((long)0), &fld);
    if(hr == S_OK)
        hr = fld->get_Value(&vTmp);
    if(hr == S_OK)
        m_invoiceID = (long)V_I4(&vTmp);

    if(hr == S_OK)
    hr = flds->get_Item(COleVariant((long)1), &fld);
    if(hr == S_OK)
        hr = fld->get_Value(&vTmp);
    if(hr == S_OK)
        m_vendorID = (long)V_I4(&vTmp);

    hr = flds->get_Item(COleVariant((long)2), &fld);
    if(hr == S_OK)
        hr = fld->get_Value(&vTmp);
    if(hr == S_OK)
        m_itemID = (long)V_I4(&vTmp);

    hr = flds->get_Item(COleVariant((long)3), &fld);
    if(hr == S_OK)
        hr = fld->get_Value(&vTmp);
    if(hr == S_OK)
        m_units = (long)V_I4(&vTmp);

    return hr;
}
```

As was discussed earlier, COleVariant is a MFC class available to simplify the use of variants. We first get the fields via the get_Fields() call that stores the fields in the flds member variable.

The individual field objects are obtained with calls to get_Item(). get_Item() takes a VARIANT, which is the field index, and an ADOField variable (fld) in which to store the result.

The first get_Item() call gets the first field object, since the index passed to it is 0. We then call get_Value() in order to get the actual value of the field. This is stored in a COleVariant variable, from which it can be converted into the correct type. V_I4, for example, takes the COleVariant and returns a long (I4 stands for 4 byte integer). The value extracted can then be stored in the variable m_invoiceID for use by the program.

This process is then repeated for each of the other fields in the table.

Finally, we have the PutData() method, which does the opposite — it puts data into the current record:

```
HRESULT PutData()
{
    HRESULT hr;
    COleVariant vTmp;   //temporary varaible
    VARIANT vt;         //temporary variable that is used to pass data via put_value

    hr = MyRecordset->get_Fields(&flds);

    if(hr == S_OK)
        hr = flds->get_Item(COleVariant((long)0), &fld);
    if(hr == S_OK)
    {
        vt.lVal = m_invoiceID;   // lVal refers to the long value in the
                                 // union making up the variant.
        vTmp = vt;
        hr = fld->put_Value(vt);
    }

    if(hr == S_OK)
        hr = flds->get_Item(COleVariant((long)1), &fld);
    if(hr == S_OK)
    {
        vt.lVal = m_vendorID;
        vTmp = vt;
        hr = fld->put_Value(vt);
    }

    if(hr == S_OK)
        hr = flds->get_Item(COleVariant((long)2), &fld);

    if(hr == S_OK)
    {
        vt.lVal = m_units;
        vTmp = vt;
        hr = fld->put_Value(vt);
    }

    if(hr == S_OK)
        hr = flds->get_Item(COleVariant((long)3), &fld);

    if(hr == S_OK)
    {
        vt.lVal = m_itemID;
        vTmp = vt;
        hr = fld->put_Value(vt);
    }
    return hr;
}
```

We first get the fields collection as we did in GetData(). For each field, we take the value we wish to pass into the field and set the variant variable, vt equal to it. vt is actually a union, so we have to specify which item (in this case, which type) we're using. The invoice field is a long value, so we select vt.lVal.

The value is actually passed into the field object, `fld`, using the `put_Value()` call. Note that we check whether the `get_Fields()` and `get_Item()` calls succeeded, by checking the value of the `HRESULT`.

> *Note that all the implementation for this file has gone into the `.h` file. This was done following the model of the OLE DB consumer rowsets, but it just as easily could have been done in a `.h`/`.cpp` model putting the implementation in the `.cpp` file.*

The Document Class

As in previous examples, we add the recordset to the document class as a member variable. We can then open it in the constructor:

```
CTestADODoc::CTestADODoc()
{
    m_TestADORec.Open();
    m_TestADORec.MyRecordset->MoveFirst();
}
```

Note that we have to move to the first record with a call to `MoveFirst()` on the `ADORecordset` object. In the destructor, we simply call the `ADORecordset::Close()` method:

```
CTestADODoc::~CTestADODoc()
{
    m_TestADORec.MyRecordset->Close();
}
```

Viewing the Data

Another important file to look at is the view class, `CTestADOView`. This is similar to the view classes we have seen earlier, with handler for the command buttons, so we can move onto the next record, the previous one, add a new record and update the database. We also have a Boolean `m_bNew` member variable to keep track of whether the user is adding a new record or merely updating an existing one.

The handler for the **New** button is basically the same as code shown in previous examples — it simply clears the form and sets `m_bNew` to true.

Shown below is the function, `OnPrev()`:

```
void CTestADOView::OnPrev()
{
    VARIANT_BOOL bEOF; //this variable holds the result of get_BOF

    // get pointer to CTestADORec class
    CTestADORec* pADORec = &GetDocument()->m_TestADORec;

    // get pointer to ADO recordset object
    ADORecordset* pMyRecordset = pADORec->MyRecordset;
```

```
pMyRecordset->MovePrevious();
pMyRecordset->get_BOF(&bEOF);

//This is where we test to make sure we're not at the beginning of the
//file before proceeding with getting the current record.  If we are
//at the beginning of the rowset we move to the first record.
if(bEOF == VARIANT_FALSE)
{
   // Get the data
   pADORec->GetData();

   // Pass data to the variables that are used to fill the form view
   m_invoice = pADORec->m_invoiceID;
   m_item = pADORec->m_itemID;
   m_units = pADORec->m_units;
   m_vendor = pADORec->m_vendorID;
   UpdateData(FALSE);
}

// If at BOF, move to first record and display message
else
{
   pMyRecordset->MoveFirst();
   AfxMessageBox("At beginning of file");
}
}
```

Here, we first move to the previous record with a call to `MovePrevious()` on the `ADORecordset` object. We then check to see if we're at the BOF, using `get_BOF()`. If everything is OK, then we get the data for the new (previous) record using the `GetData()` described above. We can then set the form variables to the values in the current record and update the form. If we are at BOF, then we simply display a warning message to the user.

The function, `OnNext()`, is basically the same as the code shown above, except for the fact that we call `MoveNext()` on the `ADORecordset` object and check for EOF rather than BOF.

In order to understand the `OnUpdateRec()` function, you need to know a bit about the concept of a safe array. The safe array class allows one to create arrays of arbitrary size. It also provides access to the COM `SAFEARRAY` member functions. The `COleSafeArray` comes from the `SAFEARRAY` data type, in much the same way as `COleVariant` is a class around the `VARIANT` data type allowing easier use of a variant. As with the `VARIANT`, the `SAFEARRY` comes out of Visual Basic. Visual Basic cannot deal with variable sized arrays as Visual C++ can, so the `SAFEARRAY` was designed to work around it.

Shown below is the implementation for `OnUpdateRec()`, which will update the data values of an existing or a new record:

```
void CTestADOView::OnUpdateRec()
{
    COleVariant vOrd, vVal;
    COleVariant vEmp, vEmp1;
    COleSafeArray saField, saVal;
    COleVariant vInd;

    HRESULT hr;

    saField.CreateOneDim(VT_VARIANT, 3);
    saVal.CreateOneDim(VT_VARIANT, 3);
    long rgIndices[1];

    UpdateData(TRUE);

    // get pointer to CTestADORec class
    CTestADORec* pADORec = &GetDocument()->m_TestADORec;

    // get pointer to ADO recordset object
    ADORecordset* pMyRecordset = pADORec->MyRecordset;

    vOrd = "itemID";
    rgIndices[0] = (long)0;
    saField.PutElement(rgIndices, COleVariant(&vOrd));

    vOrd = "units";
    rgIndices[0] = (long)1;
    saField.PutElement(rgIndices, COleVariant(&vOrd));

    vOrd = "vendorID";
    rgIndices[0] = (long)2;
    saField.PutElement(rgIndices, COleVariant(&vOrd));


    vVal = m_item;
    rgIndices[0] = 0;
    saVal.PutElement(rgIndices, COleVariant(&vVal));

    vVal = m_units;
    rgIndices[0] = 1;
    saVal.PutElement(rgIndices, COleVariant(&vVal));

    vVal = m_vendor;
    rgIndices[0] = 2;
    saVal.PutElement(rgIndices, COleVariant(&vVal));
```

```
if(m_bNew)
{
    hr = pMyRecordset->AddNew(saField, saVal);
}
else
{
    hr = pMyRecordset->Update(saField,saVal);
}
if(m_bNew)
{
    hr = pMyRecordset->MoveLast();
    pADORec->GetData();
    m_invoice = pADORec->m_invoiceID;
    UpdateData(FALSE);
    m_bNew = false;
}
}
```

At the start of the function, we create one dimensional safe arrays (using `CreateOneDim()`) for both the array of fields (saField) and array of values (saVal). Each of the arrays is of length 3 and type VARIANT. After retrieving the latest data and obtaining the pointer to the recordset, we start to fill the safe arrays.

This process is as follows. For each column in the table to be updated, vOrd is set equal to the name of the column, rgIndices[0] is set to the ordinal of the column and then these values are passed into the safe array (saField) creating a new element:

```
vOrd = "itemID";
rgIndices[0] = (long)0;
saField.PutElement(rgIndices, COleVariant(&vOrd));
```

We then set vVal to the column value, set rgIndices[0] to the same ordinal we set the column name to, and pass these values into the safe array, saVal, with a call to PutElement(), creating a new element:

```
vVal = m_item;
rgIndices[0] = 0;
saVal.PutElement(rgIndices, COleVariant(&vVal));
```

The value in rgIndices is the index of the safe array where the value (vOrd, vVal) is stored. Thus, when we are done, we should have two safe arrays, one with the column names (saField) and the second with the corresponding column values (saVal).

These arrays are then passed to the rowset, using AddNew() if we're creating a new row, or UpdateData() if we're updating a row value.

The final change that needs to be made to the view class is the addition of the OnUpdate() function. This won't be listed here as it is very simple. It just gets the data from the recordset and updates the values displayed on the form.

Note that you'll need to add a couple of calls to the application class to initialize and uninitialize COM. These can be added to the constructor and destructor:

```
CTestADOApp::CTestADOApp()
{
    CoInitialize(NULL);
}

CTestADOApp::~CTestADOApp()
{
    CoUninitialize();
}
```

Now you should be ready to try building and running the code:

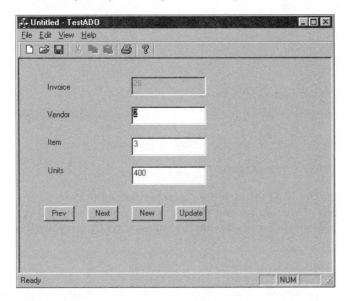

Note that in this example, we have used a recordset to handle entirely accessing a table in database. We did not explicitly have to create a connection or command object. This is part of the simplicity of ADO.

Visual C++ ADO Extensions

In ADO 2.0, Microsoft introduced a new interface, the ADO extensions, for C++ programmers. The problem this new interface is supposed to solve is the tediousness of using VARIANTs in C++. This interface permits one to bind variables to data source columns as we saw in OLE DB.

Using this approach, we would set up a binding class for our example such as the following:

```
class bindingrs : public CADORecordBinding
{
public:
    LONG m_invoiceID;
    LONG m_vendorID;
    LONG m_itemID;
    LONG m_units;
    ULONG m_inv_status;
    ULONG m_vend_status;
    ULONG m_item_status;
    ULONG m_units_status;

    BEGIN_ADO_BINDING(bindingrs)
        ADO_NUMERIC_ENTRY(1,adNumeric,m_invoiceID,10,0,m_inv_status,true)
        ADO_NUMERIC_ENTRY(1,adNumeric,m_vendorID,10,0,m_vend_status,true)
        ADO_NUMERIC_ENTRY(1,adNumeric,m_itemID,10,0,m_item_status,true)
        ADO_NUMERIC_ENTRY(1,adNumeric,m_units,10,0,m_units_status,true)
    END_ADO_BINDING()

};
```

We would then bind this to the rowset as follows:

```
bindingrs brs;

        hr->QueryInterface(__uuidof(IADORecordBinding), (LPVOID*)&bndrs)
            if(SUCCEEDED(hr))
                bndrs->BindToRecordset(&brs);
```

In this was, we can then access the data through the variables defined in the `bindingrs` class, without having to use variants. We could use the `IADORecordBinding`'s special `AddNew` and `Update()` methods, which allow one to pass the bindings class directly to the method.

Summary

The first part of this chapter went into some detail discussing the architecture of ADO, and the methods and properties of each object in the model. We then went on to see how ADO can be incorporated into C++ programs. Finally, we looked at a practical example of using ADO, and found out how it could simplify data access. One notable point was the ease of creating a recordset object, without having to explicitly set up session, connection or command objects.

In the final chapter, we'll be seeing how we can take advantage of another of the technologies under the UDA umbrella — Remote Data Services, or RDS.

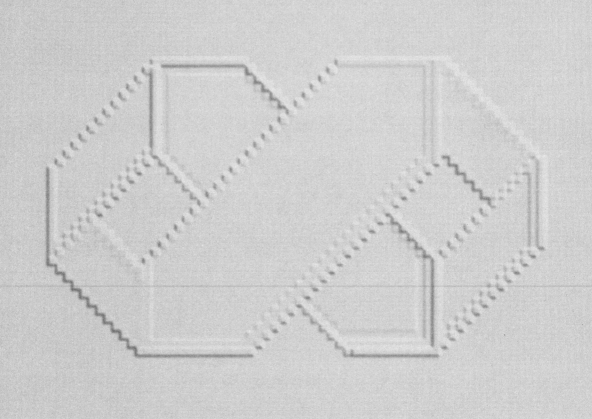

8

Remote Considerations

We cannot always assume our data will be on the same machine as the program that needs to access it. Indeed, nowadays, it is almost inevitable that you will need data that is stored on another machine, i.e. data that is **remote**. For example, the World Wide Web contains a vast wealth of information that is potentially accessible to a user over the Internet. Similarly, a company or corporation will contain important data spread over many machines networked together. The technologies covered in this book up until now, cannot, by themselves, access this data — they are specific for a local user. There has to be a technology that is specifically geared to making available to a user, data stored on a remote machine and accessible over a network. Microsoft has provided two such technologies, specifically developed for this purpose:

- ❑ Remote Data Objects (RDO)
- ❑ Remote Data Services (RDS)

The first of these, RDO, is the older of the two technologies. It has many similarities to DAO which we discussed in Chapter 3, but contains the necessary additional functionality for remote data access. While it is more limited in terms of functionality than DAO, it does have the advantage of being able to access ODBC directly, thus not requiring the Jet database engine. RDO objects will allow us to retrieve a recordset from the server and cache it on the client where it can be manipulated. Any changes made can then be transferred back to the server.

RDS is Microsoft's newer remote data access technology, and is different from RDO in that, instead of being based on DAO, is closely linked with ActiveX Data Objects. It is responsible for transferring ADO objects between client and server machines. RDS has been developed eventually to replace RDO.

We'll start this chapter with a brief overview of both RDO and RDS, and then we'll go on to look at a practical example using RDS. By the end of this chapter you will have learned:

❑   What RDO is and how it compares to DAO

❑   What RDS is and how it relates to ADO

❑   How to set up RDS on your NT machine

❑   How to access data remotely using SQL Server and RDS

Remote Data Objects (RDO)

When designing a remote data access application, there are a number of important goals that have to be achieved:

❑   Reduce network traffic.

Using a network is often very time consuming and with many networks almost full to capacity, with an unending stream of data passing to and fro, operations can be very slow and inefficient. An efficient remote access technology would reduce network transactions to a minimum by allowing batch submission of action queries such as UPDATEs and INSERTs. Such commands can be stored client-side and sent to the server in one package. Thus communication over the network only occurs as and when necessary.

❑   Limit the amount of data transferred in a query.

In other words, you can limit the number of rows a particular query will return. If a query returns an especially large number of rows, more often than not, they will not be sent across the network at once, but would be split up into chunks and sent separately, which again is costly in terms of time and the speed of the loading of the data would depend on the network traffic at the time. If you specify the maximum number of rows a query returns, you can guarantee retrieving all the required data in one go. This, again, improves performance.

❑   Take advantage of server side cursors.

Here you can delegate much of the work of processing the recordsets to the server, thereby easing the burden on the client which can utilize its resources in other ways, such as updating the UI.

❑   Allow for asynchronous queries.

This means that a new query can be begun while the previous one is still being processed.

If these criteria are all met, then we have an efficient remote access system. Needless to say, RDO fulfils these requirements.

In addition to the functionality specific for remote access, RDO has some other capabilities that DAO does not. First, it can handle stored procedures that have return values and output parameters, and as a result, can process much more sophisticated stored procedures than DAO can. Second, it can manage multiple results sets in a much cleaner manner than DAO.

The RDO Model

The RDO model consists of ten different objects, which are summarized in the table below:

RDO Object	Description
rdoEngine	This is the base of the RDO model — it is created automatically just by using RDO
rdoError	This is the error handling object
rdoEnvironment	Manages connections to a data object and also transactions
rdoConnection	Represents a connection to the data source on your remote server
rdoQuery	Represents a query, which can be parameterized
rdoColumn	Holds information about a column
rdoParameter	Represents a parameter, which is associated with a query object and can be either an input parameter, an output parameter or an input/output parameter
rdoResultset	Equivalent to a DAO recordset, representing the data returned from a query
rdoTable	Represents a table or view in the database
rdoPreparedStatement	Is maintained for backward compatibility with older version of RDO — it is replaced by the rdoQuery object

The first three objects `rdoEngine`, `rdoError` and `rdoEnvironment` are created automatically when RDO is initialized. The remainder are created by the user.

Using RDO

In Visual C++ the easiest way to use RDO is by using the RDO's data control as you would in Visual Basic. This is documented in the MSDN CD included with Visual C++.

The steps are as follows:

- ❑ Select View | ClassWizard
- ❑ Select Add Class | From a Type Library
- ❑ Select `windows/system/msrdo20.dll`

A wrapper class will be created that you can then use in your application.

RDO is rapidly being replaced by RDS as the technology used in remote data access. For this reason, we will focus on RDS for the rest of this chapter.

Remote Data Services (RDS)

RDS is a new technology which is part of Microsoft's Universal Data Access strategy. A typical RDS application is illustrated in the following diagram:

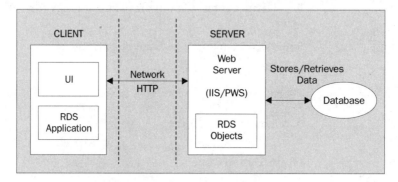

As with RDO and ADO, RDS is primarily designed for programmers of Visual Basic and Active Server Pages, i.e. those technologies that cannot easily use OLE DB. The RDS objects can be easily used in these languages. However, as we will see, RDS can also be utilized in Visual C++ applications.

RDS is a layer that works in tandem with ADO to access data on a remote server. It has the responsibility for transporting ADO recordset objects from the server where ADO lives to the client computer and thus provides for the caching of data on the client. This permits the data to be manipulated on the client, decreasing the network traffic.

RDS is also geared towards what is known as three tiered applications. These are client/server systems that are partitioned into three different levels, as shown in the diagram below:

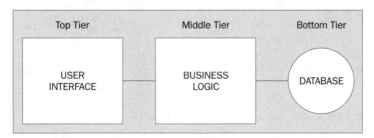

The first is the top tier which is the user interface, where the client interacts with the system. It can be either a web-based application, a traditional Windows application or any similar UI.

The second is the middle tier, which is where the **business rules** are encapsulated. There are simply rules that enforce integrity (data integrity, referential integrity, etc.) within the database. They may also synthesize or filter information. The business rules are normally contained within a COM server (as an EXE or a DLL). An alternative term for business rules is **business logic**.

The third tier is the data source itself.

Note that there are a number of ways you can implement a three-tiered architecture. First, you could have both the user interface and the business logic on the client, and the database on the server. This arrangement is known as a "fat client". Here you would typically set up an ODBC connection on the client, which would then be the means by which the layers on the client communicate to the server. There server's only job would be to supply data. All the rest of the work would be carried out by the client.

However, you could also combine the second and third tiers on the server, which would be the case if the database itself incorporated the business logic. This might be achieved if stored procedures encompass the business object. Alternatively, you might have COM objects living on the server and incorporate the business logic. In either case, all the work is carried out on the server, leaving the client free to concentrate on maintaining the user interface. This type of client is known as a "thin" client.

When using the Internet, it is now common to use an Internet server as an intermediary. For example, on the Internet server you write an ASP script that accesses the database. The client can use his or her web browser as the user interface to access the scripts on the web server. Note, you don't have to use ASP to do this — other technologies such as Perl or ColdFusion allow for the same type of operation.

An Example Using RDS

In this section, we're going to show how to access a SQL Server database on a remote computer using RDS. There's more to using RDS than just writing the right code, so let's examine what we need to use RDS, and how to configure the installations for ease of use. More specifically, we'll be looking at:

- ❑ What components and services we need to install
- ❑ How to set up the example database and make the ODBC connection
- ❑ The security issues involved in accessing a database remotely

Then we can start to write an application using C++.

Setting Up RDS

In order to try out the example from this chapter yourself, you'll need to set up RDS on your server machine. Unlike the previous examples using ODBC, DAO and ADO which rely solely on setting up an ODBC connection on the client, you have to set up an ODBC on the *server* (not the client). In addition you must set up a web server, either the Internet Information Server (IIS) or Personal Web Server (PWS), as well as RDS itself.

If you're working on NT Server and have Internet Information Server version 4.0 running, then the RDS 1.5 server components are already present. If, on the other hand, you have NT Workstation, then you'll need to install Personal Web Server together with the RDS components from NT 4 Option Pack 3. Note that we will refer to the server's web address when we make our remote calls to the server, which was the set up that was used to develop the example in this chapter, together with SQL Server for the example database.

You can install SQL Server Developer Edition, as well as the NT 4 Option Pack (for PWS and RDS), from the Visual Studio discs. If you are installing the web server separately, then you need to install RDS. You can download RDS from `www.microsoft.com/data`*.*

Internet Explorer (IE) 4.0 also provides the client version of RDS 1.5. It can also be installed as part of the Microsoft Data Access SDK 2.0. Remember that RDS is actually most commonly used with Active Server Pages, which is why it is so closely tied with IE and IIS.

Setting Up the Database

We shall be using SQL Server to set up our example database in this chapter. If you are unsure of how to do this, refer back to the OLE DB case study in Chapter 6. This is the same invoice database that we have been using in earlier examples. The script file for defining the database in SQL Server is available from the Wrox web site.

Once we have created the database, and supplied it with data, we will need to set up an ODBC connection. We have to use the OLE DB provider for ODBC as the OLEDB provider for SQL Server does not work for version 6.5. Your ODBC connection must be a *system DSN* — the reason being that the system DSN is specific to the machine and any client can use it. Select the **System DSN** tab and choose **Connection** from the list, or **Add** a new one, giving it an appropriate name. (Don't use the user DSN tab as this will create a connection that can only be used by one particular user.)

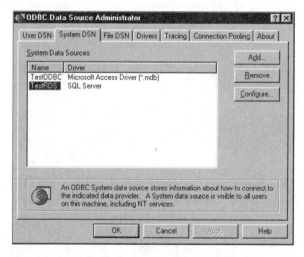

As we set up the ODBC connection, we choose whether to use NT integrated security or SQL Server security. When choosing which security to employ, there are several things to consider. First, you can use the security settings of Windows NT itself, which does not require a user to provide a user ID or password in the connection. It assumes the RDS application is being called through an account that is known to the NT machine acting as the server. This is known as using a **trusted connection**.

For SQL Server, there is an alternative — you can use its own security system, by creating a SQL Server account. Here a user ID and password must be provided, and these are set when you are creating an ODBC connection on the server as we saw above:

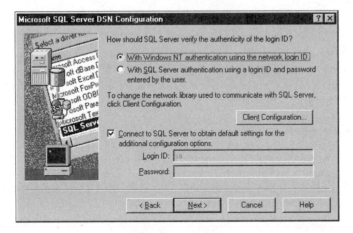

Security Issues

We need to make sure that when the client program tries to access the SQL Server database, it has the appropriate privileges to do so. If this is not set up correctly, you can have a lot of problems with authentication errors.

On the web server, you should have an account set up for an *anonymous user*, which will allow you to log on to the server without providing an ID or password. The server then grants the permissions assigned to the anonymous account. You can check out how this is set up by looking at the configuration utility for IIS or PWS — the **Microsoft Management Console**. The Microsoft Management Console is a facility provided by SQL Server to be able to view various servers, start and stop servers, perform configuration functions and so on. This is what its main UI looks like:

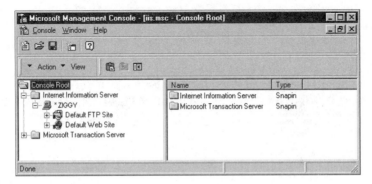

If you right-click on Default Web Site, you can bring up the properties of the web server. Select the Directory Security tab:

Select Edit for Anonymous Access and Authentication Control to bring up the Authentication Methods dialog box. You should make sure that Allow Anonymous Access is checked and press Edit to select the anonymous user account. The default should be set to IUSR_<SERVERNAME> (in my case IUSR_ZIGGY) and you can leave it as this:

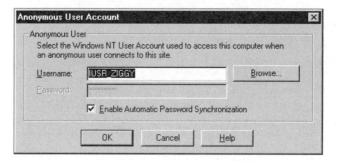

This anonymous user account is critical. We need to make sure that this user has administrative privileges under SQL Server. If this isn't the case, then RDS will return an error when the client program attempts to access the SQL Server database. So, the next thing we need to do is use the SQL Server Security manager to make sure we have these privileges set.

Remote Considerations

If you bring up the SQL Server Security manager and select sa Privilege from the View menu, then all the accounts with administrative privileges will be displayed. (Note that the abbreviation "sa" stands for "system administrator".) Select Grant New from the Security menu and the following dialog will appear:

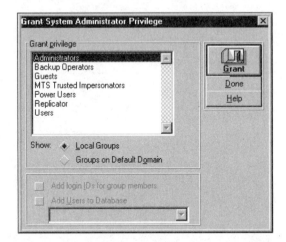

We can use this dialog to grant administrative privileges to the group Guests:

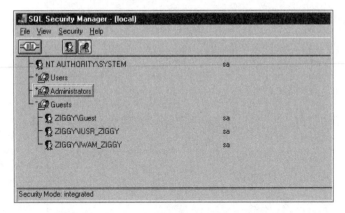

Note that the account for the anonymous user, IUSR_<SERVERNAME>, should now be included in the list of groups with administrative privileges. This means that we can access and update our SQL Server database remotely.

Developing a C++ Application to Use RDS

Now it's time to develop a client-side C++ application which we will use to access our SQL Server database remotely. However, unlike the previous examples we've seen, there is quite a bit more work to be done. RDS was designed for use with Visual Basic and other Automation servers and as such needs to use IDispatch interface functionality rather than vtable binding. Programming RDS objects in C++ is not a trivial undertaking.

We are helped out here by Visual C++ 6.0's IntelliSense feature, which automatically provides the programmer with the methods that go along with an object.

Initializing RDS

Now we come to actually writing the code to initialize and utilize RDS components. As in previous chapters, we will be using the Visual C++ 6.0 MFC AppWizard to create an MFC project, creating the same kind of form view to display the invoice information. The project is called TestRDS, and it can be found with the code for the rest of the book on the Wrox Press web site.

Firstly, we need to add some pre-processor directives to the top of the TestRDS.cpp file. The first of the two #includes below allows us to use TCHARs, the second will provide us with all essential COM functionality.

```
#include <tchar.h>
#include <objbase.h>
```

We are also using the #import method we described in the last chapter, to make ADO functionality available to us. These three DLLs contain what we will want:

```
#import "c:\program files\common files\system\ado\msado15.dll"
                      rename("EOF", "adoEOF") rename("BOF", "adoBOF")
#import "c:\program files\common files\system\msadc\msadco.dll"
#import "c:\program files\common files\system\msadc\msadcf.dll"
```

Communicating with the Database

To communicate with the database, we need to create a new class CRdsItem to handle the interaction with the RDS objects, thus encapsulating access to the database. The header file for this class (RdsItem.h) needs to be included in TestRDS.cpp.

The initialization carried out in the constructor sets up all the connection variables and opens the connection to the database. The full code for the constructor is shown below:

```
CRdsItem::CRdsItem()
{
    HRESULT hr = CoInitialize(NULL);
    _variant_t vRes;

    bstrSvr = _bstr_t("http://VIC");
    bstrConn = _bstr_t("Provider=MSDASQL;DSN=TestRDS;uid=sa;pwd=");
    bstrSQL = _bstr_t("Select invoiceID, itemID, units, vendorID from
                                                        invoice");

    hr = pDFO.CreateInstance(_uuidof(RDS::DataSpace));

    hr = InitRDSDF(pDFO, bstrSvr, pDF);
    OpenRDSRecordset(bstrSQL);
}
```

The first line simply initializes the COM environment for us.

We then set up three BSTRs defining:

- ❑ The server — bstrSvr

- ❑ The connection string — bstrConn

- ❑ The query used for this example — bstrSQL

The server variable tells the program what server we will be making our calls to. The connection string does the same thing we've seen in previous methods, that is, it provides information on what data source to use — login information etc. The final variable, bstrSQL, provides the SQL query command. We call CreateInstance() to create an RDS DataSpace object, whose role is to maintain information about the server and server program to be invoked. A second method InitRDSDF() creates a DataFactory object, which allows you to invoke a call to the data source, supplying a query, retrieving a recordset and updating a data source. We'll see how InitRDSDF() works shortly. Finally, we call OpenRDSRecordset() to connect to the SQL Server database and execute the SQL query to obtain the recordset.

In the destructor, we clean up by closing the recordset, calling Release() on our interface pointers and uninitializing COM:

```
CRdsItem::~CRdsItem()
{
    pDF.Release();
    pDFO.Release();
    pRS->Close();
    pRS.Release();
    CoUninitialize();
}
```

The InitRDSDF() method, called in the constructor, creates an RDSSERVER.DataFactory object on the server, which is an object designed to receive requests from the client. It then gets the address of the IDispatch interface for the data factory:

```
HRESULT CRdsItem::InitRDSDF(RDS::IDataspacePtr pDFO, _bstr_t bstrSvr,
                                                    IDispatchPtr &pDF)
{
   HRESULT hr;
   _variant_t vRes;
   try
   {
      vRes = pDFO->CreateObject(_bstr_t("RDSSERVER.DataFactory"),
                                                    bstrSvr);
      hr = vRes.pdispVal->QueryInterface(_uuidof(IDispatch),
                                                    (LPVOID*)&pDF);
   }
   catch(_com_error &e)
   {
      MessageBox(NULL, e.ErrorMessage(),"Com Error",MB_OK);
   }
   return hr;
}
```

Once we have a pointer to the IDispatch interface, we can create the recordset object. The method that achieves this is OpenRDSRecordset():

```
HRESULT CRdsItem::OpenRDSRecordset(_bstr_t bstrSQL)
{
   HRESULT hr;
   _variant_t vRes;
   IDispatch* tmpPtr;
   VARIANT *pVarResult;
   DISPPARAMS dispparams;
   unsigned int puArgErr;
   DISPID dsID[1];
   pVarResult = new VARIANT;

   LPOLESTR strQuery[1] = {OLESTR("Query")};

   hr = pDF->GetIDsOfNames(IID_NULL,(OLECHAR FAR* FAR*)strQuery,1,
                                    LOCALE_SYSTEM_DEFAULT, dsID);
   if(FAILED(hr))
   {
      AfxMessageBox("Invalid function");
      delete pVarResult;
      return hr;
   }

   dispparams.rgvarg = new VARIANT[3];
   dispparams.rgvarg[2].vt = VT_BSTR;
   dispparams.rgvarg[2].bstrVal = bstrConn;
   dispparams.rgvarg[1].vt = VT_BSTR;
   dispparams.rgvarg[1].bstrVal = bstrSQL;
   dispparams.rgvarg[0].vt = VT_I4;
   dispparams.rgvarg[0].ppdispVal = 0;
```

```
dispparams.cArgs = 3;
dispparams.cNamedArgs = 0;

hr = pDF->Invoke(dsID[0], IID_NULL,LOCALE_SYSTEM_DEFAULT,
                 DISPATCH_METHOD, &dispparams, (VARIANT*)pVarResult,
                                               NULL,&puArgErr);

if(FAILED(hr))
{
   AfxMessageBox("Remote call failed");
   delete pVarResult;
   return hr;
}
tmpPtr = (pVarResult->pdispVal);

//now we can get the recordset
hr = tmpPtr->QueryInterface(_uuidof(ADODB::_Recordset), (void**)&pRS);
if(FAILED(hr))
{
   AfxMessageBox("Query interface on Recordset failed");
}
tmpPtr->Release();
delete pVarResult;
return hr;
}
```

There is quite a lot going on in this method, so let's examine it carefully section by section. Note we can not simply call the methods directly because the object lives on another server. You must use the IDispatch interface to do this, more specifically its Invoke() method. A detailed description of IDispatch can be found in any introductory book on COM.

In order to call methods on the data factory object, we need to obtain the dispatch IDs (or DISPIDs) for the methods it supports. The following line of code will get the DISPID for the query function:

```
LPOLESTR strQuery[1] = {OLESTR("Query")};
hr = pDF->GetIDsOfNames(IID_NULL,(OLECHAR FAR* FAR*)strQuery,1,
                                  LOCALE_SYSTEM_DEFAULT, dsID);
```

If this function fails, it prints a message box and exits, deleting the pVarResult pointer.

Next, we have to prepare to call to the Query() method on the data space object. To do this, we create a DISPPARAMS structure, which holds the parameters for the function that is to be invoked. An array of three VARIANTs are created, each containing the type of the parameter (vt) and the value of the parameter. Two other variables are also included: CArgs holds the number of arguments and CNamedArgs holds the number of named arguments. As we won't be using named arguments, the latter variable is set to zero.

```
dispparams.rgvarg = new VARIANT[3];
dispparams.rgvarg[2].vt = VT_BSTR;
dispparams.rgvarg[2].bstrVal = bstrConn;
dispparams.rgvarg[1].vt = VT_BSTR;
dispparams.rgvarg[1].bstrVal = bstrSQL;
dispparams.rgvarg[0].vt = VT_I4;
dispparams.rgvarg[0].ppdispVal = 0;

dispparams.cArgs = 3;
dispparams.cNamedArgs = 0;
```

We will call the `IDispatch` method `Invoke()` which carries out the query:

```
hr = pDF->Invoke(dsID[0], IID_NULL,LOCALE_SYSTEM_DEFAULT,
                    DISPATCH_METHOD, &dispparams, (VARIANT*)pVarResult,
                                            NULL,&puArgErr);
```

If this call fails, you get another error message. Finally, we get a pointer to the recordset:

```
hr = tmpPtr->QueryInterface(_uuidof(ADODB::_Recordset), (void**)&pRS);
```

The rest of the program will use this pointer to access the recordset returned as the result of the remote query and manipulate the data. Note that it is the recordset object that is manipulated and not the data source itself. Changes can be made to the recordset, but will not be reflected in the data source until the `SubmitChanges()` function is executed. We will come to this function shortly.

First, we implement a method called `DoChanges()` which will execute `SubmitChanges()` and commits alterations made to the recordset to the database itself. Its listing is as follows.

```
HRESULT CRdsItem::DoChanges()
{
    HRESULT hr;
    DISPID dsID[1];
    _variant_t pvar;
    ADODB::_RecordsetPtr pRSTmp;

    DISPPARAMS dNoArgs = {NULL, NULL, 0, 0};
    LPOLESTR strQuery[1] = {OLESTR("SubmitChanges")};

    hr = pDF->GetIDsOfNames(IID_NULL, (OLECHAR FAR* FAR*)strQuery, 1,
                                        LOCALE_SYSTEM_DEFAULT, dsID);
    if(FAILED(hr))
    {
        AfxMessageBox("Invalid function");
        return hr;
    }
```

```
   try
   {
      hr = _com_dispatch_method(pDF, dsID[0], DISPATCH_METHOD, NULL,
               NULL, L"\x0008\x0009", (BSTR)bstrConn, (IDispatch*)pRS);
   }
   catch(_com_error &e)
   {
      MessageBox(NULL, e.Description(),"Com Error",MB_OK);
   }
return hr;
}
```

The first thing we do is to call the `IDispatch` method `GetIDsOfNames()` with the function name `SubmitChanges` as one of the parameters. Once you have the DISPID of the `SubmitChanges()` function, you would normally call `Invoke()` to implement the function, which is what we did in the `OpenRDSRecordset()` method above. However there is a second way of achieving the same result, using `_com_dispatch_method()`:

```
try
{
   hr = _com_dispatch_method(pDF, dsID[0], DISPATCH_METHOD, NULL,
            NULL, L"\x0008\x0009", (BSTR)bstrConn, (IDispatch*)pRS);
}
catch(_com_error &e)
{
   MessageBox(NULL, e.Description(),"Com Error",MB_OK);
}
```

`_com_dispatch_method()` performs the remote query operation and returns a pointer to an `IDispatch` object that can be used to obtain the recordset object.

The function parameter are:

- ❏ `pDF` — the pointer to the data factory

- ❏ `dsID[0]` — the DISPID of the `Query()` function

- ❏ `DISPATCH_METHOD` — a constant telling the function that this is a dispatch method rather then one getting or setting data

- ❏ Another constant telling the function what type of value is returned — in this case it is `NULL`

- ❏ The address of the pointer that is returned — in this case `NULL`

- ❏ A string telling the function the type of parameters being passed to the `Query()` method

- ❏ The parameters themselves (the connection string and the pointer to the recordset)

The difference here is that instead of simply testing the HRESULT, we use try and catch blocks, which allows you to obtain a textual error message should the method fail. Invoke() doesn't throw COM errors in this way.

If you wish to use Invoke() in the normal way, you can alter the code to the following:

```
HRESULT CRdsItem::DoChanges()
{
    HRESULT hr;
    DISPID dsID[1];
    unsigned int puArgErr;
    _variant_t pvar;
    ADODB::_RecordsetPtr pRSTmp;

    DISPPARAMS dNoArgs = {NULL, NULL, 0, 0};
    DISPPARAMS dispparams;
    LPOLESTR strQuery[1] = {OLESTR("SubmitChanges")};

    VT_BSTR = 8;
    VT_DISPATCH = 9;

    hr = pDF->GetIDsOfNames(IID_NULL, (OLECHAR FAR* FAR*)strQuery, 1,
                                      LOCALE_SYSTEM_DEFAULT, dsID);
    if(FAILED(hr))
    {
        AfxMessageBox("Invalid function");
        return hr;
    }

    dispparams.rgvarg = new VARIANT[2];
    dispparams.rgvarg[1].vt = VT_BSTR;
    dispparams.rgvarg[1].bstrVal = bstrConn;
    dispparams.rgvarg[0].vt = VT_DISPATCH;
    dispparams.rgvarg[0].pdispVal = (struct IDispatch *)pRS;

    dispparams.cArgs = 2;
    dispparams.cNamedArgs = 0;

    hr = pDF->Invoke(dsID[0], IID_NULL, LOCALE_SYSTEM_DEFAULT,
                     DISPATCH_METHOD, &dispparams, NULL, NULL, &puArgErr);

    if(FAILED(hr))
        AfxMessageBox("Remote Call Failed");
    delete dispparams.rgvarg;

    return hr;
}
```

When we've modified the data or added a new record, we need to requery the database to obtain the most up-to-date data to display in the dialog. Specifically, when a new record has been added, we need to obtain the identity values — that is InvoiceID, the primary key — once the new record has been added to the database. These values are provided by the database itself, but since it is being accessed remotely, the new recordset on the client will not have a value for InvoiceID until the database is requeried. The method that will achieve this is called RedoQuery() and the code for this is shown below. It is essentially the same as the method we used to obtain the data initially:

```
HRESULT CRdsItem::RedoQuery()
{
   IDispatch* tmpPtr;
   ADODB::_RecordsetPtr pRSTmp;
   HRESULT hr;
   VARIANT *pVarResult;
   DISPPARAMS dispparams;
   unsigned int puArgErr;

   DISPID dsID[1];
   LPOLESTR strQuery[1] = {OLESTR("Query")};
   pVarResult = new VARIANT;
   hr = pDF->GetIDsOfNames(IID_NULL, (OLECHAR FAR* FAR*)strQuery, 1,
                                      LOCALE_SYSTEM_DEFAULT, dsID);
   if(FAILED(hr))
   {
      AfxMessageBox("Invalid function");
      delete pVarResult;
      return hr;
   }

   dispparams.rgvarg = new VARIANT[3];
   dispparams.rgvarg[2].vt = VT_BSTR;
   dispparams.rgvarg[2].bstrVal = bstrConn;
   dispparams.rgvarg[1].vt = VT_BSTR;
   dispparams.rgvarg[1].bstrVal = bstrSQL;
   dispparams.rgvarg[0].vt = VT_I4;
   dispparams.rgvarg[0].ppdispVal = 0;

   dispparams.cArgs = 3;
   dispparams.cNamedArgs = 0;

   hr = pDF->Invoke(dsID[0], IID_NULL, LOCALE_SYSTEM_DEFAULT,
    DISPATCH_METHOD, &dispparams, (VARIANT*)pVarResult, NULL, &puArgErr);

   if(FAILED(hr))
   {
      AfxMessageBox("Remote call failed");
      delete pVarResult;
      return hr;
   }
   tmpPtr = (pVarResult->pdispVal);

   //now we can actually get the recordset
   hr = tmpPtr->QueryInterface(_uuidof(ADODB::_Recordset), (void**)&pRS);
   if(FAILED(hr))
   {
      AfxMessageBox("Query interface on Recordset failed");
   }
   tmpPtr->Release();
   delete pVarResult;
   return S_OK;
}
```

This completes our code for the `CRdsItem` class. The rest of the code is pretty similar to what we've seen before — all we have to do now is add message handlers for the buttons on the form that will use the `CRdsItem` class and allow us to step through the data, modify it and add new records.

Implementing the View Class

In this section we'll complete the example by developing the TestRDSView class. We will take a look at the code we need to add for the message handlers for the **Prev**, **Next**, **New** and **Update** buttons, and also the overridden `OnUpdate()` method. Once again we include a Boolean variable `m_bNew` in the View class which is set to `true` only when the **New** button is pressed.

Note that for this particular form, we will add a new button **Send Changes** which will submit modified data across to the server.

The completed form should look like this:

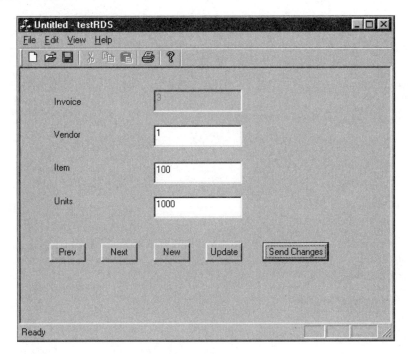

Shown below is the code for `OnNext()`:

```
void CMyTestRDSView::OnNext()
{
    _variant_t res;
    char tres[20];
    VARIANT_BOOL bEOF;
    CTestRDSDoc* pDoc = GetDocument();

    // first make sure that you have records
    pDoc->ds.pRS->get_adoBOF(&bEOF);
    if(bEOF == VARIANT_TRUE)
    {
        MessageBox("No records in the file", "File Warning", MB_OK |
                                                    MB_ICONINFORMATION);
        return;
    }

    // test for EOF
    pDoc->ds.pRS->MoveNext();
    pDoc->ds.pRS->get_adoEOF(&bEOF);
    if(bEOF == VARIANT_TRUE)
    {
        MessageBox("At end of file", "File Warning", MB_OK |
                                                    MB_ICONINFORMATION);
        pDoc->ds.pRS->MoveLast();
    }

    res = pDoc->ds.pRS->Fields->GetItem("invoiceID")->Value;
    if(res.lVal > 0)
        m_invoice = ltoa((long)res.lVal, tres,10);
    m_item = ltoa((long)pDoc->ds.pRS->Fields->GetItem("itemID")->Value,
                                                    tres, 10);
    m_units = ltoa((long)pDoc->ds.pRS->Fields->GetItem("units")->Value,
                                                    tres, 10);
    m_vendor = ltoa((long)pDoc->ds.pRS->Fields->GetItem("vendorID")->Value,
                                                    tres,10);

UpdateData(false);
}
```

The first thing we do is get a pointer to the recordset object. We then test for BOF to make sure we're not dealing with an empty recordset. If we are, we provide an error message to the user and exit. We then move to the next record and test for EOF:

```
pDoc->ds.pRS->MoveNext();
pDoc->ds.pRS->get_adoBOF(&bEOF);
if(bEOF == VARIANT_TRUE) {
    MessageBox("No records in the file", "File Warning", MB_OK |
                                                MB_ICONINFORMATION);
return;
}
```

Note that the function to test BOF is called `get_adoBOF()`. When we imported the ADO functionality, the names of the `BOF()` and `EOF()` methods were changed to ensure that there are no naming conflicts.

The next part of the code obtains all the values from the current row and copies them to the members of the view class:

```
res = pRecordset->Fields->GetItem("invoiceID")->Value;
m_invoice = ltoa((long)res.lVal, tres,10);
m_item = ltoa((long)pRecordset->Fields->GetItem("itemID")->Value,
                                                      tres, 10);
m_units = ltoa((long) pRecordset->Fields->GetItem("units")->Value,
                                                      tres,10);
m_vendor = ltoa((long) pRecordset->Fields->GetItem("vendorID")->Value,
                                                      tres,10);
```

Finally, we call UpdateData(), passing an argument of false to indicate that we want to update our form.

Now we come to the code for the OnPrev() message handler, which is similar to that on OnNext():

```
void CTestRDSView::OnPrev()
{
    _variant_t res;
    char tres[20];
    VARIANT_BOOL bEOF;
    CTestRDSDoc* pDoc = GetDocument();

    // first make sure you don't have an empty file
    pDoc->ds.pRS->get_adoBOF(&bEOF);
    if(bEOF == VARIANT_TRUE)
    {
        MessageBox("No Records in the file", "File Warning", MB_OK |
                                             MB_ICONINFORMATION);
        return;
    }

    // test for BOF
    pDoc->ds.pRS->MovePrevious();
    pDoc->ds.pRS->get_adoBOF(&bEOF);
    if(bEOF == VARIANT_TRUE)
    {
        MessageBox("At beginning of file", "File Warning", MB_OK |
                                             MB_ICONINFORMATION);
        pDoc->ds.pRS->MoveFirst();
    }
    res = pDoc->ds.pRS->Fields->GetItem("invoiceID")->Value;

    if(res.lVal > 0)
        m_invoice = ltoa((long)res.lVal, tres,10);
    m_item = ltoa((long)pDoc->ds.pRS->Fields->GetItem("itemID")->Value,
                                                      tres, 10);
    m_units = ltoa((long)pDoc->ds.pRS->Fields->GetItem("units")->Value,
                                                      tres, 10);
    m_vendor = ltoa((long)pDoc->ds.pRS->Fields->GetItem("vendorID")->Value,
                                                      tres, 10);

    UpdateData(false);
}
```

`OnNew()` is as we've seen before:

```
void CTestRDSView::OnNew()
{
    m_item = "";
    m_units = "";
    m_vendor = "";
    m_invoice = "";
    UpdateData(false);
    m_bNew = true;
}
```

The most important function in the view class is the function that either inserts a new record or updates an existing record. As with the other examples we've seen, it's called `OnUpdateRec()`:

```
void CTestRDSView::OnUpdateRec()
{
    COleVariant vOrd, vVal;
    COleVariant vEmp, vEmp1;
    COleSafeArray saField, saVal;
    COleVariant vInd;
    ADODB::_RecordsetPtr pRecordset;
    CRdsItem RdsItem;
    HRESULT hr;

    saField.CreateOneDim(VT_VARIANT, 3);
    saVal.CreateOneDim(VT_VARIANT, 3);
    long rgIndices[1];

    UpdateData(true);

    vOrd = "itemID";
    rgIndices[0] = (long)0;
    saField.PutElement(rgIndices, COleVariant(&vOrd));

    vOrd = "units";
    rgIndices[0] = (long)1;
    saField.PutElement(rgIndices, COleVariant(&vOrd));

    vOrd = "vendorID";
    rgIndices[0] = (long)2;
    saField.PutElement(rgIndices, COleVariant(&vOrd));

    vVal = atol(m_item);
    rgIndices[0] = 0;
    saVal.PutElement(rgIndices, COleVariant(&vVal));

    vVal = atol(m_units);
    rgIndices[0] = 1;
    saVal.PutElement(rgIndices, COleVariant(&vVal));

    vVal = atol(m_vendor);
    rgIndices[0] = 2;
    saVal.PutElement(rgIndices, COleVariant(&vVal));
```

```
    RdsItem = GetDocument()->m_RdsItem;
    pRecordset = RdsItem.pRS;

    if(m_bNew)
        hr = pRecordset->AddNew(saField, saVal);
    else
        hr = pRecordset->Update(saField, saVal);

    if(m_bNew)
    {
        hr = pDoc->ds.pRS->AddNew(saField, saVal);
        hr = pDoc->ds.pRS->MoveLast();
    }
    else
        hr = pDoc->ds.pRS->Update(saField,saVal);

    if(m_bNew)
    {
        m_invoice = "TBD";
        UpdateData(false);
        m_bNew = false;
    }
}
```

As we saw with ADO, we fill the appropriate safe arrays with the new or updated data, and pass them as parameters to either the recordset object's AddNew() or Update() functions depending on the value of m_bNew. The function PutElement() is responsible for storing data in the safe array. Now we come to the OnUpdate() method:

```
void CTestRDSView::OnUpdate(CView* pSender, LPARAM lHint, CObject* pHint)
{
    char tres[50];
    _variant_t res;
    CTestRDSDoc* pDoc = GetDocument();

    res = pDoc->ds.pRS->Fields->GetItem("invoiceID")->Value;
    m_invoice = ltoa((long)res.lVal, tres,10);
    m_item = ltoa((long)pDoc->ds.pRS->Fields->GetItem("itemID")->Value,
                                                          tres, 10);
    m_units = ltoa((long)pDoc->ds.pRS->Fields->GetItem("units")->Value,
                                                          tres, 10);
    m_vendor = ltoa((long)pDoc->ds.pRS->Fields->GetItem("vendorID")->Value,
                                                          tres,10);
    UpdateData(false);
}
```

Remember the OnUpdate() and OnUpdateRec() functions are only concerned with updating the recordset. We will now look at a brand new method that updates the data in the database, OnSendChanges():

```
void CTestRDSView::OnSendChanges()
{
    VARIANT res;
    char tres[10];
    CTestRDSDoc* pDoc = GetDocument();

    // we sumbit the changes
    pDoc->ds.DoChanges();

    // requery the database and display the last record
    pDoc->ds.RedoQuery();
    pDoc->ds.pRS->MoveLast();

    // if there is no invoiceID then supply one
    res = pDoc->ds.pRS->Fields->GetItem("invoiceID")->Value;
    if(res.lVal > 0)
        m_invoice = ltoa((long)res.lVal, tres,10);

    m_item = ltoa((long)pDoc->ds.pRS->Fields->GetItem("itemID")->Value,
                                                        tres, 10);
    m_units = ltoa((long)pDoc->ds.pRS->Fields->GetItem("units")->Value,
                                                        tres, 10);
    m_vendor = ltoa((long)pDoc->ds.pRS->Fields->GetItem("vendorID")->Value,
                                                        tres, 10);

    UpdateData(false);
}
```

OnSendChanges() is the method that is executed when we click on the **Send Changes** button. After getting the pointer to the document, DoChanges() is called which update the database. Then RedoQuery() gets the updated data, and in doing so returns the invoiceIDs of any new records. Finally we move to the last record and update the form. This allows us to take advantage of the RDS model in that we can make a number of changes to the recordset, but make only a single call to the server, reducing the number of network transactions to a minimum.

Now the project is complete, and you can now compile it and test it out. However, note that, when you come to adding a new record, you must supply the value of the ItemID as a multiple of 100 for the record to be entered properly.

Summary

In this chapter, we have seen two different methods for accessing remote data: RDO which was the old way of data access, which is due to be replaced by RDS. It should be emphasized that RDS, along with ADO, is part of Microsoft's Universal Data Access (UDA) strategy.

In this chapter, we accomplished the following:

- ❑ Briefly discussed both RDO and RDS
- ❑ Developed a simple example of using RDS components with Visual C++

In working through the RDS example, we discovered the following. The trickiest aspect of using RDS is actually setting up the web server and ODBC connection on that server. Also the main difference between RDS and client-based data access is that you do not just update the recordset, you have to pass the updated recordset across to the server, which requires writing much extra code.

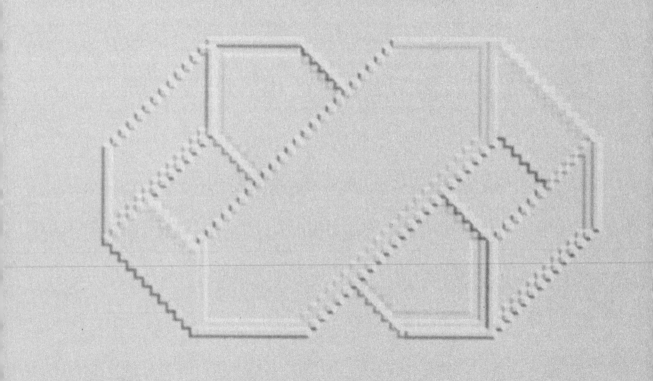

Bibliography

Database Theory

C.J.Date, *An Introduction to Database Systems, Sixth Edition*, Addison Wesley, 0-201-82458-2
C.J.Date, *An Introduction to Database Systems, Volume II*, Addison Wesley, 0-201-14474-3

Database Design

E.F.Codd
"Further Normalization of the Data Base Relational Model", Codd, E.F. in *Courant Computer Science Symposia 6, Data Base Systems (New York, May 1971)*, Prentice-Hall, 1971; "Normalized Data Base Structure: A Brief Tutorial", *Proc 1971 ACM SIGFIDET Workshop (San Diego, Nov 1971)*

The Relational Model for Database Management, Addison Wesley, 0-201-14192-2

Bibliography

Database Systems

Ron Soukup, *Inside SQL Server 6.5*, Microsoft Press, 1-57231-331-5

Alex Homer, *Beginner's Guide to Access 95*, Wrox Press, 1-874416-82-6
Cary N Prague, *Access 97 Bible*, IDG Books Worldwide, 0764530356
Maria Reidelbach and Kit Bernthal, *Access 97 for Windows : Quick Reference Guide*, DDC Publishing Inc, 1562434705

SQL

J.S.Bowman, S.L.Emerson, M.Darnovsky, *The Practical SQL Handbook, Third Edition*, Addison Wesley Developers Press, 0-201-44787-8
Joe Celko, *Instant SQL Programming*, Wrox Press, 1-874416-50-8
Joe Celko, *SQL For Smarties*, Morgan Kaufmann, 1-55860-323-9

COM

Don Box, *Essential COM*, Addison Wesley, 0-201-63446-5
Dale Rogerson, *Inside COM*, Microsoft Press, 1-57231-349-8

ATL

Richard Grimes et al, *Beginning ATL COM Programming*, Wrox Press, 1-861000-11-1
Sing Li and Panos Economopoulos, *Professional COM Applications with ATL*, Wrox Press, 1-861001-70-3
Richard Grimes, *Professional ATL COM Programming*, Wrox Press, 1-861001-40-1
Richard Grimes, *ATL COM Programmers Reference*, Wrox Press, 1-861002-49-1

MFC

Mike Blaszczak, *Professional MFC with Visual C++ 5*, Wrox Press, 1-861000-14-6

ADO

Alex Homer and David Sussman, *ADO 2.0 Programmers Reference*, Wrox Press, 1-861001-83-5

Using The Active Template Library

ATL (Active Template Library) consists of a set of class templates that implement the basic functionality of COM, thus relieving the programmer the need to implement standard COM interfaces, such as `IUnknown` and `IDispatch`.

Writing COM code used to be very hard work. Properly implementing the standard COM function `QueryInterface()` and correctly using the reference counting functions `AddRef()` and `Release()` were not trivial, and in olden days the programmer had to do it all by hand.

Microsoft developed ATL to save the programmer much time and effort by carrying out much of this routine coding automatically. In addition, ATL benefits from not having the high performance overhead of MFC; ATL components are lean and operate much faster than their MFC equivalents.

In practice, ATL is often used with MFC. Microsoft's ATL development team did provide the ability to support MFC, an option in the ATL AppWizard, allowing a programmer to use the non–COM parts of MFC: `CString`, `CMap`, `CList`, `CWnd` etc.

Thus, you are able to do the following:

- ❑ Build ATL-based COM Objects
- ❑ Use the MFC support and collection classes
- ❑ Ship the product in a single DLL

Nowadays, ATL is to writing COM components what MFC is to writing UI applications. MFC COM classes such as `COleControl` are still supported, but are not used as often as they once were.

Description of the Main Classes and Templates

This section contains much COM terminology (aggregation, apartments, threading models etc.) that have not been defined here. If you are new to COM, you should first consult the texts listed in the bibliography (Appendix A) to provide detailed explanation of these concepts. Alternatively, you could check out the first two chapters from Professional COM Applications with ATL, which are available for download from the Wrox Press web site.

There are a number of templates that are used in ATL to implement the basic COM functionality, one of which is `CComObject`. In some cases, you have a choice of which class to use to implement `IUnknown` or `IClassFactory`.

The first class template we will look at is `CComObject`:

```
template< class T > class CComObject : public T
```

The class `T` is the user-defined class that is derived from either `CComObjectRoot` or `CComObjectRootEx`. The purpose of `CComObject` is to implement `IUnknown` for an object that does not use aggregation. (Alternatively, if an object is always aggregated, the class to use instead is `CComAggObject`. If an object may or may not be aggregated, then use `CComPolyAggObject`.)

Now we'll take a look at the related class templates `CComObjectRoot` and `CComObjectRootEx`:

```
template< class T> class CComObjectRootEx : public CComObjectRootBase
```

`CComObjectRootEx<T>` handles reference counting in ATL, and is able to handle both aggregated and non-aggregated components. Any class that implements a COM server object must inherit from `CComObjectRootEx`.

There are several choices for the threading model to pass into the template in place of the parameter T:

- ❑ CComSingleThreadModel — provides a non-thread safe method for incrementing and decrementing a variable.

- ❑ CComMultiThreadModel — provides a thread safe method for incrementing and decrementing a variable. It implements AutoCriticalSection and CriticalSection to handle multithreading issues.

- ❑ CComMultiThreadModelNoCS — also provides a thread safe method for incrementing and decrementing a variable, the main difference between this model and the previous one is that no critical section is involved.

- ❑ CComObjectThreadModel — will either reference CComSingleThreadModel or CComMultiThreadModel depending on what type of threading is used by your application. It cannot reference CComMultiThreadModelNoCS.

- ❑ CComGlobalsThreadModel — similar to CComObjectThreadModel, the main difference is whether the application uses the apartment threaded model.

Note that CComObjectRoot is a typedef of CComObjectRootEx<CComObjectThreadModel>.

Next, we'll look at CComModule:

```
class CComModule : public _ATL_MODULE
```

This class implements a COM server module and is used by the ATL AppWizard, which automatically creates an instance of the CComModule class called _Module, which allows the COM module components to be accessed. It manages all the activities of the class objects including creation and self-registration.

The next class template is CComCoClass:

```
template< class T, const CLSID* pclsid > class CComCoClass
```

The class T is the COM object you are currently implementing. The second parameter pclsid is a pointer to the to the component's class ID (CLSID), which is stored in the registry. This class performs several functions. As well as getting the class ID, this class also gets the object's error information, providing the ISupportErrorInfo interface is implemented. Also, it provides the definitions for both the class factory and the aggregation model. It does this using the DECLARE_CLASSFACTORY() and DECLARE_AGGREGATABLE() macros.

Finally, we will look at `IDispatchImpl`. This template brings about the implementation of the `IDispatch` interface:

```
template< class T, const IID* piid, const GUID* plibid, WORD wMajor = 1, WORD wMinor = 0,
class tihclass = CComTypeInfoHolder > class IDispatchImpl : public T
```

This is more complicated than the classes and templates we have seen already. The six parameters are:

- ❑ `T` — the class name of component being implemented

- ❑ `piid` — the ID of the interface being implemented

- ❑ `plibid` — a pointer to the type library section for the object

- ❑ `wMajor` and `wMinor` — the major and minor versions of the type library (the default values are 1 and 0 respectively)

- ❑ `tihclass` — the class that manages all the type information (the default is `CComTypeInfoHolder`)

Module Maps

One of the key parts of ATL, as with MFC, is the use of macros to avoid the need to write a lot of routine code. There are a number of macros that are commonly used in ATL. Among them are the object map, the COM map and the connection point map.

The Object Map

The object map contains a list of objects that are implemented in the module. It is of the form:

```
BEGIN_OBJECT_MAP(<array of object definitions>)
   OBJECT_ENTRY(<CLSID of the ATL object>, <class of the ATL object>)
END_OBJECT_MAP()
```

Typically, the entry for the array of object definitions is `ObjectMap`.

The COM Map

In ATL, the COM map handles calls to `QueryInterface()`, listing one by one the interfaces that are returned. It takes the form:

```
BEGIN_COM_MAP(<class implementing the COM object>)
    COM_INTERFACE_ENTRY(<interface name>)
END_COM_MAP()
```

The Connection Point Map

A connection point is implemented by a COM object that needs to asynchronously notify its container of an event. Such objects are known as connectable objects. The connection point map provides for implementation of this functionality in COM objects. It is of the form:

```
BEGIN_CONNECTION_POINT(<Name of class implementing connection point>)
    CONNECTION_POINT_ENTRY(GUID)
END_CONNECTION_POINT()
```

Where the parameter `GUID` is the ID for the interface included in the connection point.

Creating A Project with the ATL AppWizard

Now that we've have had a brief look at the main classes and maps in ATL (there is a lot more besides), let's create a control using ATL. We start by creating an ATL project using Visual C++. Select the ATL COM AppWizard and give the project a name, in this case `smallFin`:

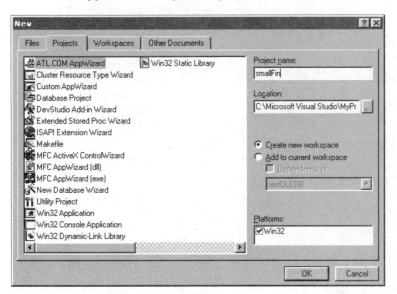

We now will select DLL as the server type:

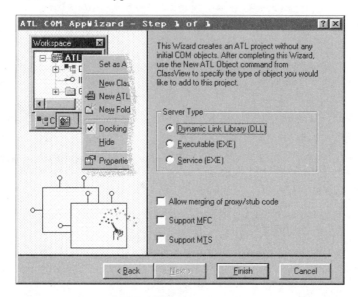

Note we do not check the **Support MFC** box as we are not going to develop a user interface. Now we press **Finish** and the next screen displays a list of the files that are going to be created:

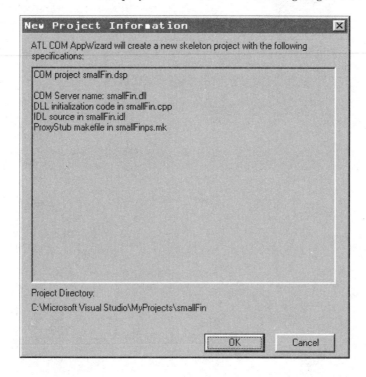

Now press **OK**. At this point several files are generated that provide the shell of the COM object. The first file that is created is smallFin.cpp. This file holds the implementation of the five standard DLL functions:

```
// smallFin.cpp : Implementation of DLL Exports.

CComModule _Module;

BEGIN_OBJECT_MAP(ObjectMap)
END_OBJECT_MAP()

extern "C"
BOOL WINAPI DllMain(HINSTANCE hInstance, DWORD dwReason, LPVOID /*lpReserved*/)
{
    if (dwReason == DLL_PROCESS_ATTACH)
    {
        _Module.Init(ObjectMap, hInstance, &LIBID_SMALLFINLib);
        DisableThreadLibraryCalls(hInstance);
    }
    else if (dwReason == DLL_PROCESS_DETACH)
        _Module.Term();
    return TRUE; // ok
}

// Used to determine whether the DLL can be unloaded by OLE
STDAPI DllCanUnloadNow(void)
{
    return (_Module.GetLockCount()==0) ? S_OK : S_FALSE;
}

// Returns a class factory to create an object of the requested type
STDAPI DllGetClassObject(REFCLSID rclsid, REFIID riid, LPVOID* ppv)
{
    return _Module.GetClassObject(rclsid, riid, ppv);
}

// DllRegisterServer - Adds entries to the system registry
STDAPI DllRegisterServer(void)
{
 // registers object, typelib and all interfaces in typelib
 return _Module.RegisterServer(TRUE);
}

// DllUnregisterServer - Removes entries from the system registry
STDAPI DllUnregisterServer(void)
{
    return _Module.UnregisterServer(TRUE);
}
```

Note that this is where the _Module object is declared, whose functions are employed in all the DLL functions:

- ❏ Init() — initializes the module's data
- ❏ Term() — releases the module's data
- ❏ GetLockCount() — returns the lock count on the module
- ❏ GetClassObject() — creates an object
- ❏ RegisterServer() — performs self registration of all the COM objects in the module
- ❏ UnRegisterServer() — unregisters the COM objects in the module

Note also the object map, the purpose of which is to list the COM objects that are included in the DLL. So far, we have not implemented any COM objects, so the map is empty.

The next file we will look at is the IDL file. At the moment it contains just the skeleton code generated by AppWizard — there are no ATL objects defined. However, it has already been set up to produce the type library that can be used by Visual Basic and other languages.

```
// smallFin.idl : IDL source for smallFin.dll

import "oaidl.idl";
import "ocidl.idl";
[
    uuid(726E8741-3760-11D2-875A-00409540508C),
    version(1.0),
    helpstring("smallFin 1.0 Type Library")
]
library SMALLFINLib
{
    importlib("stdole32.tlb");
    importlib("stdole2.tlb");
};
```

Inserting the COM Object

Now we will create a COM object to add to our DLL. Select Insert I New ATL Object... and see the
following dialog:

Select **Simple Object** and click on **Next**. The following dialog then appears:

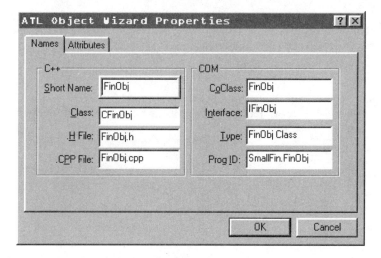

Type in the short name FinObj and the wizard will fill in the rest of the names.

Now select the **Attributes** tab. The following dialog should appear:

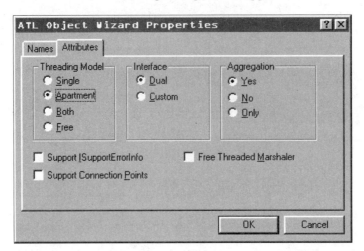

This is where we can specify what type of object we're building. By default the following three buttons are checked:

- ❑ Apartment threading model — where multiple objects can reside on a single thread
- ❑ Dual Interface — enables implementation of IDispatch, thus the object can be accessed via automation
- ❑ Aggregation — object can be aggregated

These default values suit the needs of our simple project. The three lower boxes allow for options, which we will not need — error support, connection points and free threaded marshaling. Just press **OK** to create the object.

Two new files are created: FinObj.cpp and FinObj.h, and the two original files (smallFin.cpp and smallFin.idl) supplied with new code:

In smallFin.cpp the object map is modified as follows:

```
BEGIN_OBJECT_MAP(ObjectMap)
    OBJECT_ENTRY(CLSID_FinObj, CFinObj)
END_OBJECT_MAP()
```

The IDL file is modified as follows:

```
// smallFin.idl : IDL source for smallFin.dll

import "oaidl.idl";
import "ocidl.idl";
[
    object,
    uuid(726E8750-3760-11D2-875A-00409540508C),
    dual,
    helpstring("IFinObj Interface"),
    pointer_default(unique)
]
interface IFinObj : IDispatch
{
};

[
    uuid(726E8741-3760-11D2-875A-00409540508C),
    version(1.0),
    helpstring("smallFin 1.0 Type Library")
]
library SMALLFINLib
{
    importlib("stdole32.tlb");
    importlib("stdole2.tlb");
    [
        uuid(726E8751-3760-11D2-875A-00409540508C),
        helpstring("FinObj Class")
    ]
    coclass FinObj
    {
        [default] interface IFinObj;
    };
};
```

Notice that there are two major changes made to the IDL file. First, an object is added to handle the IFinObj interface. There is nothing within the interface definition as no methods have yet been defined. Second a coclass has been added in the library definition.

Now we turn to the key file, FinObj.h, where the CFinObj class is implemented:

```
// FinObj.h : Declaration of the CFinObj

#include "resource.h" // main symbols

// CFinObj
class ATL_NO_VTABLE CFinObj :
    public CComObjectRootEx<CComSingleThreadModel>,
    public CComCoClass<CFinObj, &CLSID_FinObj>,
    public IDispatchImpl<IFinObj, &IID_IFinObj, &LIBID_SMALLFINLib>
{
public:
    CFinObj()
    {
    }
```

Note that CFinObj inherits from three class templates: CComCoClass, CComObjectRootEx and IDispatchImpl. The last is used to implement the dual interface. The parameter passed to CComObjectRootEx is the result of choosing the single apartment threading model.

We also see that the macro ATL_NO_VTABLE is also used in the class declaration. It is a definition of __declspec(novtable). The purpose of this macro is to prevent initialization of the vtable in the constructor, which prevents the creating of surplus vtables. However, while this macro provides compiler optimization, and is implemented by default, it does have the side effect of restricting when virtual function calls are made. When ATL_NO_VTABLE is used, you must not call virtual functions from the constructor or destructor. Such calls must be made in FinalContruct() and FinalRelease().

```
DECLARE_REGISTRY_RESOURCEID(IDR_FINOBJ)

DECLARE_PROTECT_FINAL_CONSTRUCT()

BEGIN_COM_MAP(CFinObj)
    COM_INTERFACE_ENTRY(IFinObj)
    COM_INTERFACE_ENTRY(IDispatch)
END_COM_MAP()

// IFinObj
public:
};
```

Next, the Wizard adds two macros, DECLARE_REGISTRY_RESOURCEID() and DECLARE_PROTECT_FINAL_CONSTRUCT(). The purpose of the first is to run the registry script file, which has a .rgs extension, the task of which is to add or remove the object from the registry. The second macro is included because we specified that our object is aggregatable. In the event of aggregation occurring, the macro prevents the object from being deleted in FinalConstruct(), where an aggregated component has its reference count incremented and decremented back to zero.

Finally, note the creation of the COM map. As was described earlier, there is where the application maps the interfaces IFinObj and IDispatch to QueryInterface().

When we come to compile this source code, two more files are generated: smallFin_i.c and smallFin.h. The smallFin_i.c file holds the definitions of the CLSIDs:

```
. . .

#ifndef CLSID_DEFINED
#define CLSID_DEFINED
typedef IID CLSID;
#endif // CLSID_DEFINED
```

```
const IID IID_IFinObj =
{0x726E8750,0x3760,0x11D2,{0x87,0x5A,0x00,0x40,0x95,0x40,0x50,0x8C}};

const IID LIBID_SMALLFINLib =
{0x726E8741,0x3760,0x11D2,{0x87,0x5A,0x00,0x40,0x95,0x40,0x50,0x8C}};

const CLSID CLSID_FinObj =
{0x726E8751,0x3760,0x11D2,{0x87,0x5A,0x00,0x40,0x95,0x40,0x50,0x8C}};
```

The smallFin.h header file contains a lot of code that holds the definition of the interfaces that our class implements.

Now let's turn our attention to the registry script. This is used along with the DLL registration functions to register or unregister the objects. Let's have a quick look at it:

```
HKCR
{
    SmallFin.FinObj.1 = s 'FinObj Class'
    {CLSID = s '{726E8751-3760-11D2-875A-00409540508C}'}
    SmallFin.FinObj = s 'FinObj Class'
    {
        CLSID = s '{726E8751-3760-11D2-875A-00409540508C}'
        CurVer = s 'SmallFin.FinObj.1'
    }
    NoRemove CLSID
    {
        ForceRemove {726E8751-3760-11D2-875A-00409540508C} = s 'FinObj Class'
        {
            ProgID = s 'SmallFin.FinObj.1'
            VersionIndependentProgID = s 'SmallFin.FinObj'
            ForceRemove 'Programmable'
            InprocServer32 = s '%MODULE%'
            {
                val ThreadingModel = s 'Apartment'
            }
            'TypeLib' = s '{726E8741-3760-11D2-875A-00409540508C}'
        }
    }
}
```

There are several keywords that the registry script uses, such as ForceRemove and NoRemove. The first tells the ATL registry functions to remove the existing key before creating this key. The second tells the ATL functions to not remove the key when the object is unregistered. The letter s, which occurs frequently in this script, stands for string. (Other scripts contain the letter d for DWORD.) Finally, note that the CLSID is registered twice with two different ProgIDs: the version independent, SmallFin.FinObj, and version dependent, SmallFin.FinObj.1, definitions. These identifiers are necessary so that other programs can use them to activate the component.

Adding Methods

Now that we have defined our object, the next step is to add methods and properties so that it can actually do something. For the purposes of this example we will add one function called CalcPV(), which will take three parameters:

- ❑ An annual payment
- ❑ The number of years
- ❑ The interest rate

From these, it calculates and returns the present value of the payment.

We will also add a property, will be the default interest rate used in the calculation.

The calculation will look like this:

```
PAYMENT = SUM [P * (1 + R)ⁿ]
```

Where P is the annual payment, R the interest rate as a fraction, and n ranges from 1 to the total number of years.

Select the **Class View** tab and right-click on the symbol for the object's IFinObj interface. Select **Add Method** and the following dialog will appear.

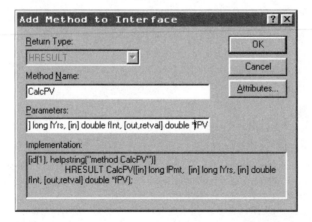

Once you've typed CalcPV in the **Method Name** box, type the following into the **Parameters** box:

```
[in] long lPmt, [in] long lYrs, [in] double fInt, [out,retval] double *fPV
```

The code is longer than the input box so you will lose sight of the first part of it. However, as you type, the code appears in full in the **Implementation** box. The three [in] parameters are variables which will contain the annual payment, the number of years and the interest rate respectively. The [out] parameter will contain the result of the calculation.

The next step is to add the interest rate. So, right-click of IFinObj and select **Add Property**. The following menu will appear:

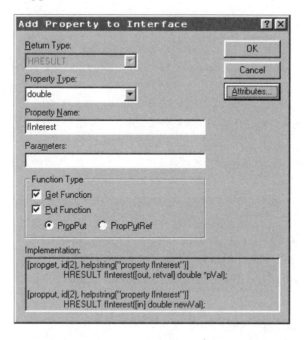

We will select the property type as double and supply the name fInterest. Two functions are created, a propput and a propget function. They will be called put_fInterest() and get_fInterest().

All that remains is to add the function implementation code and add a variable to hold the value of the property. Then we'll have a simple control.

Let's look at the changes made on adding the method and the property. First the IDL file where the IFinObj interface is defined:

```
interface IFinObj : IDispatch
{
    [id(1), helpstring("method CalcPV")] HRESULT CalcPV([in] long lPmt,
            [in] long lYrs, [in] double fInt, [out,retval] double *fPV);
    [propget, id(2), helpstring("property fInterest")] HRESULT
                            fInterest([out, retval] double *pVal);
    [propput, id(2), helpstring("property fInterest")] HRESULT
                            fInterest([in] double newVal);
};
```

The other major changes are in FinObj.h and FinObj.cpp. In FinObj.h definitions were added for the three functions:

```
public:
    STDMETHOD(get_fInterest)(/*[out, retval]*/ double *pVal);
    STDMETHOD(put_fInterest)(/*[in]*/ double newVal);
    STDMETHOD(CalcPV)(/*[in]*/ long lPmt, /*[in]*/long lYrs, /*[in]*/
                      double fInt, /*[out,retval]*/ double *fPV);
```

We also manually add a protected member variable `fIntValue` to hold the value of the
`fInterest` property:

```
protected:
    double fIntValue; //holds the interest value
```

This is initialized in the constructor:

```
CFinObj()
    {
        fIntValue = 0.05;
    }
```

Finally, we implement the three interface functions in `FinObj.cpp` as follows:

```
// CFinObj
STDMETHODIMP CFinObj::CalcPV(long lPmt, long lYrs, double fInt, double
                                                                    *fPV)
{
    long lngI;
    double fRes = 0;

    //if the interest rate is 0 then set it to the default
    if(fInt == 0)
        fInt = fIntValue;
    for(lngI = 1; lngI <= lYrs; lngI++)
    {
        fRes += lPmt*pow(1 + fInt,(double)lngI);
    }
    *fPV = fRes;
    return S_OK;
}

STDMETHODIMP CFinObj::get_fInterest(double *pVal)
{
    *pVal = fIntValue;
    return S_OK;
}

STDMETHODIMP CFinObj::put_fInterest(double newVal)
{
    fIntValue = newVal;
    return S_OK;
}
```

Note that as we use the `pow()` function in the first of the three methods, we must include the
`math.h` header file at the top of `FinObj.cpp`:

```
#include <math.h>
```

Thus we now have a simple ATL COM object. Notice how much work the Wizards have done for us. However, you still needs to understand what is generated as there will be cases where the generated code has to be modified in order to use it.

Testing the Code

You can test out this DLL with a simple VB form. If you want to try this out for yourself, you can download the code from the Wrox Press web site. The form is shown below:

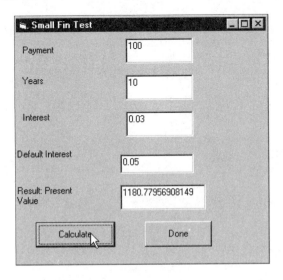

Here is the code that lies behind the form:

```
Dim sf As Object

Private Sub Calc_Click()
    Set sf = CreateObject("SmallFin.FinObj.1")
    Dim pmt1 As Integer
    Dim yrs1 As Integer
    Dim inter As Double
    Dim res As Double
    sf.fInterest = Val(defint1.Text)

    pmt1 = Val(pmt.Text)
    yrs1 = Val(Yrs.Text)
    inter = Val(int1.Text)
    res = sf.CalcPV(pmt, Yrs, inter)
    pv.Text = res
End Sub

Private Sub done_Click()
    End
End Sub
```

```
Private Sub Form_Load()
    Set sf = CreateObject("SmallFin.FinObj.1")
   defint1.Text = sf.fInterest
End Sub
```

Don't forget that in order to run this you need to add the `smallFin 1.0 Type Library` to your project references.

Conclusion

We have seen how ATL is used to build a COM object, requiring relatively little work on our part. The macros and classes defined in ATL hide a lot of the code that was previously necessary in implementing a COM object. Thus, the developer can focus almost entirely on the functionality of the object.

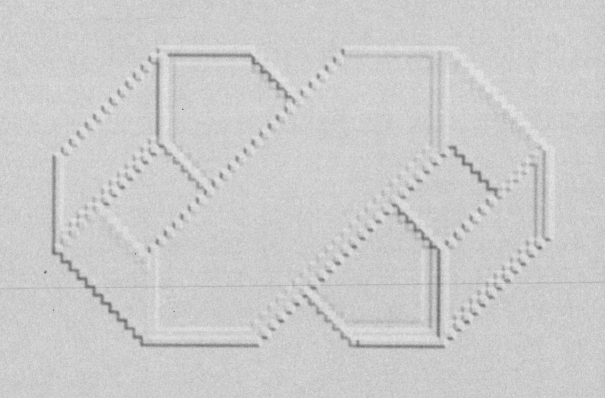

Index

Symbols

#import method
ADO, 253

A

Access
database systems, 8, 10, 13, 14, 18, 35, 37, 39, 44,
45, 53, 55, 62, 63, 67, 72, 73, 74, 102, 103, 114,
118, 171, 179, 227, 256
Entity-Relationship Model, 39
installation, 227
OLE DB
providers, 131
accessors, 188
CAccessor class, 152
CAccessorBase class, 152
CDynamicAccessor class, 153
CDynamicParameterAccessor class, 153
CManualAccessor class, 153
command objects, 135, 152
OLE DB, 135, 147, 152
rowset objects, 135
table objects, 152
ACID
atomicity, 134
concurrency, 134
durability, 134
isolation, 134
session objects, 134
Active Directory Services
OLE DB
providers, 131
Active Server Pages
see ASP
ActiveX Data Objects
see ADO

ADO, 73
#import method, 253
ADO extensions
Visual C++, 263
architecture, 235
ASP, 234
C++, 250
COM, 234
command object, 245
methods, 246
OLE DB, 245
parameter object, 249
properties, 246
compared to RDO, 73
connection object, 236
attributes, 237
ConnectionString, 237
CursorLocation, 238
IsolationLevel, 239
Methods, 240
Mode, 239
OLE DB, 236
properties, 236
error object, 247
OLE DB
providers, 247
properties, 247
field object, 247
methods, 248
properties, 248
recordset object, 248
higher level objects, 236
MFC
OLE method, 251
MFC ClassWizard, 251
OLE DB, 73, 127, 129, 146, 234
consumers, 130
providers, 234

Index

service components
shape component, 132
OLE SDK, 254
parameter object, 249
command object, 249
properties, 249
property object, 249
properties, 249
RDS, 271, 277, 286
recordset class, 254
recordset object, 240
cursor types, 240
dynamic cursor, 240
field object, 248
forward-only cursor, 241
methods, 245
OLE DB, 240
performance issues, 241
properties, 242
static cursor, 241
support objects, 247
Universal Data Access, 119, 146
Visual C++, 250
aggregate functions, 55
COUNT(), 57
GROUP BY element, 56
MAX(), 57
MIN(), 57
SUM(), 55, 56
ALTER TABLE statement, 65
syntax, 65
anomalies
addition anomalies, 20
deletion anomalies, 20
update anomalies, 20
ASP
ADO, 234
ATL
OLE DB, 150
wrapper classes, 150
ATL Object Wizard, 182
data access classes
creating, 184
OLE DB, 147, 150
consumer templates, 155
consumers, 154
atomicity
ACID, 134

B

BSTRs, 251
Btrieve
database systems, 9, 72
OLE DB
providers, 131

business logic
see business rules
business rules
RDS, 271

C

C++
ADO, 250
OLE DB, 250
CAccessor class
accessors, 152
CCommand class, 161
OLE DB, 152
CAccessorBase class
accessors, 152
CCommand class
CAccessor class, 161   ’
OLE DB, 151
CCreateContext class
MFC, 219
CDaoDatabase class
compared to CDatabase class, 105
DAO, 105
MFC, 105
CDaoQueryDef class
DAO, 106
MFC, 106
CDaoRecordset class
compared to CRecordset class, 104
DAO, 104, 107
dynaset option, 107
MFC, 104
CDaoTableDef class
DAO, 106
MFC, 106
CDaoWorkspace class
DAO, 105
MFC, 105
CDatabase class
compared to CDaoDatabase class, 105
MFC, 75
ODBC, 75, 79
CDataSource class
OLE DB, 151
CDynamicAccessor
OLE DB, 153
CDynamicAccessor class
accessors, 153
OLE DB, 153
CDynamicParameterAccessor class
accessors, 153
OLE DB, 153
CMainFrame class
MFC ClassWizard, 218
modifying, 217

CManualAccessor class
accessors, 153
OLE DB, 153
code reuse
COM, 124
column maps, 185, 188
COLUMN_ENTRY() macro, 152, 158
COLUMN_MAP() macro, 161
COM
ADO, 234
advantages, 126, 145
code reuse, 124, 125
COM components, 124, 125, 126
GUIDs, 125
IDispatch, 280
OLE DB, 123, 126, 127, 128, 145
  service components, 132
RDS, 277
SAFEARRAY, 260
throwing COM errors, 283
command objects, 133, 134, 245
accessors, 135
document class, 190
IAccessor, 141
IColumnsInfo, 141
ICommand, 141
ICommandProperties, 141
ICommandText, 142
IConvertType, 142
interfaces, 140
rowset objects, 134
session objects, 134
SQL, 134
comparison operators, 53
Component Object Model
see COM
concurrency
ACID, 134
CONSTRAINT element, 62
Control Panel
ODBC connection, 77
COUNT() function
aggregate functions, 57
CREATE INDEX statement, 64
syntax, 64
CREATE TABLE statement, 62
syntax, 62
creating reports, 219
creating rowsets
OLE DB, 221
CRecordset class
compared to CDaoRecordset class, 104
dynaset option, 81
MFC, 76
MFC ClassWizard, 80

ODBC, 76, 79, 81
snapshot option, 81
cross joins, 49, 52
not recommended, 53
SELECT statement, 52
syntax, 52
CRowset class
OLE DB, 153
CRuntime class
MFC, 219
CSession class
OLE DB, 151
CTable class
OLE DB, 151
  consumer wizard, 151
cursors
dynamic cursor, 240
forward-only cursor, 241
keyset cursor, 241
relational databases, 37
static cursor, 241

D

DAO, 72
advantages, 118
CDaoDatabase class, 105
CDaoQueryDef class, 106
CDaoRecordset class, 104, 107
CDaoTableDef class, 106
CDaoWorkspace class, 105
compared to ODBC, 103, 108, 113
compared to RDO, 269
disadvantages, 118
introduction, 102
MFC, 75, 103, 107
ODBC, 102
persistent objects, 103
QueryDefs, 114
data access classes
creating
  ATL Object Wizard, 184
exercises classes, 187
users classes, 185
Data Access Objects
see DAO
Data Definition Language
ALTER TABLE statement, 62
CREATE INDEX statement, 62
CREATE TABLE statement, 62
DROP TABLE statement, 66
SQL, 44, 62
data factory objects, 278, 280
Data Manipulation Language
SQL, 44

Index

data source objects, 133
  IDBCreateSession, 138
  IDBInitialize, 138
  IDBProperties, 138
  interfaces, 138
  IPersist, 139
  session objects, 134
data space objects, 278, 280
database systems, 8
  Access, 8, 10, 13, 14, 18, 35, 37, 39, 44, 45, 53, 55, 62, 63, 67, 72, 73, 74, 102, 103, 114, 118, 171, 179, 227, 256
  Btrieve, 9, 72
  creating, 181
  Entity-Relationship Model, 38
  flat file databases, 9
  FoxPro, 8, 101, 118
  ISAM, 8, 72, 101, 102, 103, 118
  object-oriented databases, 32
  ODBC, 73
  Oracle, 8, 10, 35, 36, 37, 39, 55, 62, 72, 73, 74, 103, 106, 118, 128, 144
  parameterized queries, 84, 94, 95, 186, 188
  QueryDefs, 35, 106, 114
  relational databases, 9, 10, 44
    anomalies, 20
      addition anomalies, 20
      deletion anomalies, 20
      update anomalies, 20
    characteristics, 11
    concepts, 12
    cursors, 37
    data normalization, 19, 26
    data redundancy, 19
    definition, 11
    denormalization, 32
    domain integrity, 37
    entity integrity, 37
    functional dependence, 20
    indexing, 33
      clustered indexes, 33, 35, 180, 198
      compound indexes, 34
      single field indexes, 34
      unique index, 33
    keys, 14
      alternate keys, 16
      candidate keys, 14, 24
      foreign keys, 15, 186, 196, 201
      intelligent keys, 17
      primary keys, 14, 17, 185, 188
      surrogate keys, 17
    normal forms, 21
      Boyce-Codd normal form, 24
      domain/key normal form, 26, 31
      fifth normal form, 26
      first normal form, 21
      fourth normal form, 25
      second normal form, 21
      third normal form, 22
    referential integrity, 18, 37, 201
    relationships, 12
      many-to-many, 13
      one-to-many, 13
      one-to-one, 13
    transactions, 37
  repeating groups, 10
    definition, 11
  SQL Server, 8, 10, 33, 35, 37, 39, 53, 55, 62, 64, 67, 72, 73, 74, 79, 103, 106, 118, 127, 128, 144, 178, 184, 227, 230, 238, 256, 272, 273, 274, 275, 277, 278
  stored procedures, 35, 84
    triggers, 36
  TableDefs, 106
DDL
  see Data Definition Language
DDV_MaxChars() macro, 194
DECLARE_DYNAMIC() macro, 83
DEFINE_COMMAND() macro, 152, 159, 161
  SELECT statement, 171
DELETE statement, 61
  syntax, 61
DLLs, 125
DML
  see Data Manipulation Language
document class
  command objects, 190
  recordset objects, 259
  rowset objects, 189, 194, 212
DROP TABLE statement, 66
  syntax, 66
durability
  ACID, 134
Dynamic Link Libraries
  see DLLs

E

Entity-Relationship Model
  Access, 40
  database systems, 38
enumerator objects, 135
error objects, 135, 247
exercises classes
  data access classes, 187

F

FAILED() macro, 166, 196
filters
  comparison operators, 53
  keywords, 53

SELECT statement, 46, 53
flat file databases, 9
forms
   updating, 212
FoxPro
   database systems, 8, 101, 118
   OLE DB
      providers, 131
FROM element, 48, 50
full outer joins, 49, 53
   syntax, 53
functions
   _com_dispatch_method(), 282
   Abort(), 229
   AddBindEntry(), 153
   AddNew(), 92, 245, 262, 264, 289
   AddProperty(), 160
   AddRef(), 126
   AddString(), 117
   AllocSysString(), 251
   BeginTrans(), 240
   BOF(), 286
   Cancel(), 141
   CanConvert(), 142
   ClearRecord(), 153, 166
   Close(), 85, 245, 259
   CoCreateInstance(), 133, 136, 256
   CoInitialize(), 136
   Commit(), 229
   CommitTrans(), 237, 240
   COUNT(), 57
   CreateAccessor(), 135, 153
   CreateInstance(), 278
   CreateOneDim(), 262
   CreateView(), 100
   Delete(), 153, 245
   DoChanges(), 290
   DoDataExchange(), 88, 89, 194
   DoFieldExchange(), 84, 96, 115
   Edit(), 92, 245
   EOF(), 286
   Execute(), 141, 246
   get_adoBOF(), 286
   get_BOF(), 260
   get_Fields(), 257, 259
   get_Item(), 257, 259
   get_Value(), 257
   GetClassID(), 139
   GetData(), 144, 255, 257, 258, 260
   GetDBSession(), 141
   GetDefaultConnect(), 82, 84, 96
   GetDefaultDBName(), 108, 115
   GetDefaultSQL(), 82, 84, 96, 115
   GetDocument(), 90, 99, 193
   GetIDsOfNames(), 282

   GetItemData(), 99
   GetNextRows(), 144
   GetParam(), 153
   GetProperties(), 138
   GetTextExtent(), 174
   GetValue(), 153
   InitInstance, 219
   InitInstance(), 101
   InitRDSF(), 278
   Insert(), 153
   InsertRow(), 166
   Invoke(), 280, 281, 282, 283
   IsEOF(), 90
   MAX(), 57
   MIN(), 57
   MoveFirst(), 196, 206, 245, 259
   MoveLast(), 245
   MoveNext(), 90, 162, 196, 245, 260
   MovePrev(), 91, 196
   MovePrevious(), 245
   OnDraw(), 225
   OnInitialUpdate(), 88, 98, 117, 174, 193, 194, 202,
      212, 213, 224
   OnOK(), 221
   OnUpdate(), 87, 93, 109, 110, 166, 193, 195, 202,
      212, 262, 285, 289
   Open(), 85, 134, 159, 161, 168, 223, 237, 240, 241,
      245, 255
   OpenDataSource(), 159, 161, 168, 185, 188, 189,
      223, 230
   OpenRDSRecordset(), 278, 279, 282
   OpenRowset(), 140, 144, 159, 160, 161, 169, 189,
      223
   put_Value(), 259
   PutData(), 255, 258
   PutElement(), 262, 289
   Query(), 280
   QueryInterface(), 137
   ReCalcLayout(), 194
   RedoQuery(), 290
   Release(), 126, 278
   Requery(), 81
   ResetContent(), 207
   ResizeParentToFit(), 194
   RollbackTrans(), 237, 240
   SetCurSel(), 207
   SetData(), 153, 166, 199
   SetDataItem(), 117
   SetFieldType(), 84, 96, 115
   SetItemData(), 98, 99, 208
   SetParam(), 153
   SetProperties(), 138
   StartTransaction(), 229
   SubmitChanges(), 281
   SUM(), 55, 56

Index

SysAllocStringByteLen(), 251
SysAllocStringLen(), 251
TabbedTextOut(), 174
TextOut(), 174
Update(), 92, 196, 199, 245, 264, 289
UpdateBatch(), 241
UpdateData(), 89, 90, 166, 262, 287

G

Globally Unique Identifiers
see GUIDs
GROUP BY element, 55
aggregate functions, 56
SUM(), 55
GUI
SQL, 67
GUIDs
COM, 125

H

HAVING element, 56
compared to WHERE element, 56
helper functions, 207

I

IAccessor
command objects, 141
rowset objects, 143
IColumnsInfo
command objects, 141
rowset objects, 143
ICommand
command objects, 141
ICommandProperties
command objects, 141
ICommandText
command objects, 142
IConnectionPointContainer
transaction objects, 145
IConvertType
command objects, 142
rowset objects, 143
IDBCreateSession
data source objects, 138
IDBInitialize
data source objects, 138
IDBProperties
data source objects, 138
IDispatch, 277, 278, 280, 282
COM, 280
recordset objects, 279

IGetDataSource
session objects, 140
IIS
RDS, 272
IMPLEMENT_DYNAMIC() macro, 83
IN keyword, 55
indexing, 33
clustered indexes, 33, 35, 180, 198
compound indexes, 34
single field indexes, 34
unique index, 33
information hiding
stored procedures, 35
inner joins, 49, 50
syntax, 50
INSERT statement, 58, 60
syntax, 58
installation
Access, 227
Installshield, 227
OLE DB
    consumers, 227
SQL Server, 227
Installshield
installation
    OLE DB
        consumers, 227
Internet
OLE DB, 145
RDS, 145, 272
Universal Data Access, 126
Internet Explorer
RDS, 273
Internet Information Server
see IIS
IOpenRowset
session objects, 140
IPersist
data source objects, 139
IRowset
rowset objects, 144
IRowsetInfo
rowset objects, 144
ISAM
database systems, 8, 72, 101, 102, 103, 118
OLE DB
    providers, 131
ISessionProperties
session objects, 140
isolation
ACID, 134
ITransaction
transaction objects, 145
ITransactionLocal, 229

ITransactionOptions
transaction objects, 145

J

joins, 49
cross joins, 49, 52
full outer joins, 49, 53
inner joins, 49, 50
left outer joins, 49, 51
right outer joins, 49, 51

K

keys
alternate keys, 16
candidate keys, 14, 24
foreign keys, 15, 186, 196, 201
    referential integrity, 201
intelligent keys, 17
primary keys, 14, 17, 185, 188
relational databases, 14
surrogate keys, 17
keywords, 54
IN keyword, 55

L

left outer joins, 49, 51

M

MAX() function
aggregate functions, 57
MFC
CCreateContext class, 219
CDaoDatabase class, 105
CDaoQueryDef class, 106
CDaoRecordset class, 104
CDaoTableDef class, 106
CDaoWorkspace class, 105
CDatabase class, 75
CRecordset class, 76
CRuntime class, 219
DAO, 75, 103, 107
Document/View architecture, 75, 85
MFC wizards, 75, 94
ODBC, 75, 79
ODBC API, 75
OLE DB, 154, 183
OLE method
    ADO, 251
User Interface, 182
wrapper classes, 75, 103

MFC AppWizard, 79, 107, 183, 254
RDS, 277
MFC ClassWizard, 80, 82, 95, 107, 109, 172
ADO, 251
CMainFrame class, 218
CRecordset class, 80
view classes, 191
Microsoft Foundation Classes
see MFC
Microsoft Management Console
SQL Server
    security, 274
Microsoft Transaction Server
OLE DB
    providers, 131
MIN() function
aggregate functions, 57
multi-valued dependency, 25

N

normal forms
Boyce-Codd normal form, 24
domain/key normal form, 26, 31
fifth normal form, 26
first normal form, 21
fourth normal form, 25
second normal form, 21
third normal form, 22

O

object-oriented databases, 32
compared to relational databases, 33
object-oriented programming, 124
ODBC, 72, 123
advantages, 101
CDatabase class, 75, 79
compared to DAO, 103, 108, 113

compared to OLE DB, 73, 127
CRecordset class, 76, 79, 81
DAO, 102
database systems, 73
disadvantages, 101
MFC, 75, 79
ODBC API, 73, 74
    MFC, 75
ODBC connection
    Control Panel, 77
OLE DB, 145
    providers, 131, 156, 184, 273
RDS, 272
sample database, 77

Index

SQL Server, 184, 274
Universal Data Access, 119, 128
ODBC API, 73, 74
MFC, 75
ODBC connection
Control Panel, 77
OLE DB, 73, 123
see also OLE DB objects
accessors, 135, 147, 152
ADO, 73, 127, 129, 146, 234
  command object, 245
  connection object, 236
  recordset object, 240
advantages, 145
ATL, 150
ATL Object Wizard, 147, 150
C++, 250
CAccessor class, 152
  CCommand class, 161
CCommand class, 151
  CAccessor class, 161
CDataSource class, 151
CDynamicAccessor class, 153
CDynamicParameterAccessor class, 153
CManualAccessor class, 153
COM, 123, 126, 127, 128, 145
compared to ODBC, 73, 127
consumer templates, 150
  ATL Object Wizard, 155
consumers, 130, 149, 154
  ADO, 130
  ADO objects, 150
  ATL objects, 154
  consumer wizard, 147, 150
    CTable class, 151
  creating, 177, 183
  definition, 149
  installation, 227
  security, 230
  source control, 227
  transactions, 229
  User Interface, 182, 191
  visibility, 230
creating rowsets, 221
CRowset class, 153
CSession class, 151
CTable class, 151
definition, 128
design goals, 129
disadvantages, 145
flexibility, 129
interfaces, 137
Internet, 145
MFC, 154, 183

performance, 129
providers, 131, 156
  Access, 131
  Active Directory Services, 131
  ADO, 234
    error object, 247
  Btrieve, 131
  FoxPro, 131
  ISAM, 131
  Microsoft Transaction Server, 131
  ODBC, 131, 145, 156, 184, 273
  Oracle, 131
  provider wizard, 147
  SQL Server, 131, 184
reliability, 129
service components, 132
  cursor engine, 132
  query processor, 132
  shape component, 132
    ADO, 132
  synchronization component, 132
templates, 147
Universal Data Access, 119, 127, 128
OLE DB objects
see also OLE DB
command objects, 133, 134, 245
  accessors, 135
  interfaces, 140
  rowset objects, 134
  session objects, 134
  SQL, 134
data source objects, 133
  interfaces, 138
  session objects, 134
enumerator objects, 135
error objects, 135
rowset objects, 133, 134, 240
  accessors, 135
  command objects, 134
  interfaces, 142
  session objects, 134
session objects, 133
  ACID, 134
  command objects, 134
  data source objects, 134
  interfaces, 139
  metadata, 134
  rowset objects, 134
transaction objects, 135
  interfaces, 144
OLE SDK
ADO, 254
Open Database Conectivity
see ODBC

Oracle
 *database systems, 8, 10, 35, 36, 37, 39, 55, 62, 72,
 73, 74, 103, 106, 118, 128, 144*
ORDER BY element, 57

P

PARAM_MAP() macro, 152
parameter maps, 186, 188
parameterized queries
 database systems, 84, 94, 95, 186, 188
Personal Web Server
 see PWS
PWS
 RDS, 272

Q

QueryDefs
 compared to stored procedures, 35
 DAO, 114
 database systems, 35, 106, 114

R

RDO, 72
 compared to ADO, 73
 compared to DAO, 269
 compared to RDS, 267
 introduction, 268
 RDO model, 269
 rdoEngine object, 270
 rdoEnvironment object, 270
 rdoError object, 270
 Visual C++, 270
RDS
 ADO, 271, 277
 business rules, 271
 COM, 277
 compared to RDO, 268
 IIS, 272
 Internet, 145, 272
 Internet Explorer, 273
 MFC AppWizard, 277
 ODBC, 272
 PWS, 272
 RDS model, 290
 SQL Server, 272, 277
  security, 275
 trusted connections, 273
 Universal Data Access, 119, 270
 Visual C++, 277
records
 definition, 9
 fields, 9

recordset objects, 240, 286, 289
 IDispatch, 279
referential integrity, 18, 37
 foreign keys, 201
relational databases, 10, 44
 anomalies, 20
  addition anomalies, 20
  deletion anomalies, 20
  update anomalies, 20
 characteristics, 11
 compared to object-oriented databases, 33
 concepts, 12
 cursors, 37
 data normalization, 19, 26
 data redundancy, 19
 database systems, 9
 definition, 11
 denormalization, 32
 domain integrity, 37
 entity integrity, 37
 functional dependence, 20
 indexing, 33
  clustered indexes, 33, 35, 180, 198
  compound indexes, 34
  single field indexes, 34
  unique index, 33
 keys, 14
  alternate keys, 16
  candidate keys, 14, 24
  foreign keys, 15, 186, 196, 201
  intelligent keys, 17
  primary keys, 14, 17, 185, 188
  surrogate keys, 17
 normal forms, 21
  Boyce-Codd normal form, 24
  domain/key normal form, 26, 31
  fifth normal form, 26
  first normal form, 21
  fourth normal form, 25
  second normal form, 21
  third normal form, 22
 referential integrity, 18, 37, 201
 relationships, 12
  many-to-many, 13
  one-to-many, 13
  one-to-one, 13
 transactions, 37
Remote Data Objects
 see RDO
Remote Data Services
 see RDS
report view class, 223
reports
 creating, 219

Index

reserved words
FROM, 46, 47
INSERT, 46
PRIMARY, 64
SELECT, 46, 47
WHERE, 46, 47
right outer joins, 49, 51
rowset objects, 133, 134, 166, 184, 240
accessors, 135
command objects, 134
document class, 189, 194, 212
IAccessor, 143
IColumnsInfo, 143
IConvertType, 143
interfaces, 142
IRowset, 144
IRowsetInfo, 144
session objects, 134
transactions, 229

S

SAFEARRAY, 260
security
OLE DB
consumers, 230
SELECT element, 47
SUM(), 55
SELECT statement, 152, 159, 169
cross joins, 52
DEFINE_COMMAND() macro, 171
filters, 46, 53
SQL, 46
syntax, 46
session objects, 133, 169
ACID, 134
command objects, 134
data source objects, 134
IGetDataSource, 140
interfaces, 139
IOpenRowset, 140
ISessionProperties, 140
metadata, 134
rowset objects, 134
sorting
ORDER BY element, 57
source control
OLE DB
consumers, 227
Visual SourceSafe, 228
SQL, 33, 43
aggregate functions, 56
command objects, 134
comparison operators, 54
Data Definition Language, 44, 62

Data Manipulation Language, 44
definition, 44
GUI, 67
keywords, 54
sample database, 45
SELECT statement, 46
SQLscript.txt, 181
tools for creating SQL, 67
SQL Server
database systems, 8, 10, 33, 35, 37, 39, 53, 55, 62,
64, 67, 72, 73, 74, 79, 103, 106, 118, 127, 128,
144, 178, 184, 227, 230, 238, 256, 272, 273, 274,
275, 277, 278
installation, 227
ODBC, 184, 274
OLE DB
providers, 131, 184
RDS, 272, 277
security, 274
Microsoft Management Console, 274
RDS, 275
SQLscript.txt, 181
stored procedures
compared to QueryDefs, 35
database systems, 35, 84
information hiding, 35
triggers, 36
Structured Query Language
see SQL
SUCCEEDED() macro, 166
SUM() function
aggregate functions, 55, 56

T

TableDefs
database systems, 106
transaction objects, 135
IConnectionPointContainer, 145
interfaces, 144
ITransaction, 145
ITransactionOptions, 145
transactions
OLE DB
consumers, 229
relational databases, 37
rowset objects, 229
triggers
stored procedures, 36
trusted connections
RDS, 273

U

Universal Data Access, 123
ADO, 119, 146
Internet, 126
ODBC, 119, 123, 128
OLE DB, 119, 123, 127, 128
RDS, 119, 270
UPDATE statement, 61
syntax, 61
updating forms, 212
User Interface
MFC, 182
OLE DB
consumers, 182, 191
view classes, 191
developing, 191
users classes
data access classes, 185

V

VARIANTs, 251
VBSQL, 72
visibility
OLE DB
consumers, 230
Visual C++
ADO, 250
ADO extensions, 263
IntelliSense feature, 277
RDO, 270
RDS, 277
Visual SourceSafe
source control
OLE DB
consumers, 228

W

WHERE element, 49, 50, 53, 95
compared to HAVING element, 56

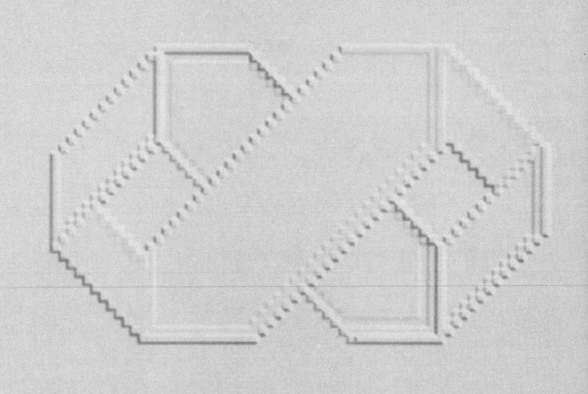

Beginning ATL COM Programming

Authors: Various
ISBN: 1861000111
Price: $39.95 C$55.95 £36.99

This book is for fairly experienced C++ developers who want to get to grips with COM programming using the Active Template Library. The Beginning in the title of this book refers to COM and ATL. It does not refer to Programming.

We don't expect you to know anything about COM. The book explains the essentials of COM, how to use it, and how to get the most out of it. If you already know something about COM, that's a bonus. You'll still learn a lot about the way that ATL works, and you'll be one step ahead of the COM neophytes.

Neither do we expect you to know anything about ATL. ATL is the focus of the book. If you've never touched ATL, or if you've been using it for a short while, but still have many unanswered questions, this is the book for you.

Professional MFC with Visual C++ 5

Author: Mike Blaszczak
ISBN: 1861000146
Price: $59.95 C$83.95 £56.49

Written by one of Microsoft's leading MFC developers, this is the book for professionals who want to get under the covers of the library. This is the 3rd revision of the best selling title formerly known as 'Revolutionary Guide to MFC 4' and covers the new Visual C++ 5.0 development environment.

This book will give a detailed discussion of the majority of classes present in Microsoft's application framework library. While it will point out what parameters are required for the member functions of those classes, it will concentrate more on describing what utility the classes really provide. You will learn how to write a few utilities, some DLLs, an ActiveX control and even an OLE document server, as well as examining Microsoft's Open Database Connectivity (ODBC) and Data Access Objects (DAO) strategies. At the very end of the book, you'll take a look at what the Microsoft Foundation Classes provide to make programming for the Internet easier.

There's a CD_ROM included which has the complete book in HTML format - now you can use any browser to read your book on the road.

Professional ATL COM Programming

Authors: Dr. Richard Grimes
ISBN: 1861001401
Price: $59.99 C$89.95 £45.99

For experienced Visual C++ programmers with experience of COM and ATL (Active Template Library) The coverage throughout, is for the latest ATL version 3.0 and as such is essential reading for getting the most out of your COM servers.

Author, Richard Grimes - famous for his definitive text on DCOM, has applied all his specialist knowledge of ATL usage in the field to give you *the* book on ATL architecture and usage. If you've ever looked at Wizard-generated ATL code and wondered what's behind it. If you've ever wondered how it works, why it's implemented in that way and the options for customising and extending it – then the answer is in these pages. You will learn all about the plumbing behind ATL via example code that will be useful in your own projects. You should read this if you wish to: debug, get the right factory, thread, marshal, use Windows classes, use connection points, sink events, build composite controls and understand the COM object wizard.

Professional COM Applications with ATL

Authors: Sing Li and Panos Econompoulos
ISBN: 1861001703
Price: $49.99 C$69.95 £45.99

This book examines how and why you should use COM, ActiveX controls and DNA Business Objects, and how these components are linked together to form robust, flexible and scalable applications.

A key part of the book is the extended case study in which we produce a distributed events calendar that fits Microsoft's Distributed interNet Applications (DNA) model. This three-tier application uses flexible browser-based controls for the client user interface, business objects on both client and server to process the required information efficiently and Universal Data Access to perform the queries and updates. It depends on the support for component-based development now available for Windows NT server.

The additions and changes to this book make it both significant and relevant to readers of the first edition, Professional ActiveX/COM Control Programming.

Beginning NT Programming

Author: Julian Templeman
ISBN: 1861000170
Price: $39.99 C$59.95 £36.99

This book is designed to lay bare the guts of NT programming. In order to do this, it concentrates on programming at a system level, using the Win32 API, rather than the Windows GUI. You'll learn about structured exception handling, how threads and processes work and how to deal with NT's filing system. You'll also learn about how to write NT Services, deal with the NT security system programmatically and implement inter-process communication.

If you're already familiar with C++, and are keen to take your first steps in writing NT system applications, or to add NT-specific features to your applications, then this is the book for you.

Professional NT Services

Author: Kevin Miller
ISBN: 1861001304
Price: $59.99 C$83.95 £55.49

Professional NT Services teaches developers how to design and implement good NT services using all the features and tools supplied for the purpose by Microsoft Visual C++. The author develops a set of generic classes to facilitate service development, and introduces the concept of *usage patterns* — a way of categorizing the roles that services can fulfil in the overall architecture of a system. The book also gives developers a firm grounding in the security and configuration issues that must be taken into account when developing a service.

To date, the treatment of NT services has been sketchy and widely scattered. This book is aimed at bringing the range of relevant material together in an organized way. Its target readership is C/C++ Windows programmers with experience of programming under Win32 and basic knowledge of multithreaded and COM programming. At an architectural level, the book's development of usage patterns will be invaluable to client-server developers who want to include services as part of a multi-tiered system.

Beginning Object Oriented Analysis and Design

Author: Jesse Liberty
ISBN: 1861001339
Price: $34.95 C$48.95 £32.49

Beginning Object-Oriented Analysis and Design is a tutorial about planning and designing a software product or project in a practical way, before getting involved with writing code. Using OOA&D, a programmer can develop a concrete blueprint or model of their software using the standard modeling language, UML. From the UML model, the programmer can successfully code the objects described. This can be done in any OO-capable language, although C++ is used as an example.

Going beyond the methodology and the modeling language, the book talks about the entire process of professional software development. *Beginning Object-Oriented Analysis and Design* is written in a straightforward manner that should be readily accessible to anyone developing software.

ADO 2.0 Programmer's Reference

Authors: David Sussman, Alex Homer
ISBN: 1861001835
Price: $24.99 C$37.95 £22.99

ADO 2.0 is the next step in Microsoft's Universal Data Access strategy. If you want flexible, easy data access, then you need to know about ADO. This reference introduces ADO 2.0 and provides a complete guide to using ADO for the rapid development of your data applications.

Who is this book for?
If you're a developer in VB, J++, C++, or web scripting languages, and you need to access data quickly and efficiently, this is the book for you. It's also ideal for users of ADO 1.5 who want to know how ADO has expanded. It's a complete reference guide to ADO 2.0, covering everything you need to know to fully utilize the power of Microsoft's data access technology in your applications.

Visual C++ Windows Shell Programming

Authors: Dino Esposito
ISBN: 1861001843
Price: $39.99 C$55.95 £36.99

The Windows shell is the user interface for Windows 9x and Windows NT 4.0, allowing execution of common tasks such as accessing the file system, launching programs and changing system-wide settings. However, it's not just about user interaction: the shell exposes programming hooks that you can use from your own applications. This book shows you how to work with and extend the functionality of the shell, from tinkering with the Shell API to writing COM objects that get loaded into the shell's address space.

Within these pages is a compendium of shell programming techniques. You'll learn how to push the Windows shell to perform complex actions, and customize it using C++ programs. There's coverage of the Shell API, the Windows Scripting Host, and shell and namespace extensions that use the shell's object model.

Beginning Visual C++6

Author: Ivor Horton
ISBN: 186100088x
Price: $49.99 C$69.95 £45.99

"I've been designing, programming and teaching people about computers for over 30 years. All of the good things I have seen flowed from a deep knowledge of the problem and the tools to deal with it. I want you to succeed at the cutting edge of Windows programming by building on a solid bedrock of C++ understanding. You'll need the discipline to work through the examples and experiment on your own, and to hang in there with me when things get tough. I'll help you, but you have to want to climb the mountain, and believe that it's worth becoming a real programmer."

Who is this book for?
This book is for anyone who wants to learn C++ and Windows programming with Visual C++ 6. Although progress will be easier if you have some experience of a programming discipline, an adept newcomer will also succeed in taming object-oriented programming and writing real Windows applications.

Instant UML

Authors: Pierre-Alain Muller
ISBN: 1861000871
Price: $34.95 C$48.95 £32.49

UML is the Unified Modeling Language.
Modeling languages have come into
vogue with the rise of object-oriented development,
as they provide a means of communicating and recording every
stage of the project. The results of the analysis and design phases are
captured using the formal syntax of the modeling language, producing a
clear model of the system to be implemented.

Instant UML offers not only a complete description of the notation and
proper use of UML, but also an introduction to the theory of object-
oriented programming, and the way to approach object-oriented application
development. This is UML in context, not a list of the syntax without rhyme
or reason.

This book is relevant to programmers of C++, VB, Java and other OO-
capable languages, users of Visual Modeler (which comes with the
Enterprise Edition of Microsoft's Visual Studio) and novice users of
Rational Rose and similar UML-compliant tools.

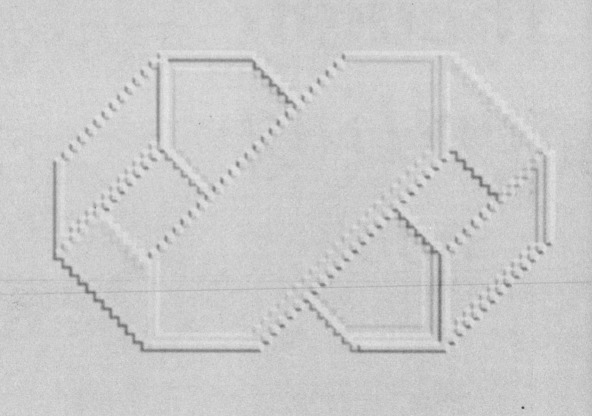